Cambridge History of Medicine
EDITORS: CHARLES WEBSTER AND CHARLES ROSENBERG

Abortion, doctors and the law:
Some aspects of the legal regulation of abortion in
England from 1803 to 1982

Abortion, doctors and the law

Some aspects of the legal regulation of abortion in
England from 1803 to 1982

John Keown

Director, Centre for Health Care Law, University of Leicester

The right of the
University of Cambridge
to print and sell
all manner of books
was granted by
Henry VIII in 1534.
The University has printed
and published continuously
since 1584.

CAMBRIDGE UNIVERSITY PRESS

CAMBRIDGE

NEW YORK   NEW ROCHELLE   MELBOURNE   SYDNEY

Published by the Press Syndicate of the University of Cambridge
The Pitt Building, Trumpington Street, Cambridge CB2 1RP
32 East 57th Street, New York, NY 10022, USA
10 Stamford Road, Oakleigh, Melbourne 3166, Australia

First published 1988

Printed in Great Britain at the University Press, Cambridge

British Library cataloguing in publication data

Keown, John
    Abortion, doctors and the law: some aspects of the legal
        regulation of abortion in
    England from 1803 to 1982. —
    (Cambridge history of medicine).
    1. England. Abortion. Law, 1803–1982
    I. Title
    344.204'419

Library of Congress cataloguing in publication data

Keown, John
    Abortion, doctors and the law.
    (Cambridge history of medicine).
    Bibliography: p.
    Includes index.
    1. Abortion — Law and legislation — Great Britain —
    History.   I. Title.   II. Series.   [DNLM: 1. Abortion,
    Legal — history — England. HQ 767.5.G7 K37a]
    KD3340.K46   1988   344.41'0419   88-2604
    344.104419

ISBN 0 521 34574 X

PN

To my mother and father
and to Paul, Day, Do, Mart and Christiana

Contents

Table of Cases

Table of Statutes

Acknowledgements

I should like to thank all those who helped to make this book possible. I am especially grateful to John Finnis and Mavis Maclean, who supervised the thesis on which the book is based.

I should also like to thank those who so kindly gave up their time to be interviewed; the researchers (especially Peter Bartrip and Robert Dingwall) and staff (especially Noël Blatchford and Jenny Dix) of the Centre for Socio-Legal Studies, Oxford; the Economic and Social Research Council, who funded my research; Margaret Pelling, Joan Austoker, Irvine Loudon, and Charles Webster of the Wellcome Unit for the History of Medicine, Oxford; Juliet Cheetham; the staff of the Bodleian Law Library and the Radcliffe Science Library (particularly Theo); Susan Sternberg and Sandi Irvine of Cambridge University Press and the many others – too many to mention individually – who provided assistance and encouragement.

I remain, of course, solely accountable for the accuracy of the book.

Introduction

Much has been written, particularly over the last twenty years, on the subject of the law of abortion.[1] The bulk of the literature, however, has been concerned with the desirability or otherwise of legal reform, has addressed the subject in the broad context of moral, philosophical, political and sociological considerations, and has related largely to the law in the United States.[2] Remarkably little academic attention has been given to the development and scope of the law in England, and research that has considered English law has tended to concentrate on the political dimensions of the relaxation of the law by the Abortion Act 1967 (see Appendices, p. 168), and in particular the role played in that relaxation by the Abortion Law Reform Association.[3] Not only is research into the development of the law sparse but also the question of the influence both of the medical profession on its development and of the law on the practice of abortion by the profession has been largely ignored. This text seeks to make a contribution to the remedying of these deficiencies.

The book spans the period 1803 to 1982 and considers certain aspects of the development of the law, with particular reference to the influence of the medical profession (that is, registered medical practitioners and their predecessors, the 'regular' as opposed to uneducated practitioners) on its enactment and the degree to which the law has influenced the practice of abortion by the profession. It does not, therefore, present either a comprehensive history of the law itself or a socio-political history of its development. Nor does it address directly the legal status of the unborn child,[4] the rights and duties of its parents and the doctor in the provision of abortion,[5] the degree to which the Abortion Act 1967 has achieved its aims, or the vexed question of the desirability of reform. Rather, adopting a socio-legal perspective, it considers what the scope of the prohibition of abortion has been and focusses on aspects of professional influence on the evolution of that prohibition and of professional practice thereunder.

Against the background of the common-law prohibition of abortion, Chapters 1 and 2 trace the passage of the anti-abortion statutes in the nineteenth century, culminating in the Offences Against the Person Act 1861, and consider the influence of the medical profession on their enactment. Chapter 3 discusses whether this law prohibited, either in theory or in practice, the performance of abortion by the medical profession before 1938. Chapter 4 examines the extent of the profession's influence on the shape and enactment of the Abortion Act 1967, and Chapter 5 how extensively the Act has been interpreted by medical practitioners to allow abortion. Chapter 6 looks at the reaction of the profession to proposals to amend the Act restrictively. The concluding chapter of the book suggests a possible explanation, from a sociological perspective, of the influence of the profession on the development of the law relating to abortion, and its interpretation of that law in its performance of abortion.

The medical sources for this thesis were largely the following: works listed in the *Index Catalogue of the Library of the Surgeon-General's Office* (first four series); and in *Index Medicus* 1903–1982; the *Lancet* 1824–1862 and 1898–1982; the *British Medical Journal* 1857–1862 and 1898–1982; works in the stack lists of the Radcliffe Science Library (1517 d,e,f; 162 d,e,f); and interviews conducted with the following: Dr E. G. Daw F.R.C.O.G. (15 November 1984); Dr P. J. Huntingford F.R.C.O.G. (20 February 1985); Sir John Dewhurst F.R.C.O.G. (21 February 1985); Professor R. W. Taylor F.R.C.O.G. (11 March 1985); Dame Josephine Barnes F.R.C.O.G. (11 March 1985); Dr S. A. Bond M.R.C.S. (12 March 1985); and Sir John Peel F.R.C.O.G. (18 March 1985). A further interview, on the enforcement of the Abortion Act 1967 and the Abortion Regulations 1968, was carried out on 3 April 1985 with two officers of the Department of Health and Social Security: Mr Moutrie (a Department solicitor) and Mr Kirby (who is in charge of the inspection of premises approved under the Abortion Act 1967).

1

The first statutory prohibition of abortion: Lord Ellenborough's Act 1803

This chapter focusses, against the background of the common-law offence of abortion, on the enactment of the first statutory prohibition of abortion in Lord Ellenborough's Act 1803 (43 Geo III c. 58).

1.1 Abortion and the common law

During the late seventeenth, the whole of the eighteenth, and early nineteenth centuries, English and American women were totally free from all restraints, ecclesiastical as well as secular, in regard to the termination of unwanted pregnancies, at any time during gestation. (Cyril C. Means Jr)[1]

Abortion and the ecclesiastical courts 1200–1600
Whether the common law prohibited the destruction of unborn life has been, and remains, a controversial question, an exhaustive examination of which would be beyond the scope of this chapter. However, it will be contended here, *pace* Professor Means, that the weight of available authority supports the view that the common law prohibited abortion, at the latest, after the fetus had become 'quick' or 'animated'. Animation was believed to occur when the fetus 'quickened' in the womb. An incident of the second trimester of pregnancy, quickening marks the first maternal perception of fetal movement. In associating the origin of life with quickening, the law betrayed both pragmatic and metaphysical influences. The former concerned the need to prove, in any prosecution for abortion, that the woman had been pregnant and that the fetus had been killed by the abortifacient act. Evidence of quickening would clearly facilitate prosecution. The metaphysical influence upon the law was the popular theory, originated by Aristotle and perpetuated by Galen, that human life began at the point of 'animation'. This

theory was espoused by the canon law of the Christian Church and thence it found its way into the developing common law.[2]

In 1971, Means proposed the thesis that women in England between 1327 and 1803 (and in the United States between 1607 and 1830) enjoyed a common-law liberty to procure abortion.[3] He did not only contend that the common law placed no restriction on abortion; earlier he had maintained that the statutory prohibition of abortion in the nineteenth century was motivated by a desire to preserve maternal, rather than fetal, life.[4]

His thesis of a liberty to abort, whether the fetus died before or after birth, is based largely on two anonymous cases. The first he calls '*The Twinslayer's Case*' (*Anonymous* 1327), where a writ was issued for the arrest of one D, who had allegedly beaten a woman advanced in pregnancy whereby one of the twins she was carrying died instantly and the other soon after birth. The report states that D appeared 'and pled not guilty, and for the reason that the justices were unwilling to adjudge this thing a felony, the accused was released to mainpernors and then the argument was adjourned sine die'.[5]

The second authority Means names '*The Abortionist's Case*' (*Anonymous* 1348), wherein the defendant, who had been indicted for killing a child in its mother's womb, escaped conviction on the grounds that the indictment failed to state a baptismal name and that it was difficult to know whether he had killed the child.[6] Means also cites Sir William Staunford (1509–1558) and William Lambard (1536–1601), who observed that a child, until it is born, is not a creature *in rerum natura* and may not therefore be a victim of homicide.[7]

However, it has been countered that the failure to convict in the above cases can be attributed not to the lawfulness of abortion but to problems of procedure and proof. The argument runs that a closer reading of the reports reveals that in the 1327 case the proceedings were adjourned not because the writ charged a non-existent offence but because the defendant had been arrested on an unrelated charge, and that in the 1348 case the failure to convict was expressly attributed not to the permissibility of abortion but to the procedural defect of the absence of a baptismal name and to the practical difficulty of determining the cause of the child's death.[8] Some support for this argument may be provided by the fact that the existing legal authorities pointed to the criminality of abortion.

In the thirteenth century, Bracton wrote that to kill a fetus which was 'formed or animated' amounted to homicide.[9] This was echoed by his commentator, Fleta, who also specified the liability of the pregnant woman.[10] The disagreement between these authorities on the one hand and Staunford and Lambard on the other is not irreconcilable: the former borrowed from the canon law in their expositions of the developing common law whereas the latter were concerned solely with 'Pleas of the Crown'. Moreover, the latter merely denied that abortion was homicide, not that it was some lesser form of offence.[11]

The better interpretation of the authorities appears to be that the common-law courts, although not denying abortion to be a secular offence, were content to allow the exceptional difficulties of proof that it posed to be resolved in an ecclesiastical forum.

Evidence for this view is furnished by the research of Professor Helmholz into infanticide in the Province of Canterbury in the fifteenth century.[12] He establishes that both infanticide and abortion were punished by the ecclesiastical courts. He concludes that to speak as some writers have done about a 'common law freedom of abortion' is unwarranted if the phrase implies that one could cause the death of a fetus with impunity, and he adds that the fact that the royal courts – which assumed that local and ecclesiastical courts would take cognisance of a great deal of unlawful conduct – did not regularly punish a particular type of conduct does not establish that such conduct was permissible at common law.[13]

It appears that the offence of abortion was, as with some cases of infanticide,[14] left to the church courts solely with the pragmatic aim of facilitating prosecution: in the church courts the administration of the *ex officio* oath allowed even self-incriminating evidence to be given, whereas in the royal courts prosecution was hedged about with procedural technicalities, which compensated for the severe penalties inflicted upon conviction for felony.[15] Partly on account of such penalties juries would probably have been reluctant to convict, particularly if the mother herself were indicted.

The exercise of jurisdiction over abortion by the common-law courts 1600–1803

The unsettling effect of the Reformation on the ecclesiastical courts and their decline in the seventeenth century – reflected in the abolition of the *ex officio* oath in 1661 – rendered them less able to exercise effective control over abortion.[16] How did the common-law courts respond to this development? If, as has been suggested, they allowed the church courts to deal with the offence solely to facilitate prosecution, an increasing exercise of royal jurisdiction would be expected when the church courts could no longer discharge this function satisfactorily. This is precisely what the evidence suggests.

Several authorities, culled from sources such as the records of the Courts of Assize and the reports of inquests, indicate an increasing exercise of royal jurisdiction over abortion in the seventeenth century. This trend was, perhaps, presaged by the early case of *R.* v. *Lichefeld* (1505). The defendant was alleged to have 'feloniously entertained' one Joan Wynspere, knowing that she had taken poison to destroy her unborn child, shortly before her death from the effects of the poison.[17]

The full facts of the case are recorded in the report of the inquest into Wynspere's death, which was held on 5 January 1504 at Basford before Richard Parker, the coroner. The report appears in a series of Nottinghamshire coroners' inquests from 1485 to 1558 as translated by R. F. Hunnisett. It reads:

On 12 Dec. 1503 Joan Wynspere of Basford, 'syngilwoman', being pregnant, at Basford drank divers poisoned and dangerous draughts to destroy the child in her womb, of which she immediately died. Thus she feloniously slew and poisoned [toxigavit] herself as a suicide and also the child in her womb. On that day she possessed a gown worth 12d., a coat worth 6d., a vest worth 4d. and a small chest worth 6d. Thomas Lichefeld of Basford, clerk, then feloniously entertained her at Basford, knowing that she had committed this felony.[18]

Hunnisett adds:

This inquest, which was on view of Joan's body only, was delivered to the gaol delivery justices at Nottingham on 20 March 1504 and into King's Bench in Trinity term. In Hilary term 1505 Thomas Lichefeld appeared in King's Bench and pleaded that the indictment of him was insufficient since the principal, to whom he was accessory, was dead, as manifestly appeared by the indictment, and without her he should not have to answer. This plea was accepted and he went sine die.[19]

Clearly, had abortion fallen exclusively within the jurisdiction of the ecclesiastical courts, the defendant could simply have contended

that he could not have 'feloniously entertained' Wynspere 'knowing
that she had committed this felony' if she had not in fact committed
an offence. Yet the inquest found that she had feloniously killed
herself and her unborn child and this was the premise on which the
indictment against Lichefeld was framed.[20]

By the beginning of the seventeenth century, however, there are
authorities which reveal more clearly the protection which the
common-law courts were prepared to extend to the unborn child.
In March 1602, the case *R. v. Webb*[21] was tried at Southwark
Assizes, before Francis Gawdy J. and Serjeant William Daniel. The
indictment ran:

The jurors for our Lady the Queen present, that Margaret Webb, lately of
Godalmyn, spinster, on the tenth day of August, in the forty-first year of
the reign of our Lady Elizabeth [1599] by the grace of God Queen of
England, France and Ireland, and defender of the faith, with force and
arms, and at the aforesaid Godalmyn in the aforesaid county, not having
the fear of God before her eyes, but moved and seduced by the instigation
of the devil, once ate the poison called 'rattesbane' with the intention of
spoiling and destroying the infant in the womb of Margaret herself and
thus the aforesaid Margaret, by reason of eating the aforesaid poison,
spoiled and destroyed then and there the infant in her womb, as a
pernicious example to all the malefactors offending in like manner, against
the peace of our Lady the Queen, her crown and dignity.[22]

The report of the case adds that the defendant was pardoned by a
general pardon, though whether before or after conviction is not
clear.[23] Two main conclusions may be drawn from this case.
Firstly, the case is further authority for the proposition that abortion
was an offence at common law. Although the report is brief and
there is neither argument nor citation of authority, the case was
heard by a strong court: Gawdy J. became Chief Justice of Common
Pleas in 1605,[24] and Serjeant Daniel, described by Lord Burleigh as,
'a vearie honest, learned, and discreat man', was appointed a judge
of the same court in 1604.[25] It is unlikely that the bench, together
with any counsel and both grand and petty juries, would have acted
under a misapprehension as to the court's jurisdiction to hear the
case. The second main conclusion is that, since Webb herself was
indicted, the case undermines the thesis that a woman enjoyed a
common-law liberty to abort. Further, her prosecution suggests
that the predominant rationale of the law against abortion was the

preservation of fetal life, though the prohibition would also tend to deter women from exposing themselves to the risks of interrupting pregnancy.

R. v. Webb concerned abortion resulting in stillbirth, but it would be reasonable to conclude that if the courts were prepared to grapple with the difficulties of proof inherent in such cases then, *a fortiori*, they would also have been willing to exercise jurisdiction over cases of abortion where fetal death occurred after live birth, and was attributable to injuries sustained *in utero*. There is, indeed, evidence to support this conclusion. In the year before Webb's Case the court of Queen's Bench heard an action for trespass and assault brought against one Sims for beating a woman advanced in pregnancy with the result that her child died after it had been born alive.[26] Fenner and Popham JJ. upheld the submission that this was murder, and their judgement reflects the pivotal significance of considerations of proof:

if it be dead born it is no murder, for non constat, whether the child were living at the time of the batterie or not, or if the batterie was the cause of the death, but when it is born living, and the wounds appeare in his body, and then he dye, the batteror shal be arraigned of murder, for now it may be proved whether these wounds were the cause of the death or not, and for that if it be found, he shall be condemned.[27]

The court in R. v. *Webb* went further, and was prepared to entertain an indictment which alleged abortion resulting in stillbirth. Webb's Case therefore supplements *Sims's Case* and both cases, together with R. v. *Lichefeld*, indicate the willingness of the royal courts to exercise jurisdiction over the offence of abortion. Two further cases reveal that the exercise of this jurisdiction continued in the following century.

In August 1732, one Eleanor Beare was not only indicted for abortion but was actually convicted of the offence. The trial was held at Derby Assizes and was reported, apparently *verbatim*, in the *Gentleman's Magazine*.[28] The indictment contained three counts. The first charged an attempt to persuade one Nicholas Wilson to poison his wife and giving him poison for that purpose. The second and third charged abortion. The second count read:

Indicted a second time . . . for a misdemeanor, in destroying the foetus in the womb of Grace Belfort, by putting an iron instrument up into her body, and thereby causing her to miscarry.[29]

The third count ran:

Indicted a third time, for destroying the foetus in the womb of a certain woman, to the jury unknown, by putting an iron instrument up her body, or by giving her something to make her miscarry.[30]

The defendant pleaded not guilty. Counsel for the Crown opened the prosecution on these two counts with an address to the jury on the severity of the offence charged. He declared:

Gentlemen, you have heard the indictment read, and may observe, that the misdemeanor for which the prisoner stands indicted, is of a most shocking nature; to destroy the fruit of the womb carries something in it so contrary to the natural tenderness of the female sex, that I am amazed how ever any woman should arrive at such a degree of impiety and cruelty, as to attempt it in such a manner as the prisoner has done; it has really something so shocking in it, that I cannot well display the nature of the crime to you, but must leave it to the evidence: It is cruel and barbarous to the last degree.[31]

He called Grace Belfort, upon whom the instrument had allegedly been used. It emerged that she had been a servant of the accused and that during her service had had intercourse with a man after they had been drinking at her mistress's house. Subsequently, her mistress asked her if she was pregnant, to which she replied that she thought she was. Belfort testified that the defendant offered 'to clear me from the Child, without giving me Physick', if she could obtain 30 shillings from the father.[32] Shortly after, the witness added, the accused passed an instrument, resembling an iron skewer, a considerable way into her body and the following day she miscarried.[33] Belfort's testimony was supported by that of other witnesses. One woman said that she had slept with Belfort and had noticed the symptoms of a miscarriage on the bed, and a man that he had heard the accused say that she had once been paid five pounds to go to Nottingham to procure abortion.[34] The judge observed that as the second count of the indictment had been so plainly proved, there was no need to proceed to the third. The report concludes:

His Lordship summed up the evidence in a very moving speech to the jury, wherein he said, he never met with a case so barbarous and unnatural. The jury, after a short consultation, brought the prisoner in guilty of both indictments, and she received sentence to stand on the pillory, the two next market-days, and to suffer close imprisonment for three years.[35]

A second eighteenth-century case which reveals the exercise of jurisdiction over abortion by the secular courts is *R. v. Turner*.[36]

The defendant, a Warsop weaver, was tried for abortion on 10 October 1755 at the Nottinghamshire General Quarter Sessions convened at East Retford. The indictment charged him with a misdemeanor,

in persuading and procuring Elizabeth Mason to take and swallow a certain quantity of arsenick mixed with treacle in order to kill and destroy a male bastard child by him begotten on her body and which she was then quick with.[37]

The brief report of the case states that Turner pleaded not guilty and was acquitted.[38]

That abortion was punishable in the royal courts well before the first statutory prohibition of the offence in 1803 is apparent not only from the above cases, but also from the leading contemporary treatises. Sir Edward Coke (1552–1634), in his *Third Institute*, classified abortion resulting in stillbirth as 'a great misprision', and abortion resulting in death after live birth as murder.[39] Serjeant Hawkins (1673–1746), Sir William Blackstone (1723–1780), Sir Edward Hyde East (1764–1847) and Sir William Russell (1785–1833) all followed Coke and, it should be noted, were clearly aware of the authorities cited by Professor Means in his attempt to undermine Coke's exposition of the law.[40] One further authority, cited by both Hawkins and East in support of Coke, is Hale's Summary of the Pleas of the Crown (1682).[41] Its treatment of abortion echoes that found in Coke's *Third Institute*. To the question, 'What [is] the person killed?' is written the reply:

It must be a person *in rerum natura*. If a woman quick with child take a potion to kill it, and accordingly it is destroyed without being born alive, a great misprision, but no felony; but if born alive, and after dies of that potion, it is murder. The like if it dies of a stroke given by another in like manner.[42]

By contrast, in his more comprehensive *History of the Pleas of the Crown*, written in 1685, Hale states that abortion resulting in stillbirth is 'a great crime' but, relying on *The Twinslayer's Case*, denies that abortion resulting in death after live birth is murder.[43]

It would appear, however, that the opinion of Coke prevailed. It was cited in the case of *Millar* v. *Turner* (1748), where the question arose whether a child *en ventre sa mère* was a child living at the time specified in certain marriage articles.[44] Hardwicke L.C. observed: 'the destruction of him is murder; which shews the [law] considers

such infant as a living creature . . . .'.[45] This dictum doubtlessly
refers to the case where the child dies after live birth. That indictments for murder were in fact framed in such circumstances is borne
out by the inclusion of two such indictments as precedents in the
Lex Coronatoria, published in 1822.[46] The first charges the husband
of a pregnant woman with assaulting her by kicking 'in and upon
the belly of her' so that her child 'received divers mortal bruises in
and upon his arms, belly, legs, and thighs', was 'brought forth . . .
alive' and died from its injuries the day after its birth.[47] The second
indictment is of particular interest as it charges the mother herself.[48]
Clearly, the opinion of the judges in *Sims's Case* had become
established law by the early nineteenth century, at the latest, as had
Coke's opinion as to abortion resulting in stillbirth. Indeed, in 1802
the Crown Office drew up an indictment which charged abortion
resulting both in live birth and in stillbirth. The first three counts
charged one E.F. with violently assaulting and administering drugs
to one A.B., who was 'big and pregnant' with child, with intent to
'kill and murder' the said child, with the result that the child was
born alive and, like its mother, became 'distempered in body'. The
second and third counts charged similar offences. The fourth count
charged violent assault and the introduction of an instrument,
rendering the woman 'distempered in body', with intent to cause
her to miscarry and bring the child forth dead.[49]

The 'freedom to abort': de jure and de facto
The authorities considered above, assessed in the light of the
pragmatic constraints and theological influences upon the common
law, lead to the conclusion that the common law prohibited abortion and did so predominantly for the protection of fetal life.
Nevertheless, there may well have been a significant freedom *de
facto* to abort for those either sufficiently ignorant or desperate to
risk the dangers of mortality and morbidity. The task of detecting
and prosecuting such a 'victimless' crime could hardly have been
easy, and perhaps this helps to account for the dearth of reported
cases.

Referring to the period 1540 to 1720, one historian states that it is
clear that on certain social levels both abortion and contraception
were familiar.[50] Another writes that these were the most frequently
used methods of fertility control in the Elizabethan era.[51] Similarly,
Quaife, in his study of illicit sex among the Somerset peasantry in

the seventeenth century records his impression that attempted abortion was widespread and often successful but that many girls refrained from it for fear of its physical dangers.[52]

1.2 The statutory restriction of the abortion law: Lord Ellenborough's Act 1803

In 1803, the prohibition against abortion was revised by Lord Ellenborough's Act (43 Geo. III c. 58). There has as yet been no wholly satisfactory explanation of the restriction of the abortion law by this Act, which is perhaps understandable in view of the apparent absence of any popular or religious outcry over abortion before it was passed. However, by drawing largely on legal, medico-legal and hitherto undiscovered Parliamentary materials, three possible reasons for the restriction of the law can be suggested here: the desire of the Chief Justice, Lord Ellenborough, to clarify the law; a perception of abortion as a social problem; and condemnation by eminent medical practitioners of the moral significance which was attached to quickening.

The clarification of the law
The offence of procuring abortion at common law was, as the conflict of authorities suggests, not clearly delineated. Throughout the nineteenth century, legal opinion would continue to differ over the existence and definition of the offence.

In *R.* v. *Russell* (1832) the defendant was indicted as an accessory before the fact to the suicide of one Sarah Wormsley. She had died as a result of swallowing white arsenic which she had taken to produce abortion. The question arose whether she was, therefore, *felo de se.* Crown counsel relied on three grounds in his submission that she had died as a result of an unlawful act, the third being that it was a common-law misdemeanor for a woman to take any substance with intent to procure abortion.[53] Lord Tenterden C.J. asked whether there was any authority to support this proposition, to which counsel replied: 'No; but the act itself is one, having in it all the ingredients of crime. It is against the law of God, injurious to the individual, and prejudicial to the state'.[54] Eight of the twelve judges who decided the case held that the deceased was *felo de se*, but without specifying the ground for their ruling.[55] However, in *R.* v.

Gaylor (1857), involving similar facts, there appears this more helpful dictum of Pollock C.B.: 'A woman taking a drug to procure abortion may be guilty of an offence at common law, but not so if she were not pregnant at the time'.[56] Still, in *R. v. Whitchurch* (1890), where a woman was charged with conspiring to procure her own miscarriage, the contention made by counsel for the defence that it was not an offence to procure abortion at common law was not challenged either by the judge, Wills J., or by the strong court for which he stated a case.[57]

These cases help to illustrate the fact that even in more recent times the definition and very existence of the offence of abortion at common law have been shrouded in doubt. The vagueness in the law which must have confronted Lord Ellenborough may well have been compounded by the indictment drawn up by the Crown Office in Michaelmas Term 1802, which was undeniably circuitous.[58] Moreover, since this Office was the department responsible for conducting the ministerial business of the Court of King's Bench, it would not be unreasonable to infer that Ellenborough, who had been sworn in as Lord Chief Justice the previous March, would have been aware of the uncertainty in the law which was implied by the form of the indictment. Moreover, both the wording of the Bill introduced by Ellenborough in 1803 and the amendments made thereto support the view that the prohibition of abortion at common law was perceived to be vague and inadequate.

Ellenborough's Malicious Shooting Bill was introduced into the House of Lords in March 1803. The Bill incorporated certain provisions of a previous Bill, the Irish Chalking Bill, and sought to render the law relating to several existing misdemeanors more precise, consistent and effective by converting them into specific statutory felonies. Before the significance of the Act can be properly assessed, it will be necessary to consider the relationship between the two Bills as well as the amendments made to Ellenborough's measure during its passage through the legislative process.

The Irish Chalking Bill and the Malicious Shooting Bill[59]. The long title of the Chalking Bill read; 'An Act to prevent malicious cutting and wounding, and to punish offenders called Chalkers, in Ireland'. The Bill provided that if, after 10 April 1803, any person or persons in Ireland should with any knife or other offensive weapon wilfully, wantonly, and maliciously cut or stab, or with a pistol or pistols, or other fire arms, wound, or attempt to wound, any person or persons in the face or head, or in any limb or member, or in any part of the body, with intent in so doing to murder, rob, or maim, or with an intent to disable or disfigure him, her or them . . .

then they would be guilty of felony and suffer death without benefit of clergy.

The House of Lords resolved itself into a Committee upon the Bill on Thursday 17 March.[60] Lord Auckland, a supporter of legal uniformity between Ireland and Great Britain, questioned why the Bill should be limited to Ireland.[61] Lord Chancellor Eldon felt that consideration of the measure ought to be postponed: there was no adequate definition of 'chalking' and the House did not have before it sufficient information to allow it to legislate only for Ireland.[62] Information supporting the need for legislation was, however, provided by other speakers. The Archbishop of Dublin said that he did not know whether the incidence of 'chalking' in Great Britain warranted the extension of the proposed measure but assured the House that it was very prevalent in Ireland.[63] Lord Carleton agreed about the necessity for the measure. He informed the House that the Bill had been introduced by the Attorney-General for Ireland into the House of Commons, which, satisfied of its necessity, had passed it, and he assured his peers that the offence which the Bill sought to punish 'prevailed to an alarming degree in Ireland'.[64]

Lord Ellenborough, however, was highly critical of the Bill as it stood. He said that it had been brought before the House without any evidence and that its wording 'abounded with unnecessary phrases and with absurdities'. He was, moreover, of the view that every penal law ought to apply throughout a kingdom and he certainly believed that the Bill should apply to England. He therefore urged its postponement to allow time to consider how this might be effected.[65] The Bill was duly deferred, and shortly after Ellenborough returned with his own proposal for reform in the shape of the Malicious Shooting Bill, which received its first reading on 28 March.[66] The long title of the Bill read:

An Act for the further prevention of malicious shooting, stabbing, cutting, wounding, and poisoning, and also the malicious setting fire to buildings; and also for repealing a certain Act, made in the first year of the late King James the First, intituled, 'An Act to prevent the destroying and murdering of bastard children', and for substituting other provisions in lieu of the same.

The preamble set forth the reasons for the introduction of the Bill but without any express reference to abortion:

Whereas divers cruel and barbarous outrages have been of late wickedly and wantonly committed in divers parts of the United Kingdom of Great Britain and Ireland, upon the persons of divers of His Majesty's subjects. . . . And whereas certain other heinous offences, committed with intent to destroy the lives of His Majesty's subjects by poison, or with intent by burning to destroy or injure the buildings, and other property of His Majesty's subjects, or to prejudice persons who have become insurers of or upon the same, have been of late also frequently committed; but no adequate means have been hitherto provided for the prevention and punishment of such offences. . . .

The Bill comprised two clauses. The first contained the proposed prohibition on abortion:

if any person or persons . . . shall either in England or Ireland wilfully, maliciously, and unlawfully shoot at, or attempt to discharge any loaded fire arms, at any of His Majesty's subjects, or shall . . . stab, cut, wound, or in any manner maim or disable any limb, member, or part of the body whatsoever . . . with intent in so doing, or by means thereof, to murder, or rob, or to main, disfigure, or disable . . . or *shall wilfully, maliciously, and unlawfully administer to, or cause to be administered to or taken by any of His Majesty's subjects, any deadly poison, or other noxious and destructive substance or thing, with intent* such His Majesty's subjects thereby to murder, or *thereby to cause and procure the miscarriage of any woman, then being quick with child;* or shall . . . set fire to any house . . .

they would be guilty of felony, punishable by death without benefit of clergy.

During the first reading of the Bill, Ellenborough declared that the Bill aimed,

to generalize the law with regard to certain penal offences, and to adapt it equally to every part of the united kingdom. Among other provisions, he had introduced several to meet the defects and difficulties that now lay in the way of conviction for several offences of the most criminal nature.[67]

The long title and preamble of the Bill, together with Ellenborough's explanation of its purpose, make it clear that he was focussing not on the creation of new offences but on the removal of inconsistencies from existing ones. Hence, assault with intent to murder, which was only a misdemeanor, was to be made as punishable as assault with intent to rob, which was a capital felony. He remarked: 'the crime surely was more atrocious in the case where it was now least punishable'. By the same reasoning, the administration of poison with intent to murder was to be made capital whether the attempt was successful or not. Another provision, he continued, was directed against abortion and sought to prohibit

administering poisonous drugs to women for the purpose, and with the intent, of procuring abortion, which, at present, is only punishable where actual abortion of the living child is effected.[68]

Again, Ellenborough clearly felt attempted abortion to be equally deserving of punishment, whether the attempt proved successful or not, and his Bill consequently proposed to make the offence consist simply in the intentional administration of the substance rather than the actual procurement of the miscarriage. His proposal had the advantage of facilitating prosecution by relieving the Crown of the burden of proving that the defendant's act had caused the fetus's death, and a medical journal later stated that this was precisely the proposal's objective.[69]

That improved enforcement of the law was a central aim of the Bill is confirmed both by the preamble's reference to the lack of 'adequate means' of prevention and punishment, and by the drafting of the second clause, which sought to alleviate the burden of proof which the statute 21 Jac. I c. 27 had imposed on a mother charged with murdering her bastard child. This Act of 1623 had reversed the common-law presumption of stillbirth and provided that, if a woman concealed the death of her illegitimate issue so that it might not be known whether it had been born alive, she should suffer death for murder unless she could prove stillbirth. However, the sympathy of both judges and juries for defendants prosecuted under this statute led to a divergence between legal theory and practice. Ellenborough wanted to remedy this situation. He sought to relieve judges, who were forced to bend the law by admitting even the most tenuous evidence of stillbirth, of their difficulties in such cases.[70]

The preamble to the second clause refers to the doubts as to the true meaning of the Act of 1623 and notes that 'the same has been found in sundry cases difficult and inconvenient, to be put in practice . . .'. Clause 2 therefore proposed to repeal the Act and to bring the law into line with current practice by enacting a similar piece of legislation qualified by the requirement that the Crown would have to adduce 'probable evidence' that the deceased child had been born alive.

Ellenborough commended the Bill to the House as a measure designed to render the law more consistent and to assimilate the laws of Great Britain and Ireland. He trusted that it would secure all the objectives of the Chalking Bill and effect many desirable amendments to the law relating to murder and fraud in both countries.[71]

Lord Auckland drew the debate to a close by remarking that capital offences were already so numerous that they ought not to be increased without great deliberation. Nevertheless, even he was ready to admit that 'the crime[s] enumerated by the noble and learned Lord called for severe and exemplary punishment'.[72]

Whereas the Chalking Bill had been a limited response to a particular problem, Ellenborough's Bill represented the first attempt to clarify the law relating to offences against the person in a comprehensive manner. It dealt with a greater range of offences and applied to both Ireland and England. That he should select the ill-defined crime of abortion for clarification is understandable. What is less clear is whether he foresaw the ways in which the wording of the Bill appeared to narrow the scope of the offence. Firstly, it is doubtful whether the words 'any person or persons' were sufficiently wide to render the pregnant woman herself liable to prosecution. Secondly, the words 'any deadly poison, or other noxious or destructive substance or thing' would not appear to have prohibited abortion by beating, instrument, physical exertion, manual manipulation, or by a combination of such methods.[73] Thirdly, the words 'wilfully, wantonly and maliciously', which appeared in the Chalking Bill, were replaced by 'wilfully, maliciously and unlawfully', perhaps implying that abortion might be lawful in certain circumstances. In spite of these apparent restrictions of the crime's scope, the abortion provision in cl. 1 would be enacted unamended.

Amendments to the Malicious Shooting Bill. Other parts of Ellenborough's Bill were, however, to undergo significant amendment before its enactment. On 29 April the Bill was considered by a Committee of the Whole House. Although the debate was not officially reported, a brief report does appear in *The Times* of 30 April, to the effect that several amendments moved by the Bill's sponsor had been accepted. The amendments relating to the offence of abortion were the most radical. The long title of the Bill now specifically referred to 'administering things and using means to procure the miscarriage of women', and the preamble now included abortion among the 'heinous offences' which the Bill sought to prohibit. More importantly, a new clause had been added to punish abortion before quickening. It was designed, in the words of its preamble, for cases where 'the woman may not be quick with child at the time, or it may not be proved that she was quick with child . . .'. It provided:

if any person or persons . . . shall wilfully and maliciously administer to, or cause to be administered to, or taken by any woman, any medicines, drug, or other substance or thing whatsoever, or shall use or employ, or cause or procure to be used or employed any instrument or other means whatsoever, with intent thereby to cause or procure the miscarriage of any woman not being, or not being proved to be, quick with child at the time of administering such things or using such means . . .

the offender would be guilty of a misdemeanor punishable at the court's discretion by either a fine, imprisonment, the pillory, whipping, or a combination thereof, or by transportation for a maximum of fourteen years.

This amendment clearly proposed a considerable extension of the scope of the offence. In contrast to cl. 1 it prohibited attempts to procure abortion before quickening, and its prohibition on potional abortion embraced 'any medicines, drug, or other substance or thing whatsoever'. Moreover, the use of 'any instrument or other means whatsoever' was to be proscribed. This created an anomaly in the Bill in that it prohibited instrumental attempts before but not after quickening.[74]

Although the offence of pre-quickening abortion was broader in these respects than that of post-quickening abortion, it was nevertheless regarded as a less serious offence, being classed only as a misdemeanor rather than a felony. This is possibly accounted for by the relative uncertainty inherent in proving attempted abortion in the early stages of pregnancy and the popular belief that abortion procured before quickening did not destroy a human being.

The addition of this new clause indicates that the House paid particular attention to the crime of abortion, and the fact that the drafting of the clause differed materially from that of cl. 1 suggests that someone other than the Bill's sponsor was responsible for its introduction. This possibility is reinforced by the fact that Ellenborough was not given to innovation. Indeed, as both legislator and judge he displayed an extreme conservatism. As Chief Justice of King's Bench between 1802 and 1818 he religiously followed precedent: in *Ashford* v. *Thornton*, for example, he upheld the right to trial by battle.[75] Moreover, had he himself drafted the new clause, the punishment would probably have been capital, as it was for all the offences contained in the first clause. It may have been, therefore, that his concern about the law of abortion was shared, and perhaps even surpassed, elsewhere in the House. Not all the Lords, however, gave unreserved support to the Bill as a whole. Lord Alvanley expressed concern at the number of offences which the Bill proposed to make capital and he trusted that its sponsor would allow it to be recommitted. Ellenborough assured him that he would move its recommitment to ensure that it received 'minute deliberation'.[76]

The Bill was considered on recommitment on 9 May.[77] The offence of pre-quickening abortion was elevated to the status of a felony, and the final clause, dealing with child murder, was radically altered. Henceforth, trials of women for the murder of their bastard issue were to proceed and be governed by the same rules of evidence as applied in other murder trials, though a proviso – which was to be enacted as a fourth section – declared that if it appeared that a woman who had been acquitted on such a charge had 'by secret burying or otherwise' endeavoured to conceal the birth of the child, the court was empowered to imprison her for a maximum of two years.

Again, it seems unlikely that Ellenborough himself designed such a sweeping revision of the law, and perhaps this amendment represents an attempt by the House, or concerned elements within it, to improve the efficacy of the law protecting the child after birth and to safeguard innocent mothers from conviction, thereby complementing the first and second clauses, which sought to ensure the safety of the unborn child and to protect women from hazardous interference. The Bill was read for the first time in the House of Commons on 18 May and on 13 June was committed to a Committee of the Whole House.[78] On 16 June it was passed with minor amendments. Two days later the Lords agreed to the Bill as amended and on 24 June it received the Royal Assent.

Although the Act thoroughly revised the offence of abortion, there is no evidence that Ellenborough intended to depart from its predominant rationale of protecting the fetus.[79] On the contrary, the available evidence points the other way. The abortion provision in cl. 1 was embedded among provisions relating to homicide, and the penalties for these offences were all equally severe. Moreover, if Ellenborough's predominant aim was the protection of women from dangerous interference, why was pregnancy an element of the offence and why, when interference would be hazardous at all stages of gestation, was the offence punishable more severely after the fetus had quickened? Further, the abortion provisions were complemented by the final clause relating to infanticide, and this fortifies the view that the primary aim of these sections was the protection of children. Moreover, Glanville Williams has observed that the Act represents a metaphysical pronouncement by Parliament that the fetus is a human life deserving of protection from the moment of impregnation.[80] Finally, this interpretation of the predominant policy of the Act is reinforced by the fact that Lord Ellenborough was renowned for his strict Christian morality. Contemporaries commended him not only as a wise reformer of the law, but also as 'a [f]earless advocate of religion, and a determined assertor of public and private morals'.[81] All this is not to suggest that the protection of the fetus was the sole aim of the Act, for the statute would simultaneously operate to safeguard women from hazardous attempts at abortion and to relieve many unfortunate mothers from the rigours of 21 Jac. I c. 27.

Just as Ellenborough's proscription of abortion can, at least partly, be understood in terms of his moral philosophy, so can the extension of capital punishment by the Act be appreciated in terms of his philosophy of punishment. He subscribed to Paley's view that the extreme penalty should be provided for many offences, if executed in only a few.[82] With Lord Eldon, he led the Lords in its opposition to Samuel Romilly's campaign to reduce capital punishment. He urged that leniency would encourage crime and maintained that transportation was looked upon as no more than a 'summer's airing in an easy migration to a milder climate'.[83]

Ellenborough largely succeeded in clarifying the law on abortion. However, the fact that he picked this rather than other confused areas of the law for clarification suggests that it was a particular cause of concern. The remainder of this chapter considers why this may have been the case.

The perception of abortion as a growing problem

The fact that both Houses of Parliament supported without any real hesitation the tightening of the legal prohibition on abortion suggests that the pre-existing law was felt to be inadequate to suppress the practice. Although there appears to be no evidence to suggest widespread alarm, either among public or clergy, about an increase in abortion there is at least some evidence that the practice was believed to be widespread. The preamble to the Act refers to all the offences it contains as having been 'of late frequently committed'. Moreover, in 1836 Archer Ryland's *Crown Circuit Companion* attributed the Act's proscription of abortion to the fact that it had been 'of frequent occurrence, and in many instances productive of loss of life not only to the foetus but to the mother . . . .'.[84] Evidence as to the perceived frequency of the crime is also provided by other sources.

In 1799 John Burns, a Glasgow surgeon, wrote that 'drastic purges' were 'too frequently employed' for the purpose of procuring abortion.[85] In the same year an anonymous tract on prostitution declared that it was not possible to calculate the numbers of pregnant women who took reputed abortifacients.[86] Eleven years earlier Dr Samuel Farr had written:

It is to be lamented . . . that whilst this crime, which is practised generally by the most abandoned, *escapes unpunished*, a poor deluded creature, in the case of infant murder, whose shame highly extenuates her guilt, should suffer death. . . .[87]

It is clear, therefore, that at least in certain quarters, abortion was regarded as of frequent occurrence and the common law as having failed to suppress it. Whether this perception was accurate is a difficult question requiring further research. It is noteworthy, however, that one historian, McLaren, has concluded that concern for the protection of maternal health and family welfare from excessive childbearing could have led many to contemplate abortion; that there existed a wide range of techniques from pessaries to potions which were believed to be effective abortifacients, and that the popular belief that the fetus was not alive until quickening allowed women to regard abortion as legitimate.[88] If accurate, this does tend to verify Ellenborough's perception that abortion had been 'of late frequently committed' and to validate the concern which was expressed over its incidence. A perception of abortion as a widespread problem would not, therefore, have been groundless and may help to explain its statutory prohibition in 1803. Interestingly, McLaren also states that the eighteenth century witnessed increasing hostility towards abortion, reflecting an increasing assumption by laymen and doctors of their right to interfere in women's childbearing.[89] Moreover, any disquiet over abortion may well have been exacerbated by eminent medical authorities, who denied any qualitative distinction between life before and after quickening.

The influence of the regular medical practitioner on the Act

In 1803 the 'regular' or educated practitioners of medicine lacked the centralised organisation necessary to exercise a direct professional influence on the restriction of the law against abortion. Although local medical societies existed towards the end of the eighteenth century, and although the General Pharmaceutical Society of Great Britain was formed as early as 1794, and can be regarded as marking the beginning of the movement for medical reform, the Provincial Medical and Surgical Association (which became the British Medical Association in 1855) was not formed until 1832. This did not, however, prevent some regulars from openly criticising the popular belief that human life did not begin until quickening, and calling for the suppression of irregulars.

The scientific extension of legal principle. While Ellenborough's statutory declaration of the criminality of abortion after quickening was partly attributable to the lawyer's concern for clarity in the law, the criminalisation of pre-quickening abortion may partly have been attributable to the medical man's concern that fetal life should be protected by the law at all stages of gestation.

In the eighteenth century, the phenomenon of generation was being approached on an increasingly scientific basis, as was medicine generally. According to popular opinion, the fetus was animated or came to life at some stage after the beginning of pregnancy but this belief was challenged in the latter half of the eighteenth century by Samuel Farr, M.D. In 1788, his *Elements of Medical Jurisprudence* (an abridged translation of the *Elementa Medicinae Forensis* published by Faselius in 1767) appeared. This first English work on medical jurisprudence advocated the theory of immediate as opposed to mediate animation. Farr wrote:

life begins . . . immediately after conception. Hence those seem to err, 1st. who would persuade us, that the foetus acquires life when it is so particularly active, that the mother becomes sensible of its motions. 2d. Those who think that life does not begin till the seventh or the fourteenth day, or even till a month after conception. And 3d. Those who suppose that a foetus, as long as it continues in the womb, where it does not breathe, cannot be called a living animal.[90]

With specific reference to the abortion of embryos he wrote:

as such beings might live, and become of use to mankind, and as they may be supposed from the time indeed of conception, to be living animated beings, there is no doubt but the destruction of them ought to be considered as a capital crime.[91]

His objection that whereas the depraved mother guilty of abortion escaped punishment, the hapless mother guilty of infanticide was executed, has been noted above.[92] This objection was echoed in a paper written by the eminent William Hunter M.D., Physician Extraordinary to the Queen, which was read in July 1783.[93] In this influential paper, entitled 'On the uncertainty of the signs of murder in the case of bastard children', Hunter argued powerfully in mitigation of most acts of child murder. In the majority of cases, he maintained, the mother was overcome by an 'unconquerable sense of shame'[94] and was 'overwhelmed with terror and despair'.[95] He roundly criticised as unjust the Act of 1623 for condemning women to death on inadequate evidence, and he described vividly the type of situation in which they might be falsely accused.

Moreover, the very year which saw the repeal of this statute by Ellenborough's Act also witnessed the publication of Dr Thomas Percival's celebrated work on medical ethics, in which the author echoed Hunter's criticism. 'This law', he wrote, 'though humane in its principle, is much too severe in its construction'.[96] No less significantly, he condemned abortion as homicide and berated the popular view, albeit rooted in antiquity, that the fetus was merely *pars viscerum matris*:

> false it must be deemed, since no female can be privileged to injure her own bowels, much less the foetus, which is now well known to constitute no part of them. To extinguish the first spark of life is a crime of the same nature, both against our Maker and society, as to destroy an infant, a child, or a man; these regular and successive stages of existence being the ordinances of God, subject alone to his divine will, and appointed by sovereign wisdom and goodness as the exclusive means of preserving the race, and multiplying the enjoyments of mankind.[97]

Abortion and quackery. The intensity of the disapprobation of abortion by such regulars may have been influenced by the practice of abortion by their irregular competitors such as midwives. Although it should be remembered that the distinction between the two types of practitioner is not always clear ('at each end of the spectrum the two are easily distinguished; in the centre they mingle imperceptibly'[98]), surveys carried out by the societies formed by regulars to promote their interests showed irregular practice to be widespread. It appears that the bulk of surgeons and apothecaries, who sought greater recognition, were alarmed at its extent.[99] Abortion may well have been one aspect of irregular practice. McLaren concludes, from his study of quack literature in the eighteenth century, that, although the vast majority of abortions at that time were self-induced, professional abortionists existed[100] and advertised their services.[101] If so, this would have provided regulars with an added incentive to support the statutory restriction of the law in 1803.

Conclusion

This chapter has sought to give an account of the enactment of Lord Ellenborough's Act against the background of the pre-existing law. The first part of the chapter contended, contrary to the thesis of Professor Means, that abortion was an offence known to the common law. Section 1.2 indicated that the statute broadened the

offence by criminalising pre-quickening abortion and it also out-
lined three possible reasons for its enactment, namely: clarification
of the law; perception of abortion as a social problem; and criticism
by regular medical practitioners of the significance attached to
quickening. It also underlined the key role of Lord Ellenborough in
translating these reasons for reform into a piece of legislation which
appropriately bears his name. Finally, by suggesting the influence
and interests of the emerging medical profession, the chapter
furnishes a perspective for the analysis of subsequent nineteenth-
century legislation regulating abortion, which will be considered in
the next chapter.

2

Anti-abortion legislation 1803–1861 and medical influence thereon

This chapter considers the scope of Lord Ellenborough's Act and its successors, which were enacted in 1828, 1837 and 1861, and examines their prohibition of abortion in the light of contemporary medical opinion.

2.1 Anti-abortion legislation 1803–1861

Lord Ellenborough's Act was, it will be recalled, severe. Section 1 punished with death 'any person or persons' who administered 'any deadly poison, or other noxious and destructive substance or thing' with intent to procure the miscarriage of 'any woman, then being quick with child'. Section 2 went further and punished, with a variety of non-capital penalties, 'any person or persons' who administered 'any medicines, drug, or other substance or thing whatsoever' or who used 'any instrument or other means whatsoever, with intent thereby to cause or procure the miscarriage of any woman not being, or not being proved to be, quick with child at the time of administering such things or using such means . . . .'. Only s. 2, therefore, punished instrumental attempts. This anomaly was removed by the next statute to deal with abortion, Lord Lansdowne's Act 1828.[1] Section 13 of the Act, which replaced ss. 1 and 2 of Ellenborough's Act, extended the prohibition on post-quickening abortion to include attempts involving 'any instrument or other means whatsoever'. Moreover, the strict penalties for abortion, whether before or after quickening, remained substantially unchanged, although in the case of the latter the accused was no longer deprived of benefit of clergy and, on conviction for the former, the court could no longer fine or condemn to the pillory. Capital punishment for post-quickening abortion was not repealed until the successor to Lansdowne's Act, the Offences Against the

Person Act (O.A.P.A.) 1837.[2] This Act, however, not only abolished the death penalty for abortion; it also abrogated the long-standing distinction between pre- and post-quickening interference. Section 6 provided:

whosoever, with intent to procure the miscarriage of any woman, shall unlawfully administer to her or cause to be taken by her any poison or other noxious thing, or shall unlawfully use any instrument or other means whatsoever with the like intent, shall be guilty of felony, and being convicted thereof shall be liable, at the discretion of the court, to be transported beyond the seas for the term of his or her natural life, or for any term not less than fifteen years, or to be imprisoned for any term not exceeding three years.

Clearly, although the offence was no longer capital, the punishment was far from lenient.[3] This remained the case in 1861, when the next O.A.P.A. updated the offence to its present form. Under s. 58, abortion is punishable by a maximum of life imprisonment. Further, the section explicitly provides that a woman, if pregnant, can incur liability for attempted self-abortion. The Act also goes beyond its predecessor by creating, in the form of s. 59, the offence, punishable with five years of imprisonment, of obtaining or supplying means knowing that they are intended to be used contrary to s. 58.[4]

It is evident, therefore, that from 1803 to 1861 the statutory offence of abortion was gradually extended and attracted consistently severe punishment. Attempted abortion after quickening was, between 1803 and 1837, punishable by death. So too was any felonious attempt which resulted in the woman's death.

2.2 The influence of medical opinion on the law 1803–1861

The above overview of the law of abortion in this period reveals the sweeping and severe nature of the English legislation. What accounts for these characteristics? It is suggested below that the gradual extension of the law and its persistent severity can be seen not only as a reflection of the harshness of the contemporary criminal code as a whole but also as a response to proposals for reform, advanced by the emerging medical profession, which were incorporated into a programme of consolidation of the criminal law. The first statute to materialise as a result of this drive to rationalise the law was Lord Ellenborough's Act, whose prohibition of abortion followed condemnation of the practice by medical men. When this Act's successors were being enacted, medical practitioners were becoming more organised and consequently increasingly capable of exerting influence on the framing of the law through the expression of expert, professional opinion.

Lord Lansdowne's Act 1828

The most significant amendment to the abortion law made by this Act was, it will be recalled, the prohibition of instrumental abortion after quickening. However, this amendment was not the sole purpose of the Act. Its sponsor, the Marquis of Lansdowne, a former Home Secretary, explained on second reading that his Bill was designed to simplify the law by consolidating and amending some fifty-six statutes. Like Ellenborough before him, he sought to make the law more logical and consistent. With respect to abortion he proposed,

to apply the same punishment for administering poison, or using any instrument to procure abortion in a woman found not to be quick with child, as when the woman was quick with child.[5]

The law as it stood, he continued, distinguished between the two cases.[6] This proposal seems to express a desire to abrogate the distinction based upon quickening. However, in view of the survival of this distinction in s. 13 of the Act, Lansdowne should perhaps be interpreted as expressing an intention to extend the prohibition on the use of instruments to interference after quickening. As this clause was discussed neither in Committee[7] nor on third reading,[8] the Parliamentary reports fail to clarify this ambiguity.

The Bill was steered through the Commons by Mr Peel, who echoed Lansdowne's underlying aim. As the laws stood, he declared, they were 'obscure and intricate', and the aim of the proposed Bill was to simplify and clarify them.[9] He added that the amendments proposed by the Bill had been considered desirable for some years by persons whose knowledge of the subject, and experience, entitled their opinions to respect.[10] Did these authoritative individuals include medical men? There is some evidence that they may well have done. As early as 1810, Ellenborough's Act was criticised by the *Edinburgh Medical and Surgical Journal* for failing to prohibit instrumental abortion after quickening, while punishing with death the use of potional means, which were less effective. The criticism followed the report of a trial in which this lacuna had resulted in an acquittal, and ran:

we cannot avoid remarking the apparent inconsistency of the law of England, in having no statute to punish its actual perpetration by the only certain means of effecting it, whilst it punishes by death, without benefit of clergy, the attempting it by means which are very seldom effectual.[11]

This criticism was recalled in an article on criminal law published in the *Legal Examiner* for 1832–1833, which is, moreover, suggestive of the influence of medical opinion. Having described the lacuna as 'remarkable', the journal continued:

Now medical men found great fault with this statute, on the ground that medicines administered internally, rarely produced abortion, when the child is what is vulgarly called quickened. But the effect can be infallibly secured by instruments.[12]

In the light of such criticism, the removal of the anomaly in 1828 is understandable. Moreover, the influence of medical opinion seems even more apparent in the amendment of the abortion law by this Act's successor.

The Offences Against the Person Act 1837

The amendment of the abortion law effected by this Act was more radical. It abolished both the distinction between interference before and after quickening and the capital penalty affixed to the latter. As with the Acts of 1803 and 1828, the parliamentary debates disclose an intention to consolidate the law relating to offences against the person. They also reveal a concern to reduce the number of capital felonies. This concern is hardly surprising in the light of the report of the Criminal Law Commissioners in 1836, which stated that the provision of the death penalty for extensive classes of offences – often with little moral resemblance – rendered convictions difficult to secure and therefore weakened its deterrent effect.[13] In 1837 they reported their proposals to reduce capital punishment to the Home Secretary, Lord John Russell.[14] With specific reference to ss. 11–13 of Lansdowne's Act, they pointed out that the law was constantly frustrated by the reluctance of prosecutors to prefer a capital charge and of juries to convict, and by the readiness of the judges to interpret the law in the defendant's favour.[15] Capital punishment was, in other words, proving more of a hindrance than a help to conviction for these offences. As for s. 13, the Commissioners recommended not only a reduction of the prescribed punishment but also the abolition of the quickening distinction. They wrote that this would remove an evidential difficulty and obviate discussion of a question which was inevitably surrounded by considerable doubt.[16]

The doubt arose because the legal definition of quickening had been equated with its definition in medicine, which was based on the woman's first perception of the movement of the fetus.[17] Such a subjective criterion could do little to facilitate the onerous task of prosecution. The Commissioners therefore proposed the following replacement for s. 13:

Whosoever, with intent to procure the miscarriage of any pregnant woman, shall unlawfully administer to her, or cause to be taken by her, any poison or other noxious thing, or shall unlawfully use any instrument or other means whatsoever, with the like intent . . .

should be liable to transportation for not less than fifteen years, or imprisonment for a maximum of ten years and a minimum of five.[18]

Russell followed the Commissioner's proposal in relation to abortion and the O.A.P. Bill reproduced their draft section with the minor change that the maximum period of imprisonment was reduced to five years.[19] This, along with several other reforming Bills, was introduced into the House of Lords by Lord Denman. On second reading, he said that the great underlying principle was that crime should be visited with certain punishment.[20] The Bills were designed to meet the criticism that the existing law failed to recognise moral gradations between offences,[21] and they sought to make the criminal law as simple and as lenient as possible.[22] Lord Lyndhurst lent his support to the Bills, although he pointed to several inconsistencies, one of which related to abortion. He said that as the O.A.P. Bill stood,

it must be proved, to constitute the offence, that the woman was actually pregnant at the time; but surely it would be admitted, that if the man thought she was with child, and administered the drugs with the view to procure abortion, the moral guilt of the offence was the same.[23]

The report continues: 'He did not, however, believe that this change was intentionally made. It occurred *per incuriam*'.[24] In fact, the change was probably made in full knowledge of the authorities and was, probably, an accurate statement of the existing law. Pregnancy was not only an essential ingredient of post-quickening abortion but, after *R.* v. *Scudder* (1828),[25] it also had to be proved when pre-quickening interference was alleged. Nevertheless, Lyndhurst's objection prevailed and the requirement of pregnancy was dropped. Another amendment was the reduction of the penalty of imprisonment from five years to three.[26]

As enacted the Bill was shorter than Lansdowne's, comprising only thirteen as opposed to thirty-eight sections, but its effect on the law of abortion was more radical: s. 6 of the Act not only abolished the quickening distinction but replaced the death penalty with a maximum punishment of transportation for life, or three years' imprisonment. These amendments reflect the general objective of the Bill to render the law relating to offences against the person simpler and more lenient, and thereby to facilitate its enforcement. Is there any evidence that medical opinion influenced these changes?

A survey of the leading contemporary works on both obstetrics and medical jurisprudence[27] shows that none accepted as scientifically sound the popular belief that quickening marked the inception of fetal life. Some went further and expressly called for reform of the law relating to abortion (and to the reprieve of pregnant women from execution), which had long enshrined this belief.

As early as 1794, Dr Denman (father of the Lord Chief Justice who steered the Bill of 1837 through the House of Lords, see p. 30) wrote:

it is not now suspected that there is any difference between the aboriginal life of the child, and that which it possesses at any period of pregnancy, though there may be alteration in the proofs of its existence, by the enlargement of its size, and the acquisition of greater strength.[28]

In 1799, Burns stated that the fetus was alive before quickening which, for him, merely marked the acquisition of action by its voluntary muscles.[29] Other understandings of the phenomenon of quickening were, however, evident in later medical writings. In 1810, for example, the *Edinburgh Medical and Surgical Journal* announced: 'During no period of gestation does any sudden revolution or change take place; and what is called quickening, is merely the motions of the child becoming sensible to the mother'.[30] In the same year, an alternative explanation of the phenomenon was put forward. It was suggested that the sensation experienced by the mother might be due not to fetal motion but to a sudden rising of the uterus from the pelvic to the abdominal cavity.[31] This view enjoyed the support of such an eminent authority as Dr Paris.[32]

Whichever account was the more accurate, both undermined the significance which lay opinion and the law ascribed to quickening. Some medical men were moved to point this out and criticised the statutes of 1803 and 1828 for the importance they attached to a phenomenon whose physiological and moral significance had been exploded by the advance of medical science. In 1836 Professor Thomson, a leading authority on medical jurisprudence, said that the significance of quickening in Ellenborough's Act was 'extraordinary' in view of the late period at which the Act was passed and represented 'a singular instance of the difficulty of rooting out prejudice from the mind . . .'.[33] He concluded:

This distinction with respect to the periods in which criminal abortion is effected, demonstrates, very strongly, the necessity of lawyers and statesmen consulting medical men, prior to framing Acts which involve physiological questions.[34]

Thomson echoed other authorities in his criticism of the law. Obstetricians Charles Severn and Michael Ryan both supported reform of the law to bring it into line with advances in medical knowledge. Referring in 1831 to s. 13 of Lansdowne's Act, Severn wrote: 'the difference which the law makes in the nature of and punishment awarded to crimes involving precisely the same degree of moral turpitude, is arbitrary and unfounded . . .'.[35] He continued that the child was not viable before quickening nor for some months afterwards and yet was as truly quick or living before its movements were perceived by the mother as at the sixth or seventh month of gestation. Its destruction at any stage was, therefore, murder, and he expressed the belief that an 'enlightened legislature' would probably remedy the defect in the law.[36] Commenting upon the same section Dr Ryan was even more critical. In 1836, his text on legal medicine stated that, while the aim of the section was 'humane and excellent', it was based on erroneous physiological principles and abounded with absurdities: it enacted that the fetus was not alive until quickening, when in fact its life began at conception.[37] Here he echoed Beck, who maintained that both reason and physiology showed the fetus to be alive from that moment and who had consequently declared that laws which punished early abortion with less severity were both immoral and unjust.[38]

The disappearance of the word quickening from the law of abortion in 1837 suggests that the exhortations of obstetricians such as Severn and medico-legal authorities such as Thomson did not go unheeded. That their opinions penetrated legal circles is revealed by an article in the *Legal Examiner* for 1832 in which regret was expressed that Lansdowne's Act had preserved the 'absurd distinction' based on quickening.[39] It declared:

It is consonant neither with philosophy nor justice, for when we have ascertained that the destruction of life is equal in both cases, how palpably absurd it is to punish one with death, the other only with transportation.[40]

The Offences Against the Person Act 1861
It will be recalled that ss. 58 and 59 of the O.A.P.A. 1861 further extended the offence of abortion. The three innovatory features of these sections were the confirmation of the ruling *R. v. Goodhall*[41] (1846) that pregnancy was not a necessary element of the offence when committed by a third party; the express prohibition of attempted self-abortion by a pregnant woman; and finally, the creation of a new statutory misdemeanor of obtaining or supplying means knowing that they are intended to be used to procure miscarriage. How much were these changes due to the process of consolidation and how much to the influence of medical opinion?

The amendment of the law which dispensed with the need to prove pregnancy was undoubtedly influenced by the process of consolidation. In 1846 the Commissioners for Revising and Consolidating the Criminal Law, who had been appointed the previous year, produced their second report.[42] It contained a draft consolidation Bill, and article 15 of its seventh section proposed to extend the law to punish attempts whether or not the woman was with child.[43] The commentary upon the amendment explained its rationale:

The old law required that the woman should be 'quick with child.' The latest Act upon the subject omits these words. Some doubt prevails on the point, whether under the present law it is not necessary that the woman should be pregnant. It is desirable to remove this doubt. . . .[44]

Perhaps the Commissioners were unaware of the fact that the word 'pregnant' had been dropped from the original O.A.P. Bill of 1837 at the instigation of Lord Lyndhurst, which implied that the legislature did not intend pregnancy to be an ingredient of the offence.[45] If they were unaware of this significant amendment, the available case law on the interpretation of the resulting Act would have done little to clarify the ambiguity: decisions went both ways.[46]

Turning to the second significant aspect of this section, namely its express prohibition of attempts by a pregnant woman herself to procure her own miscarriage, there is also evidence to suggest that this innovation resulted from the work of the Commissioners. Article 15 of their draft Bill provided the model for this prohibition:

Every woman being with child, who, with intent to procure her own miscarriage, shall maliciously administer to herself any poison or other noxious thing, or use any instrument or other means whatsoever . . .

would be guilty of an offence.[47] This part of Article 15 is reproduced, almost word for word, in s. 58. This accretion to the law of abortion would, therefore, also appear to be attributable to uncertainty, this time concerning the liability of the woman who attempted to abort herself. This uncertainty had been evident in a case decided only five years before the passage of the 1861 Act.[48] The statutory specification of her liability would clarify the law. Nor would this clarification necessarily represent a radical amendment of the law: it will be recalled that self-abortion was an offence at common law.[49] As none of the statutes before 1861 dealt expressly with the liability of the woman, this common-law liability presumably survived. Consequently, s. 58 was, at least in this respect, more akin to clarification than amendment. This may also help to account for the limitation of the offence to women who were in fact pregnant for, as Pollock C.B. stated in 1857: 'A woman taking a drug to procure abortion may be guilty of an offence at common law, but not so if she were not pregnant at the time'.[50] Other factors which may have resulted in this apparent inconsistency in the section include the greater difficulties of proof surrounding attempted self-abortion and the fact that the non-pregnant woman who attempted to abort herself could only harm herself, not another.

As for the third and most striking extension of the abortion law by the 1861 Act, namely the statutory prohibition of supplying or obtaining the means of abortion, the question again arises whether it is explicable in terms of the process of clarification. Section 59 was modelled on a provision contained in the unsuccessful O.A.P. Bill 1859,[51] which was itself a product of the process of consolidation. Moreover, the enactment of s. 59 can at least partly be understood as an attempt to clarify the law relating to the supply of abortifacient means, which recent case law had shown to be unclear. Although in 1857 it had been decided in *R. v. Wilson*[52] that one who knowingly supplied a noxious substance to a woman who then took it to procure miscarriage could be convicted of causing a substance to be taken,[53] it was by no means clear that this applied to instrumental means. Further, the existing law neither prohibited the procurement of means by the woman or a third party nor did it cover the case where the woman refrained from using means which had been supplied. Finally, the new offence would provide an alternative to a charge of homicide where the means supplied proved fatal.[54]

Granted that the above three amendments effected by ss. 58 and 59 can be understood as products of the process of clarification and amendment initiated by Ellenborough's Act in 1803, the question remains whether the form and enactment of these sections were at all influenced by medical opinion. The evidence suggests that medical opinion played a significant role in influencing the amendments themselves and the general clamp-down on abortion which they represent.

Each of the amendments will be analysed from this perspective. This analysis will suggest, firstly, the impact of medical opinion on the restriction of the law from 1803 to 1861 and, secondly, that this opinion was inspired by a concern for the protection of fetal (and maybe maternal) life and the furtherance of professional interests.

Medical concern over maternal mortality and morbidity. Section 58 was the first statutory provision unequivocally to prohibit attempted abortion on pregnant and non-pregnant women alike. Such a prohibition not only relieves the prosecution of the burdensome task of proving pregnancy but also protects women, pregnant or not, from potential danger. This may have been one of the objectives of the legislation. Significantly, the hazards of attempted abortion were continually stressed by medical and medico-legal authorities from before the enactment of Ellenborough's Act.

Writing as early as 1799, John Burns stressed the particular dangers associated with the use of purgatives during pregnancy.[55] Fifteen years later his warning was repeated.[56] He wrote that, although purgatives were very often taken to produce abortion, when abortion did follow, the mother could seldom survive.[57]

Similarly, Severn wrote that when, unusually, abortion was successfully effected, 'the mother most frequently is involved in the ruin, and falls a miserable victim to her own execrable and heartless depravity'.[58] Medical opinion continued to warn of the dangers of maternal mortality and morbidity from abortion right up to the enactment of ss. 58 and 59. Writing in 1857, Dr William Hinds concluded that abortion was sometimes fatal, and often associated with severe, if not permanent, injury.[59]

Medico-legal authorities were no less cautionary. In 1815 O. W. Bartley warned that attempted abortion often proved suicidal.[60] Underlining the particular hazards of instrumental attempts, he cited a case where a woman had fallen victim to an abortionist who had introduced a stiletto, and added:

Every woman who attempts to promote abortion, does it at the hazard of her life; if this were generally known it would in all probability deter them from such a proceeding, except that they are in a state of consummate depravity.[61]

The following year, the 'father' of medical jurisprudence, George Male, listed several methods and stressed that none was safe:

Abortion may be procured by violent means, as blows on the abdomen, stimulating the uterus into action, or causing inflammation or profuse haemorrhage, or by the introduction of sharp instruments into the uterus itself, by means of which, the membranes are ruptured; and if the operator is unskilled, the head of the child is so much wounded as to occasion its death: the mother, also, generally falls a sacrifice, as this crime is usually committed by ignorant people, who, directing the instrument improperly, wound the uterus.

He continued that certain medicines taken directly into the stomach would also often cause abortion, but warned that there was no drug which would induce miscarriage in those not predisposed to it without acting violently on their system and probably endangering their lives.[62] He was echoed in 1821 by John Gordon Smith who wrote that in general abortion produced ill-health and suffering and that attempted abortion often succeeded only in killing the mother.[63] In 1825, Theodric Beck's text[64] provided a thorough treatment of both the methods of abortion and their dangers. Beck classified the methods as 'general' and 'local'; the former, such as venesection, acting on the woman's constitution and the latter, such as the introduction of instruments, on the uterus itself.[65] With all these methods, he stressed, the life of the mother was as endangered as that of the child.[66] In short, he wrote that all methods were uncertain, always endangered the life of the mother, and sometimes proved fatal to her and not to the child.[67]

Similarly, in 1836 Ryan's work stated that there was no medicine or abortive means which produced abortion and nothing but abortion, and which did not endanger the lives of both mother and infant.[68] Moreover, the use of mechanical means, either to irritate the cervix uteri or to pierce the fetal membranes, bore out the truth of the aphorism *Saepe, suos utero quae necat, ipsa perit.*[69]

In the same year, Professor Thomson reiterated his colleagues' view that if drastic medicines were used to procure abortion, they would be as likely to destroy the mother as the fetus.[70] Moreover, mechanical means, which he believed to be as popular as drugs, also exposed the woman to as much danger as the child.[71]

In 1844 A. S. Taylor, one of the most distinguished nineteenth-century authorities on legal medicine, added the weight of his opinion to the view that mechanical means generally proved fatal, at least in the hands of unskilled operators, though he conceded that they were more effective than medicinal means.[72] The latter, however, he believed to be more popular but he pointed out that on the rare occasions they had proved successful it was generally at the expense of the mother's life.[73]

The consensus of medical and medico-legal opinion from the turn of the century to the enactment of ss. 58 and 59 was, therefore, that the induction of abortion, whether by drugs or instruments, was a hazardous procedure involving a high risk of mortality and morbidity and a low possibility of success. There is no reason to believe that those in legal and legislative circles were unaware of this. Indeed, in one case Coleridge J. (as he then was) specifically referred to Taylor's opinion on the dangers of abortion.[74] Moreover, the *Legal Examiner* published an article in 1832 which reveals not only that the belief that abortion threatened the woman's life had filtered outside medical circles, but also that it was believed to help to explain the statutory prohibition of the practice. The article declared that it was confirmed by every writer on medical jurisprudence that abortion always exposed the woman to imminent danger, and that it therefore followed that abortion should be illegal.[75] It continued that even if the fetus were regarded as having a separate existence this argument was unaffected:

The reason assigned for the punishment of abortion is not that, thereby an embryo human being is destroyed, but that it rarely or never can be [e]ffected by drugs without the sacrifice of the mother's life.[76]

This view, though somewhat qualified elsewhere in the article,[77] exaggerates the solicitude of the law for the safety of the woman at the expense of its concern to protect the fetus. If the law regarded the woman as the victim of the offence, why did it prohibit self-abortion?

Medical concern for fetal life. Apart from jeopardising the life of the mother attempted abortion directly threatened the fetus. Section 58 expressly prohibited attempted self-abortion by a pregnant woman. This offence, it will be recalled, was known to the common law and, as Chapter 1 concluded, the primary aim of the law was the protection of fetal life, even to the extent of punishing the woman who attempted to procure her miscarriage unaided.[78] Is there any evidence that this concern to safeguard fetal life, which culminated in s. 58, was influenced by medical opinion?

Significantly, medical men throughout this period continued to berate abortion as an evil indistinguishable from infanticide and calling for severe punishment. They invoked their scientific knowledge, enhanced by advances such as the discovery of the ovum in 1827,[79] to support their contention that the destruction of the fetus at any stage of pregnancy was immoral and should be prohibited by law.

In 1807, Burns's work on abortion expressed a representative view: 'Whoever prevents life from continuing, until it arrive at perfection, is certainly as culpable as if he had taken it away after that had been accomplished'.[80] Similarly, Severn wrote in 1831 that abortion was a 'detestable species of murder' and declared: 'abortion wilfully produced is equally abhorrent to morality, at whatever period of gestation'.[81] The immorality of abortion was asserted with no less vigour by medico-legal experts. In 1815 Bartley asserted his conviction that the life of the embryo began at the moment of impregnation.[82] He added: 'There are in the catalogue of human vices, few more heinous . . . so heinous that the utmost power of exaggeration cannot add to its deformity. It is murder . . .'.[83] He concluded that even if a woman and her accomplice failed in their attempt to procure her abortion, they should both be liable to a charge of murder, for it was an 'unnatural crime' and could not be viewed, even by the most abandoned, without horror.[84] Shortly after, Male joined in the condemnation of abortion at any stage of gestation. Rejecting the popular view that fetal life began at quickening, he wrote: 'it is probable that the foetus is animated at the moment of conception, and the crime committed then, is morally as great as at any other period of pregnancy'.[85] Similarly, in 1821 John Gordon Smith criticised abortion on the ground that it accomplished the destruction of a human being.[86] The chorus of condemnation included the authoritative voice of Beck. Citing Dr Farr, his text stated in 1825 that abortion, whether before or after quickening, could be considered 'no less than murder'.[87] Ryan concurred. In 1836, the chapter on abortion in his text opened:

Abortion is justly considered a heinous crime – as it is the murder of the foetus in the womb, or in other words, of a human being.[88]

He concluded:

I therefore completely agree with Pervical, Beck, and almost the whole profession, that embryocide and foeticide ought to be equally punished with death.[89]

The O.A.P.A. 1837 repealed the death penalty for the offence but nevertheless followed medical and medico-legal opinion in abolishing the quickening distinction (which perhaps suggests that such opinion was more influential when it was perceived to relate to an area in which medical expertise was more relevant). Medical opinion continued to condemn abortion after 1837 and, interestingly, some practitioners expressly criticised self-abortion. In 1848 Dr Radford wrote that self-abortion was possible; condemned the woman who effected it as entertaining worse feelings for her offspring than the lowest animal; and called for legislation to prohibit it.[90] Abortion concerned such regular practitioners, however, not only because they regarded it as a threat to female and fetal safety but also because it provided a source of employment for their irregular competitors.

Professional concern over unprofessional practice. The above expressions of concern for both fetal and maternal life, emanating as they did from the leading medical and medico-legal authorities of the day, could only have encouraged the enactment of the anti-abortion legislation from 1803 to 1861 and, in particular, the extension of the offence to self-abortion by pregnant women and to attempts upon non-pregnant women. Moreover, they may also help to explain the singular severity of the law. It remains, however, to consider whether the most striking of the three amendments made in 1861 – the creation of s. 59 – was also influenced by the expression of professional concern.

There is substantial evidence that medical men were concerned not only for the welfare of the potential victims of abortion but also to further the process of establishing and consolidating their status as a profession. This process, which will be described in the final chapter, could only have been hindered by abortion, which provided an outlet for irregular practitioners such as herbalists and midwives. By turning away women seeking abortion, the regulars risked driving them to their less qualified yet more accommodating competitors, perhaps permanently. Increasingly restrictive legislation on abortion and on the obtaining and supplying of abortifacient means would serve not only to safeguard fetal and female life, but would also hinder irregulars from capitalising on the demand for a service which ethical precepts prevented the regulars from satisfying.

The evidence which indicates that professional condemnation of abortion was at least partly self-interested is two-fold. Firstly, the condemnation of abortion and of the trade in abortifacients was often linked – increasingly so around 1861 – with the failure of the legislature to proscribe unqualified practice. Secondly, there is evidence which casts doubt on the absoluteness of the regulars' respect for fetal life. Some evidence, which will be presented in Chapter 3, reveals that the destruction of the fetus, both before and even during birth, was condoned by the bulk of regulars when it was considered to be medically indicated. Other evidence reveals that some regulars were prepared to act unethically and to destroy the fetus for non-medical reasons.[91] For the present, it is proposed to consider the evidence which indicates that regulars, perceiving a demand for abortion, were concerned that patients might be lost to unqualified competitors unless strict laws were enacted to suppress the practice. That medical men perceived a demand for abortion is evident from their medical and medico-legal texts, which suggest that many women regarded abortion as morally acceptable – at least before quickening – and were unaware that it was a serious criminal offence.

In declaring that abortion was an increasing problem before 1861, medical men bemoaned the reluctance of many women to accord due respect to fetal life, at least before they had experienced quickening. In 1807 Burns's work on abortion declared: 'many people at least pretend to view attempts to excite abortion as different from murder, upon the principle that the embryo is not possessed of life'.[92] Similarly, eight years later Bartley wrote that it had been too generally believed, especially among the 'uninformed and ignorant', that life only began when the embryo became a fetus.[93]

One explanation for this differential evaluation of human life was advanced by Hutchinson, who pointed out that until the mother experienced the sensation of quickening, she did not regard the fetus as human life. He argued that human affections were influenced by sensory impressions and applied this reasoning to the mother's evaluation of the unborn child:

the foetus in the womb has never made such impressions on the mother; and hence it is often found, that a woman of the best moral dispositions has but little tender affection for her infant until she has contemplated it for some time, or until she has been suckled by it.[94]

This low estimation of fetal life was, moreover, exacerbated by the dangers to which it was exposed by the process of birth.[95]

Regulars' texts also claimed that many women believed that abortion was not even criminal. Dr Ryan declared:

The general opinion now entertained by those unacquainted with physiology is that the foetus is not alive until after quickening, that is, not until it stirs in the mother's womb; and therefore that it is no crime, according to popular inference, to cause abortion before quickening.[96]

He described two recent cases in which women had applied to him for abortion and had expressed such a belief.[97] Again, in 1846 Taylor's *Manual of Medical Jurisprudence*, referring to potional abortion, stated that it could not be doubted that the crime was very frequent, adding: 'Applications are continually made to druggists by the lower classes for drugs for this purpose. The applicants appear to have no idea of the criminality of the act'.[98] Similarly, in 1848 Dr Thomas Radford objected that the offence was not regarded as highly criminal as its heinousness deserved, and he maintained that this 'mischievous opinion' had partly, if not entirely, arisen from a mistaken view of the vital condition of the embryo. He urged: 'Penal laws against this crime exist, but do not prevent its commission. In order to render them effectually preventive, they should be consistently framed, and based on justice'.[99] In 1857, Dr Hinds claimed that ignorance of the law was not confined to the lower orders: even respectable people who sought abortion from medical men seemed 'astonished when made aware of the highly felonious nature of the purpose and agency they seek'.[100]

If they believed that there was common ignorance of the criminality of abortion and moral acceptance of the practice in certain quarters, particularly before quickening, it is hardly surprising that medical men should have perceived abortion as a widespread problem. This perception is particularly evident in the contributions to medical journals around the middle of the century, which confirm that they regarded it as very prevalent. In 1844 a practitioner contributing to the forerunner of the *British Medical Journal* wrote that the crime was not only 'constantly occurring' but was on the increase.[101] Again, in another journal, a comment appended to a report of an abortion trial at Nottingham Assizes declared that there was a 'very general impression' in that town that 'the grave crime . . . has long been, and is, committed . . . to a very great extent and that numerous deaths from it have recently occurred'.[102] In 1848 Dr Radford observed that 'diabolical acts' involving the destruction of children before and after birth were 'perpetrated to a great extent' in contemporary England.[103] In the following year, Taylor's *Manual* stated of instrumental abortion: 'There is every reason to believe that this crime is very frequent; but its perpetration is secret'.[104]

A growing concern among regulars over the practice of illegal abortion in the decade preceding the enactment of ss. 58 and 59 is suggested by successive editions of Taylor's works. In the first edition of his *Manual*, published five years before the third edition in which the above comment appeared, he had rejected the allegation made by a French obstetrician, Devergie, that English midwives earned a living from the use of instruments designed to puncture the fetal membranes.[105] Yet by 1849 he had, as the quotation reveals, somewhat modified his opinion. Five years later, he had largely conceded Devergie's point:

Devergie speaks of such instruments being well known in England, and of English midwives deriving a living from the practice of this crime. . . . Although this must be regarded as exaggerated statement, it cannot be denied that within the last few years many cases have transpired which show that the crime is frequently perpetrated by persons who basely derive a profit from the practice; and for one case that comes to light probably a dozen are effectually concealed.[106]

In this decade, too, the voice of the medical press calling for the legislature to eradicate both the growing practice of abortion and irregular practice generally became more strident. In 1853, an editorial in the *Lancet*, provoked by the prosecution of two irregulars for abortion, proposed legal intervention to check the increasing problem. It roundly condemned unqualified practitioners:

The trust reposed in the practitioner of medicine is one of the most sacred that can be confided to man. . . . To behold the teachings of science perverted from their legitimate purpose, and made to subserve the foul ends of infamy and vice, is a spectacle which has rarely disgraced the annals of our beneficent profession. . . .

'But', it continued:

there hangs upon the skirts of our noble profession a pestilent race ever ready to pander to vice, and who seem to wield the broken scraps and fragments of medical knowledge, picked up in the by-ways of life, with no other purpose than illicit gain, and with no other effect than ruin and misery to their victims.[107]

It then pointed to the trade of criminal abortion as 'one of the worst consequences of the free scope afforded to illegal practice in this country . . .'.[108] It protested:

It is not to be endured that the defect of our laws or their lax administration should tolerate the reckless assumption of medical practice by the ignorant and the unprincipled, who by parading the false insignia and titles of our profession are thus confounded in the eyes of the public with honourable men, and permitted to vilify and discredit an honourable profession.[109]

Those who spoke lightly, it added, of 'free trade in medicine' should reflect upon its consequences to society such as the fostering of fraud and barbarous crimes.[110] An editorial later in the year lamented that the law did not require the registration of either stillbirths or premature births who did not survive. It asked:

Who can calculate the fearful extent to which embryonic life is sacrificed? Who can estimate the amount of crime which is annually perpetrated against the infant yet unborn?[111]

The prevalence of these 'widespread and systematic atrocities' was glimpsed from time to time when the woman herself fell victim.[112]

Abortion was not only common, it was commercialised:

Is not the horrible truth patent to everyone, that . . . the *practice is a system, a regular trade?* Can we conceal from ourselves that if the practice of procuring criminal abortion be pursued as a trade that it is carried on to a frightful extent?[113]

The solution, declared the journal, lay in reform of the law, though not so much the tightening of the prohibition on abortion as the suppression of irregular practitioners, whom they blamed for the increase in the offence. How was this 'flagitious traffic' to be arrested? The journal answered:

We have, in the first place, again to express our reluctant opinion that society and the Legislature, which foster and sanction the illegitimate and irresponsible practice of medicine, are deeply to blame. If the practice of medicine in every form by the unskilled, the illiterate, the unscrupulous, be tolerated, is it not hypocrisy to wonder that the appliances of medicine are systematically perverted to the foulest and most abominable ends?

The first remedy, it continued, was to allow no-one to practise whose qualifications had not been competently approved and whose conduct was not guaranteed by his education, his social position, and the controlling influence of his profession.[114] The second remedy was to extend the Registration laws to premature births and stillbirths.[115]

An editorial later in the year highlighted both the 'terrible extent' of abortion and its commercialisation; told of the circulation of handbills advertising houses where abortion could be procured, and declared that only the ignorant would dispute that the offence was increasing.[116]

Professional pressure did lead to the enactment of the Medical Act 1858 which, *inter alia*, established a register of qualified practitioners, but this did not satisfy the regulars' demand for the proscription of unqualified practice.[117] Hopes were expressed at the time that the Act might alleviate the problem of abortion. One journal, commenting on the conviction of a foreign irregular for abortion, expressed the hope that the Act would prevent such 'low foreign adventurers' from practising nefariously in England.[118] Referring to a similar case, the *Lancet* declared that it would be a great public service if the new Medical Council were to sweep such imposters from the professional platform.[119]

However, it is evident from later articles in the same journal that the Act did not eradicate the practice of abortion by irregulars. In March 1861, commenting upon the case of *R. v. Goddard*, where a midwife was convicted of murdering a woman who died from an operation to procure abortion, the journal protested that the crime was committed under such circumstances as should alert the legislature to the dangerous laxity which permitted even the most ignorant and worthless to engage in the practice of medicine. It continued:

Under the cloak of the practitioner of medicine, which the shameful connivance of our laws permits every charlatan to wear, this and other offences against society are perpetrated by the most ignorant and vilest of men. For this, and the consequent diffusion of incalculable immorality and vice, those are greatly responsible who, in a spirit of pseudo-liberality, take up the insane cry of free trade in medicine.[120]

Shortly after, it referred to three similar cases which, it felt, pointed to 'a most disgusting and horrible practice, which is extremely prevalent . . .'.[121] The failure of the law to prohibit unqualified practice allowed those calling themselves 'herbalists', 'regular doctors' and 'midwives' to pursue, year after year,

one of the most despicable, loathsome, and enormous of human crimes. . . . The trade of abortionist . . . has become a regularly established, money-making business, carried on by both sexes. . . .[122]

The journal's uncompromising demand for legislative action, made in March 1861, while the O.A.P. Bill was passing through Parliament, merits quotation in full:

Surely the evil has now become frequent and glaring enough to make society shrink from venturing nearer to the horrible abyss which threatens to engulf so many more and an increasing number of victims. The practice of feticide *must be put a stop to*; the trade of the abortionist *must have an end*. If quacks are to be allowed to continue, they must at any rate not be permitted to practise feloniously or with nefarious intent. If midwives are to be permitted to assist the poorer female in the hour of labour, they must give some guarantee that they will refrain from interference of every kind before that hour actually arrives. There must be no tampering with 'female complaints' – no sale or administration of drugs for 'removing female irregularities and obstructions' – no connivance of any kind between recognised midwives and 'botanic doctors.' The whole system is bad – the system of allowing any ignorant knave to practise what delusion or bestiality he chooses, and any ignorant old woman to term herself a midwife. It is evidently amongst these people that the active instruments of mischief lie.[123]

It continued:

The code of medical ethics, the high sense of honour pervading the legitimate ranks of the profession, as well as the ordinary rules of morality, effectually prevent, of course, all pandering upon the part of medical practitioners, either to the depraved sentiments of the higher classes, or to the criminal desires of the lower ranks. The evil lies at the door of a loathsome parasitical race which preys upon the follies and vices of mankind. They are slayers of the body and polluters of the mind. They are of the hybrid growth of rampant, barefaced charlatanry, and vicious desires. Society may talk as much as it likes of free trade in medicine, may patronize herbalists, bone-setters, uncertificated midwives, joint-rubbers, pill-makers, and nostrum vendors of all kinds. But it may be assured that in so doing it is nourishing a serpent at its heart, whose venomous fangs are ever ready to dart poison of some kind into its circulating current, not the least deadly of which is the practice of procuring abortion by the use of instruments, upon the one hand, and by the administration of improper drugs upon the other – a practice which is getting to infect this land in so virulent a manner as must soon call for some direct interference of the Legislature for the purpose of arresting the crying shame.[124]

In the light of the above barrage of medical opinion, the tightening of the abortion law in 1861 and in particular the enactment of s. 59 are readily understandable. That the legislature was not influenced by that opinion to the extent of prohibitng all unqualified medical practice reflects, as had the Medical Act, the strength of the prevailing ethos which favoured a *laissez-faire* approach to the regulation of medical practice, and suggests limits to professional influence, particularly when the profession's motives were not wholly disinterested. However, the legislature's enactment of ss. 58 and 59 can be seen as a response to the profession's demand that, if the law was not going to suppress irregular practitioners, then it ought at least to check their growing trade in abortion. Even this more modest response to the problem would, of course, redound to the benefit of the regulars, for while it would not proscribe their competitors it would at least throw a further obstacle in their way by extending the prohibition on a procedure which, according to the regulars, they were finding increasingly profitable.[125]

Whether the regulars' assertions as to the incidence of criminal abortion by irregulars, the attitudes of laymen to it, and the failure of the law to suppress it were accurate is, like the incidence of abortion before 1803, a question requiring further research. It is possible that the outcry merely reflects anxiety about their professional status.[126] There is, however, some historical evidence available which suggests that their assertions may not have been groundless.

Some historians have stated that abortion was widespread throughout the last century. F. B. Smith has concluded that ordinary people clearly accepted abortion as a normal means of limiting their offspring and avoiding family difficulties; that it was probably very common; and must have been a main means of family limitation.[127] Whether these conclusions, like those relating to the extent of abortion before 1803, can be any more than impressionistic is arguable, not least when his final conclusion rests on articles which in fact focus not on procured but on spontaneous abortion.[128]

Sauer, in his more detailed analysis, divides the last century into three periods.[129] He concludes that between 1800 and 1840 abortion was, because of its physical dangers, probably uncommon and that what abortion there was seems to have been largely unsystematic, with abortions being attempted by the woman herself rather than by professional abortionists, who were rare.[130] From 1840 to 1880, he continues, while abortion may have been increasing, its incidence must have remained relatively low: the persistently high incidence of infanticide suggesting that the dangers of abortion were still feared by some of even the most desperate as a painful and dangerous procedure.[131] From 1880 to 1900, however, a desire to limit the number of children, together with the development of anaesthesia and antisepsis, seem to have led to a rise in abortion and a fall in infanticide such that by the end of the century the latter was no longer regarded as a problem.[132]

Conclusion

This chapter has traced the increasingly restrictive development of the law against abortion between 1803 and 1861. It has suggested that the extension of the law was influenced to a significant degree by the emerging medical profession's condemnation of abortion over this period and by its recommendations for reform. The successful implementation of these recommendations appears to have been due not only to the increasingly authoritative position of the profession as a social group, and to the scientific prestige with which their criticisms of the law were increasingly clothed, but also to the fact that they coincided with the steady consolidation of the law relating to offences against the person. The chapter has also suggested that the regulars' outspoken opposition to abortion throughout this period was motivated by a concern for fetal and possibly maternal life and also by a desire to advance their own interests at the expense of those of their irregular competitors.

3

Abortion in legal theory and medical practice before 1938

In Chapters 1 and 2 it was suggested that the passage and shape of the anti-abortion enactments from 1803 to 1861 were influenced by regular medical practitioners who relentlessly urged the need for suppression by the law of a practice which threatened not only fetal and maternal welfare but also the interests of their profession.

However, there is reason to approach the regulars' expressions of concern for fetal life with caution. Just as it would be simplistic to assume that their condemnation of abortion was purely altruistic, so too would it be superficial to conclude that they regarded fetal life as inviolable.

3.1 Medical abortion and the law 1803–1938

On 27 April 1938 a girl of fourteen was raped. She was taken to see Dr Joan Malleson, a member of the medico-legal council of the Abortion Law Reform Association, who contacted a fellow council member, Dr Aleck Bourne, obstetric surgeon to St Mary's Hospital. He replied:

I shall be delighted to take her in at St. Mary's and curette her. I have done that before and shall not have the slightest hesitation in doing it again. I have said that the next time I have the opportunity I will write to the Attorney-General and invite him to take action.[1]

On 31 May, the girl was taken to see Dr Bourne by her mother. A letter of consent to the proposed operation was then obtained from her father. Bourne then saw Dr Wingate, a resident obstetric officer at St Mary's and informed him of his reasons for operating, namely that the girl was under the age of consent and had been raped. On 6 June she was admitted to the hospital. A pregnancy test proved positive. On 14 June Bourne performed the operation. He then related the facts of the case to a Chief Inspector Bridger, who had come to the hospital in an attempt to prevent the operation, and told him 'I want you to arrest me'.[2]

The trial opened at the Central Criminal Court on 18 July. The judge, Macnaghten J., upheld a defence submission that the indictment for abortion should be amended to include the word 'unlawfully': the Crown would have to establish that Bourne's use of the instrument was unlawful. Bourne entered a plea of not guilty. The Attorney-General, for the Crown, conceded that if an instrument were used to procure an abortion which was necessary to save the life of the mother, he would not submit that such a use was unlawful.[3] Under examination, Bourne testified that his decision to operate was based mainly on the threat of 'mental and nervous injury', which was extremely difficult to cure. He explained: 'It would have been a source of nervous, psychoneurotic, and other troubles, and there would perhaps have been secondary physical illnesses all her life'.[4] Under cross-examination, he testified that he had never intended to operate before considering whether she was a suitable case and that he had not sought a second opinion as he was usually applied to himself in such cases. He denied that there was a clear distinction between danger to life and to health, as there were many cases in between where health was depressed to such an extent that life was shortened.[5]

In his closing address, counsel for Bourne submitted that there was no evidence to throw doubt on the proposition that without the operation the girl's health was likely to be greatly prejudiced for the rest of her life.[6] However, the Attorney-General contended that there was a basic distinction between saving life and preserving health, and that the operation had not been performed to save life.[7] Did Bourne's motive, he asked, of removing possible mental ill-health, render the operation lawful?[8]

In his summing-up, Macnaghten J. distinguished between the case before the court, which involved a skilful surgeon performing an abortion openly and charitably, in the belief that he was discharging his duty, from the secret termination of pregnancy performed for gain by an unskilful operator.[9] He also contrasted s. 58 of the Offences Against the Person Act 1861 with s. 1(1) of the Infant Life (Preservation) Act 1929 (I.L.(P)A.), which prohibited the destruction of a child capable of being born alive but which contained a proviso allowing its destruction in good faith for the purpose only of preserving the life of the mother. He ruled, however, that the meaning of this proviso was imported into s. 58 by the word 'unlawfully',[10] and directed:

the burden rests on the Crown to satisfy you beyond reasonable doubt that the defendant did not procure the miscarriage of this girl in good faith for the purpose only of preserving her life.[11]

Rejecting the view that a clear line could be drawn between danger to life and to health he said, 'life depends on health, and it may be that health is so gravely impaired that death results'.[12] There were, he added, divergent views with regard to the performance of abortion. There might be some women who wanted abortion, but the desire of a woman to be relieved of her pregnancy was no justification for the operation. There were also religious views that it should never be performed, but they did not represent the law either. The law lay between these two extreme views and permitted abortion for the purpose of preserving the life of the mother.[13] The preservation of life was, however, to be construed in a 'reasonable sense':

if the doctor is of opinion, on reasonable grounds and with adequate knowledge, that the probable consequence of the continuation of the pregnancy will be to make the woman a physical or mental wreck, the jury are quite entitled to take the view that the doctor who, under those circumstances and in that honest belief, operates, is operating for the purpose of preserving the life of the mother.[14]

These general considerations had to be applied to the facts of each case.[15] In the present case, the evidence showed that the continuance of the pregnancy and birth must cause 'great mental anguish' and would be likely to result in a 'normal, decent girl' becoming a 'mental wreck'.[16] He added, however:

The law of this land has always held human life to be sacred, and the protection that the law gives to human life it extends also to the unborn child in the womb. The unborn child in the womb must not be destroyed unless the destruction of that child is for the purpose of preserving the yet more precious life of the mother.[17]

Moreover, the defence was available only to members of the medical profession, and no doctor would venture to operate without consulting some other doctor of high standing.[18] Bourne was acquitted.

The summing–up in this case has been widely regarded as carving an exception out of the previously unyielding s. 58, and as establishing, for the first time, the lawfulness of therapeutic abortion. For example, a recent thesis declares that it 'made an important and far-reaching change in the law by permitting an exception to be made in some cases for therapeutic abortion'.[19] It continues:

there had been no legal definition of, nor judicial discussion expressly about, circumstances in which abortion could be deliberately and legally procured. Our conclusion must be that this case brought about a great change in the law by judicial 'declaration'.[20]

This view is based on the belief that the prohibition of abortion by s. 58 was absolute and was so regarded by the courts until 1938. This belief is, however, inconsistent with certain judicial and extra-judicial pronouncements.

In *R. v. Collins* (1898)[21] a medical man was charged at the Central Criminal Court with the murder of a woman upon whom he had allegedly used an instrument. In his summing–up, Grantham J. said that there was no doubt about the meaning of the law: any person who with intent procured the miscarriage of a woman by the unlawful use of an instrument was guilty of a felony. He added, however:

It could well be understood that there were cases where it was necessary, in order to save the life of a woman, that there should be forcible miscarriage, and a properly qualified doctor had to say when that time had arrived. That was not unlawful.[22]

This dictum is noteworthy not only for its explicit recognition of the lawfulness of therapeutic abortion, but also for its limitation of the defence to qualified doctors and the apparent absence of any requirement that the doctor's opinion be based on reasonable grounds or be confirmed by that of a second doctor. Grantham J. was not alone in recognising the lawfulness of therapeutic abortion. Some forty years before, a case involving similar facts had been tried: *R. v. Wilhelm* (1858).[23] The chief medical witness for the Crown testified that in some cases of pelvic contraction it was both necessary and customary to procure abortion. He added, however, that the instrument which the defendant had used upon the woman in question was not one which would be used for this purpose and he denied that there was evidence of contraction in the woman.[24] In his direction to the jury, Bramwell B. apparently conceded the possibility of a lawful abortion. He said:

if a person attempted to procure the abortion of a woman, without lawful cause for so doing[,], he would be guilty of a highly unlawful act.[25]

To convict, he added, they had to be satisfied that the defendant had used 'an unlawful instrument for an unlawful purpose'.[26] Unfortunately, the judge did not specify what might qualify as a 'lawful cause', but the recognition of the lawfulness of therapeutic abortion is, nevertheless, implicit. Moreover, in 1929 McCardie J., summing-up in an abortion trial, said that not all operations to terminate pregnancy were unlawful. Certain operations were legal and necessary in the last stages of pregnancy to save the life of the mother and, if possible, the life of the child. There was, moreover, a stage before that when an operation to bring away the fetus might be legal: if the fetal sac burst, blood poisoning might ensue if the fetus were not removed.[27]

These cases indicate that, long before 1938, therapeutic abortion was judicially approved, both tacitly and expressly. That the defence was not raised until *R. v. Bourne* is due less to doubts as to its validity than to the reluctance of prosecutors to question medical discretion. This is reflected in the report of an inquest, held in 1933, into the death of a woman after an abortion performed at the King Edward VII Hospital.[28] Her doctor testified that he had advised the abortion because the woman weighed sixteen stone (102 kg) and her general condition made it highly dangerous to go to term. Similarly, the obstetric physician to the hospital testified that her condition made abortion far safer than going to the seventh month and that, although he had performed similar operations with success 'scores of times', the patient had died during surgery designed to remove the uterine contents which remained from a previous operation. The report of the coroner's direction to the jury reads:

The coroner reminded the jury of the law whereby the induction of abortion for any other reason than to avert danger to life was a crime. Any felonious intent in this case could, of course, be ruled out.[29]

The jury returned a unanimous verdict of death by misadventure.

Approval of therapeutic abortion before *Bourne* was not confined to statements from the bench. There were several reported statements of approval from eminent judges speaking in an extra-judicial capacity which provide authoritative confirmation of the lawfulness of abortion before 1938. Before we focus on their forthright statements, which were made over a decade before *Bourne*, it is worth noting that the question of the lawfulness of abortion had already been the subject of counsel's opinion.

In 1895 the Royal College of Physicians sought the opinion of Sir Edward Clarke Q.C. and Mr Horace Avory (as he then was) on certain questions relating to the law of abortion. One question asked whether the law prohibited the procurement of abortion or the destruction of the child during labour for the purpose of saving the life of the mother and, if so, whether a practitioner who by declining to destroy the child allowed the woman to die was blameless. The College also enquired as to the best mode of procedure, if amendment of the law were desired. Counsel's reply, which was later published, was as follows:

We are of opinion that the law does not forbid the procurement of abortion during pregnancy, or the destruction of the child during labour, where such procurement or destruction is necessary to save the mother's life.[30]

They added that if they were right in their views, no alteration of the law would probably be desired.[31] This opinion provides further authority for the lawfulness of abortion in certain circumstances. It is, however, vulnerable to criticism; not for going too far, but for not going far enough. Firstly, the destruction of the child during delivery was not an offence known to law and hence did not require a defence. Secondly, in relation to the destruction of the child before delivery, it is arguable that the criterion of saving the woman's life was too restrictive. This argument is based not on the judicial dicta cited above but on extra-judicial dicta which favoured a more relaxed criterion and greater leeway for clinical freedom.

In 1927, at a joint meeting of the Medico-Legal Society and the section of obstetrics of the Royal Society of Medicine, Mr Justice Humphreys drew a distinction between criminal and non-criminal abortion. By the latter, the report of the meeting explains, he meant:

the steps taken by a qualified medical man to get rid of a condition in his patient which he considered, using the best of his skill and ability, and of course honestly, on medical grounds and on medical grounds alone, to be dangerous to the safety of the patient. He used the word 'safety' advisedly, because the purely medical question was not one with which the law was concerned. No doctor who had used the best of his skill and judgment in the sole interest of his patient need imagine for a moment that the law would call him to account.[32]

The sole concern of the doctor was, he stressed, the medical rather than the social or economic welfare of his patient. The golden rule was that he was not entitled to consider the prospect of social disgrace or a diseased child, but only 'the health and future of his patient on medical grounds'.[33] He added: 'When a doctor in the exercise of his discretion had decided to induce abortion there was no question of law or ethics'.[34] It would, he continued, be an impertinence for one with no medical knowledge to express any views upon which conditions justified the induction of abortion by a doctor.

His interpretation of the law is clearly more generous than that of Macnaghten J., who chose to base his direction upon the proviso to a subsection in an Act passed after this meeting. Although Humphreys J. does refer to abortion as an 'extreme step', he does not limit its performance to the preservation of the woman's life but speaks of 'the health and future' of the patient as the basic criterion. Although he ruled out social, economic and eugenic indications *per se*, he did not prohibit the consideration of such factors in the overall assessment of the threat which continuation of the pregnancy posed to the patient's 'health and future'. Nor did he lay down a requirement of consultation or stipulate that the doctor's belief in the advisability of the operation had to be based on reasonable grounds. In short, he conceded a considerable degree of discretion to the medical practitioner who acted in good faith.

The meeting was summed up by Lord Justice Salter. Not only did he too express the opinion that abortion could be lawfully performed – this was, he said, implied by the word 'unlawfully' in s. 58 – but he went even further than his brother judge in declining to rule out abortion performed for a eugenic indication. He remarked:

A very difficult case might arise if it were found during the pregnancy that one or other patient were suffering from a disease usually inherited.

The report continues:

He thought the mother should have more say than anybody else, but it was going rather far to say that to effect abortion should be lawful in any case where the mother desired it.[35]

He could see no logical distinction between a woman's having a right to abort and her having a right to expose her newborn child. Moreover, he echoed Humphreys J. in rejecting social or economic indications:

If abortion were ever sanctioned outside the strictly medical area for economic or social reasons, he would have great fears. Even where it was restrained within the medical area, he would fear the growth of a large class of compliant doctors who would be easily persuaded that there were sufficient medical reasons. . . .[36]

These revealing extra-judicial comments were, it should be stressed, made long before the case of *Bourne* and even before the enactment of the I.L.(P)A 1929.

Shortly before *Bourne*, the lawfulness of therapeutic abortion was again the subject of extra-judicial comment. In February 1938 Mr Justice Humphreys chaired a debate, which took place under the auspices of the Fellowship of Medicine, on the need for abortion law reform. He again referred to the lawfulness of the procedure. He dealt first with the preservation of the woman's life, and the report of the proceedings runs:

Mr. Justice Humphreys said that he could only give his private opinion, though he thought his fellow judges would not differ from his view, that a medical man who in these circumstances terminated the pregnancy was committing no offence against the law. Criminal statutes, like other statutes, must be construed reasonably. To his mind it was unthinkable that the criminal law could have been so stupid as to have provided that a medical man in an effort to save life was committing a criminal offence.[37]

On the question of whether abortion was justified to improve health, he preferred to remain silent. Summing-up the debate, he broached the question of non-therapeutic indications. Commenting on the view expressed by a Dr Oxley who, opposing the motion for reform of the law, had urged that the doctor should, while not recognising 'sociological' or 'eugenic' indications, nevertheless safeguard both the life and the health of his patient, Humphreys J. remarked:

Dr. Oxley has said – I do not say I agree or disagree, but it is what a brave man would say and would practise – 'Consider your patient, consider nothing but your patient's welfare, and if you come to the honest conclusion that your patient's welfare demands that you take a certain course, take it, and run the risk of somebody taking a different view.' I am quite sure that Dr. Oxley would agree with me in this, that it should not be done in a hole-and-corner way, because in that case people may doubt your *bona fides*. You should get your brother physicians or surgeons around you, you should get a thoroughly qualified hospital nurse to come and attend whatever it is you are going to do, you should let the whole world know what you are doing and why you are doing it. Otherwise the man who carries out an abortion which in certain conditions might be a criminal offence is a fool.[38]

With respect to the lawfulness of a given indication, he said:

When somebody puts a concrete case to me, and gives me the history of the patient, saying that the doctor found out this, that, or the other, and came to the honest conclusion that it was essential that an operation should be done, then I do not think that the jury would disagree with the view that the judge would take of the matter, and it would be a view favourable to the doctor. But until you can get some form of words as simple as the words 'for the purpose of saving life,' I hesitate to say that the doctor is entitled to perform an operation for procuring miscarriage merely to make the patient more healthy, because I do not know what you are proposing.[39]

Although displaying an understandably cautious reluctance to enunciate an abstract principle permitting abortion in the interests of health as well as for the preservation of life, Humphreys J. nevertheless betrays a willingness to regard such an operation as lawful when earthed in the realities of a particular case and supported by the honest belief of a practitioner in its necessity.

The above extra-judicial dicta reinforce the contention that even before *Bourne* therapeutic abortion to preserve the woman's life was lawful. The evidence also suggests that the preservation of health would also have constituted a lawful cause, and there is no evidence that health was confined to the patient's physical as opposed to her mental condition. Further, even a eugenic indication may have sufficed, though this is more doubtful. Finally, some of the above dicta indicate that a doctor had nothing to fear from the law if he acted openly and in the interests of his patient. If this were so, then the lawfulness of particular indications must, in practice, have been more a matter for medical than forensic determination.

In is in the light of the above evidence, rather than medico-legal mythology, that the significance of *Bourne* should be assessed. In this light, the case appears not so much as an example of radical judicial legislation as of conservative exposition of the law. What led Macnaghten J. to this restrictive construction of the statute? The answer would appear to lie in the fact that none of the above authorities was cited in court: the case was argued on the inaccurate assumption that there was a virtually complete absence of authority. This led the judge to pray in aid the proviso to s. 1(1) of the I.L.(P)A. 1929. That the proviso was an inappropriate basis for the direction seems clear, for s. 1 deals with the destruction of the fetus in late as opposed to early pregnancy and there are sound policy reasons for circumscribing the former more closely than the latter. First, a late abortion would be performed only when the mother's life was in danger. This was because of the relatively greater risks associated with the procedure at that stage of gestation and because the conditions warranting the destruction of the fetus would tend to present a more imminent and serious threat to the woman's life than those occurring in early pregnancy. Second, late abortion would not only destroy a fetus but would probably deprive a child manifestly capable of being born alive of the chance of life. These reasons militate against Macnaghten J.'s equation of the therapeutic destruction of the fetus in early and late pregnancy. It is respectfully submitted that his reliance on the proviso was not only unwarranted but also unnecessary. The lawfulness of therapeutic abortion had even been recognised by those concerned with the enactment of the 1929 Act and this recognition could not have been based on a proviso which they had yet to enact.

In debate on the Bill, Lord Hailsham declared:

one knows that it is necessary sometimes to procure abortion for the sake of the mother of the unborn child, and I have never heard that any doctor has been embarrassed, or has hesitated, in the discharge of that duty, by reason of the knowledge that if he was not acting in good faith then he would be guilty of a criminal offence.[40]

Macnaghten J.'s focus on the proviso is even more surprising when it is recalled that the only authority cited during the trial – *Russell On Crimes* – favoured a broader therapeutic exception. As early as 1909 this work, referring to s. 58, had maintained that the word 'unlawfully' excluded from the section acts done in the course of proper treatment in the interest of the life or health of the mother.[41] The judge's limitation of the defence to abortions performed to save the mother's life, even in the extended sense of preventing her from becoming a physical or mental 'wreck', appears therefore to be too restrictive. Further, he confined the defence to 'members of the medical profession', and they were advised to consult before operating. Moreover, the doctor's belief that the operation was necessary apparently had to be supported by 'reasonable grounds' and 'adequate knowledge'.[42] Again, the judge's reference to the deterioration of health as a 'likely' or 'probable' consequence[43] is more exacting than a requirement that the termination be merely 'for the purpose' of preserving her health. Finally, Macnaghten J. indicated that if the woman died as a result of the doctor's conscientious refusal to abort, he might be liable for manslaughter by negligence.[44] Consequently, the doctor was constrained to steer between the Scylla of unwarranted intervention and the Charybdis of careless inaction.

It has been argued that in the light of the authorities, the bulk of which were not cited at the trial, Macnaghten J.'s direction was too restrictive in law. This argument is supported by two subsequent cases which dealt with the same question. In the first, Morris J. (as he then was) ruled that the question was not whether the doctor's belief as to the necessity for termination was correct, but whether it was honestly held.[45] In the second, Ashworth J. held that the defence applied not only to operations performed to save life but also to preserve health, both physical and mental.[46]

3.2 Abortion in medical practice before 1938

It has been contended above that, well before *Bourne*, authorities for the legality of therapeutic abortion were in existence, albeit largely overlooked by both legal and medical professions. Did this effective absence of explicit legal sanction for the operation prevent its performance by medical men? If so, then the radical significance traditionally attributed to the case might be more apposite in relation to medical practice than to legal theory. This hypothesis is, however, inconsistent with the evidence of obstetrical writings which indicate that therapeutic abortion was performed even before Ellenborough's Act and that, well before *Bourne*, was being undertaken for increasingly extensive indications, including the preservation of mental health.

The first myth to dispel when considering the practice of therapeutic abortion from the beginning of the last century is that it was not performed at all. This myth has been perpetuated to the present day, even by distinguished medical authorities. In 1966 no

less eminent a body than the Special B.M.A. Committee on
Therapeutic Abortion declared:

In 1861 the operation of therapeutic abortion was not an accepted medical
procedure, and there was no question of excepting from the provisions of
the statute medical operations carried out in good faith.[47]

The persistence of this opinion is remarkable when it is appreciated
that the available evidence, contained in contemporary obstetrical
writings, testifies to the performance of abortion well before 1861
and its acceptance by the bulk of the medical profession. Some of
the indications for the operation contained in these writings will be
described against the backcloth of the profession's relative evaluation of fetal and maternal life.

However strident the demands of the medical profession before
1861 for increasingly strict legislation to safeguard the fetus from
the unqualified abortionist, it is clear from the medical literature
that even qualified practitioners did not regard fetal life as worthy of
unconditional respect. Indeed, the evidence indicates that medical
men were quite prepared to sacrifice the fetus to protect the life of
the mother. This was so even at delivery: the destruction of the child
during labour by lessening its skull was far from uncommon. In the
eighteenth and nineteenth centuries many women suffered from
pelvic deformity, whether as a result of fracture or poor diet, which
rendered natural delivery at full term hazardous.[48] Two alternatives
were the Caesarian section and craniotomy. The dangers of the
former to the woman were, until the beginning of the present
century, considerable. This left craniotomy as the safer option, and
it was performed with such frequency that some practitioners
expressed concern at the number of children thereby destroyed.
Nevertheless, professional opinion appears, almost universally, to
have regarded the life of the mother as more valuable than that of the
child. In cases of irreconcilable conflict, therefore, the welfare of the
mother prevailed. For example, in his lectures on midwifery
delivered in 1827, Dr Blundell rejected the view that craniotomy
was only justified when the child was already dead. He added:

With the dogmas of the divine, it is not in my province to interfere, and I
am glad of it; without, therefore, babbling about theology and syringes, I
may be permitted to remark, that in British midwifery, the life, nay, the
preservation of the patient from the graver lesions to her person, is to be
looked upon as paramount to every consideration relating to the foetus;
and when these require the sacrifice, craniotomy becomes justifiable.[49]

Many children had, he feared, been destroyed simply on account of the facility of the operation.[50]

The fact that obstetricians were not averse to the procedure is further illustrated by the objection in 1844 of an eminent practitioner, Dr Radford, that the 'murderous operation' was resorted to with excessive frequency.[51] It was, he wrote, only justifiable when the life of the mother was threatened by a medical condition, whether temporary or permanent.[52] If permanent, he argued, the justification would only extend to one such destructive operation though he conceded that according to the standards of contemporary obstetric practice, successive children could be destroyed, 'whatever number should be begot'.[53] He urged:

We ought invariably to consider this operation as one of necessity, and not one of election; Divine law not permitting us to sacrifice foetal life, and Human law not sanctioning the practice.[54]

Craniotomy, he argued, should be replaced as the operation of election by the Caesarian. Although conceding that the available statistics indicated that the maternal mortality for the latter was greater – 45 out of 49 dying in one series – he questioned whether the figures were attributable to the dangers of the operation itself or to other factors such as the poor constitution of the patients or their weak condition, particularly when they had endured a protracted labour or an attempt to deliver by craniotomy.[55] If the operation were properly performed and proper after-care instituted, he maintained, both the maternal and infant mortality rates would fall below those attributable to craniotomy.[56]

However, as Radford himself admitted, his views were 'very contrary to those held by the majority, if not the whole of the profession in Great Britain and Ireland'.[57] The orthodox opinion was exemplified by Francis Ramsbotham. In 1867 his text on obstetrics stated that there were only two operations designed to destroy fetal life which were approved by the profession: one was abortion, in those 'very rare' cases of extreme pelvic deformity preventing the birth of a viable child or where some irritation dependent on pregnancy placed the woman's life in 'imminent jeopardy'.[58] The second was craniotomy, which he defended as the lesser of two evils. He dismissed the objections of those who insisted on proof of fetal death before operating:

Some, indeed, horrified at this arbitrary destruction of the child, have laudably contended that the proceeding is not justified unless it be dead:

they argue, and with truth, that human life is held at the will of one Supreme Being alone, – and that, unless forfeited to the laws, to no human hand is delegated the power of destroying it. Strong and valid would these objections be, if once the operation were performed wantonly, or without grave and deep consideration; but it is never had recourse to except for the purpose of saving life, or preventing future misery. Did the mother perish, the foetus within her must perish likewise; and in this country, we consider the mother's life as paramount. . . .

He continued, echoing Blundell, that the destruction of the child was warranted not only to preserve the woman's life but also to protect her from dreadful lesions of sloughing and laceration which, though not fatal, would nevertheless make her future life one of unmitigated wretchedness.[59]

Explaining the greater esteem in which the life and health of the mother were held, he pointed out that she, unlike her unborn child, was bound to the world by many social, moral and religious ties; had feelings, affections, hopes and fears; and was involved in relationships of interdependency. Whereas her death left a void, the unborn child in dying suffered no agony of mind and had neither feelings nor dependents: its existence centred almost exclusively on itself.[60] He concluded:

We are surely justified, in a political, if not in a moral point of view, in preferring the preservation of the strong to the weak, the healthy to the diseased, and the mother of a family to the unborn foetus, provided one or other must in all probability be sacrificed. From these considerations, we prefer, whenever we have a choice, the mother's safety to the infant's life.[61]

This overriding concern for the safety of the mother also explains the reluctance of the profession as a whole to resort to the Caesarian, unless craniotomy had been tried unsuccessfully. The Caesarian's high maternal mortality rate, attributable to shock, haemorrhage, and sepsis, was – as even the proponents of the operation conceded – very high.[62]

However, as Radford pointed out, the dangers associated with craniotomy were far from negligible. Moreover, whereas the Caesarian offered at least a chance of survival to the fetus, craniotomy spelt its destruction. Clearly, if pregnancy in a woman suffering from pelvic contraction could be terminated before full term, the grave problems associated with these procedures would be averted, particularly if termination could be delayed until the fetus was viable. Hence the emergence, even before Ellenborough's Act, of the induction of abortion and of premature labour, procedures which were designed to terminate pregnancy before and after viability, respectively. The obstetrical literature of the last century reveals that, well before 1861, both procedures were recognised operations and were, moreover, increasing in popularity as ways of avoiding resort to the more drastic alternatives. Although the main focus of attention here will be on the induction of abortion it will be considered alongside the induction of premature labour, not least because obstetricians often dealt with them together, not infrequently failing to distinguish between them.

An early reference to the induction of premature labour was made by Denman. In 1794, he wrote that a Dr Kelly had informed him that in 1756 the most eminent medical men of the day had assembled in London to consider the morality and advantages of the procedure. It met, records Denman, 'with their general approbation'.[63] It appears that both Kelly and Denman had themselves safely induced premature labour by puncturing the fetal membranes.[64] The latter declared that the utility of this 'perfectly safe' procedure rested on the existence of a disproportion between the head of the child and the pelvis of the mother, or on foreseeable fetal death, and its morality on the policy of trying to save the child, which would otherwise be lost, while doing nothing to prejudice the health of the mother.[65]

It would, however, be a mistake to conclude that the operation was practised solely to preserve the lives of viable children, for in cases of severe pelvic deformity it was not possible to extract a fetus which had attained seven months' growth. Consequently, labour would have to be induced before then if the dangers of craniotomy and the Caesarian were to be avoided. In 1801 induction before viability was described in a paper written by a Bolton surgeon, James Barlow, entitled 'On the advantages and disadvantages of inducing premature labour, with a view of superseding embryulcia, the section of the symphysis pubis, and the Caesarian operation'.[66]

The induction of labour after, rather than before, viability appears to have commanded more medical attention, perhaps because of its advantages to both mother and child and its wider application: when gravid women were seen by medical men they were not internally examined until the seventh month of pregnancy, when the child was more likely to have attained viability.[67] In 1841,

Francis Ramsbotham listed the indications for induction after viability as pelvic contraction, a history of fetal death at a certain stage of pregnancy, and diseases which placed the woman's life in immediate jeopardy.[68] Should, however, induction be performed, either before or after viability,

to screen an individual from the just reproaches of the world, or to cast into oblivion the evidence of the gratification of a criminal passion, then, indeed, is murder committed in law and reason. . . .[69]

He had himself induced labour on forty occasions between 1823 and 1834.[70] Although only half the children had been born alive, he defended the morality of the operation on the ground that it offered the child at least a chance of life and also preserved the mother from danger.[71] In 1867, his text stated that induction before viability was approved when the woman's life was in danger and to save her from the dangers of craniotomy or the Caesarian. The woman should, however, be warned against further pregnancies: no doctor would be justified in aborting her indefinitely.[72]

A paper delivered by Dr Tyler Smith entitled 'On the abolition of craniotomy from obstetric practice' provides an illuminating description of the status of the induction of labour shortly before the passage of the O.A.P.A. 1861.[73] He observed that practitioners unanimously condoned the procedure in cases of moderate pelvic deformity.[74] He added that it was scarcely, if at all, more dangerous than an accidental premature labour and he noted that far more than half of the children were born alive.[75] Even when induction was performed before viability, thereby leaving the child with no possibility of survival, the operation was generally condoned:

With scarcely an exception, British accoucheurs recognise the propriety, in cases of high distortion where it is impossible for a viable child to pass, of inducing premature labour in the early or middle months of pregnancy.[76]

He had previously referred to the procedure as one which had 'gradually advanced to the rank of one of the most important operations in obstetrics'.[77] With regard to technique, he preferred the douche, as puncturing the fetal membranes contributed to the high infant mortality rate of 50% associated with induction. He maintained that the douche was particularly apt before the fifth month. After this stage, the membranes could be punctured with 'tolerable facility' and the immediate relief afforded by this method rendered it appropriate in cases such as excessive vomiting, convulsions, oppression of the circulation and respiration, and insanity.[78] Reluctant to devalue the life of the child, however, he stressed that its sacrifice in cases of extreme pelvic deformity was an exception to the obstetrical axiom that the treatment which most certainly assured the safety of the child was also the safest for the mother.[79]

The attraction of premature induction of labour as an alternative to the more drastic alternatives could only have been enhanced by improvements in the techniques available to effect delivery. Yet in spite of these improvements and the increasing popularity of induction it had, as Tyler Smith objected, by no means yet ousted craniotomy from cases of difficult labour. Why?

In a paper delivered to the Royal Medical and Chirurgical Society in 1854, Dr Lee cautioned that the safety, efficacy and morality of induction were still questioned by many foreign and English practitioners.[80] In addition to these reservations, there are also practical explanations for the failure of induction to render destructive operations obsolete. As Tyler Smith indicated, in cases of pelvic deformity the disproportion between the fetal head and the pelvis might not become apparent until labour had commenced.[81] Further, as Dr Radford pointed out, women in the lower ranks usually employed midwives, and a medical man would not normally be consulted until labour had been in progress for some time and a serious impediment to its completion diagnosed.[82] Again, even if the disproportion were detected in time, and induction advised, the woman might refuse.[83]

Although induction had not, therefore, replaced craniotomy by the time the 1861 Act was passed, it was nevertheless well established and apparently gaining in popularity. Moreover, the indications for the operation had expanded. Whereas the original indication had been pelvic deformity, Tyler Smith listed ten indications of which this was but one. The remainder included ovarian tumours, haemorrhages from the uterus or other organs, excessive vomiting, convulsions, insanity, and cases with a history of stillbirth at full term.[84]

The popularity of induction after viability is also suggested in Taylor's *Manual*, which referred to 'the common practice of inducing *premature labour*, in certain cases of disease, of deformity of the pelvis, and in cases of excessive vomiting from pregnancy'.[85] Induction before viability was, however, less frequent: he wrote that it was uncommon in England.[86] Similarly, in 1883 Tidy wrote that it was indeed a very unusual case where the necessity for inducing labour in the earlier months of pregnancy, before viability, could be justified.[87] That Tidy's caution was pragmatic rather than moral is suggested by his comment elsewhere that the only reasonable arguments against induction were not medical, but were the religious objections, advanced by Catholics, against destroying infant life.[88] Consequently, when the operation was performed after viability, even these objections lost their force.[89]

However frequent the procedure may have been, the evidence of contemporary obstetrical texts indicates that induction, both before and after viability, was an accepted medical procedure in the last century even before the passage of the 1861 Act. Professional ethics condoned the operation if it was dictated by the necessity of preserving the life of the mother or, if possible, that of the child.

This strict approach still prevailed at the end of the century. In 1889 Dr Rentoul stressed that the sole object of the operation was the preservation of the mother's life when otherwise both she and the child would die.[90] In 1898, the *Lancet* agreed that it could only justifiably and legally be performed to preserve her life:

The fundamental principle, we should say, is this: when the patient's life is *necessarily* exposed to great danger if the pregnancy is allowed to continue it is proper to terminate it after *adequate consultation*.[91]

Accordingly, it condoned induction in cases of pelvic contraction where the mother declined to undergo the Caesarian, or there was pernicious vomiting or renal insufficiency.[92] It cautioned, however, that non-medical indications were ruled out by the law: neither inconvenience which might be caused to private plans for the future nor even the real hardship which was caused, especially to the children, by the fertility of persons unable to support a family were considerations entitled to the slightest weight as the law stood, and the journal did not feel that such cases gave rise to any difficulty.[93]

Even a threat of suicide was regarded as insufficient on the ground that the mother's threat to do wrong would not improve the doctor's position if he consented to do wrong; were it otherwise, the law against abortion would be a dead letter.[94] The prospect of mental illness was also rejected as an indication. If the patient was mentally irresponsible, the appropriate course was to place her under observation or restraint.[95]

This restrictive approach may appear surprising in the light of the increasing safety of the operation due to anaesthesia and antisepsis but a countervailing influence appears to have been the need for a relatively fixed criterion which would allow the practitioner to perform abortion in the more serious cases while enabling him to resist those applications he felt undeserving. The *Lancet* revealed that medical men were often asked to abort in circumstances which did not satisfy the law. The practitioner, it urged, ought to resist these requests. Even if the wishes of the patient, her husband and her friends were strongly in favour of abortion, and even at the risk of giving offence, the doctor ought to form his opinion on the medical aspects of the case with due regard to the requirements of the law.[96]

The frequency of such requests is confirmed by the very fact that the journal felt it advisable to remind practitioners of their obligations, and was attributed by the journal to a 'good deal of ignorance on the part of some women about the right and wrong of the matter' which in turn was traced to the persistence of the belief that in the early stages of pregnancy the child was not yet alive.[97] Atkinson agreed that the doctor should refuse illegitimate requests and he recommended the use of the law to this end:

He must refuse to aid a mother in illegally limiting her family. Indeed, if such seductive approaches are made, the proposers should be warned fully of the felonious nature of their desires; they should be summarily dismissed, preferably after the words of the penal act have been recited to them slowly and deliberately.[98]

Some practitioners, however, undoubtedly yielded to these requests. In 1894 the fourth edition of Taylor's *Principles*, edited by Dr Stevenson, conceded that the crime was frequently perpetrated for profit by irregular and even by regular practitioners and that for every case that came to light probably many were successfully concealed.[99] This lent support to Dr Rentoul's call, made five years earlier, for a re-evaluation of fetal life by the profession. Medical abortion had, in his opinion, been greatly abused.[100] He wrote that, for a considerable time, there had been a strong feeling that many in the profession did not have a due regard for fetal life and did not sufficiently impress its sacredness for fear of giving offence to patients or for want of moral courage.[101] He declared that the moral law on abortion had also to be the only medical law and that the wilful killing of a human being at any stage of its existence should be censured in the most forthright manner.[102] He called for a code of practice, both to guide the practitioner and to reaffirm that the saving of life was his highest calling.[103]

Professor Ranken Lyle went even further. In a paper published in 1926 he envisaged an ideal of doing nothing to interfere with conception, generation or parturition which would be detrimental to the survival of 'a single unit of humanity', for any reason whatever.[104] He noted that improvements in medical science had already rendered induction obsolete in cases of tuberculosis and heart disease, and continued that it was the intrinsic duty of the medical profession to preserve human life from conception to death.[105] Any surgical interference with the ovum or even the prevention of conception was, he maintained, inconsistent with this duty. Observing that the maternal and infant mortality rate associated with the Caesarian was then almost nil, he urged that the induction of abortion for medical reasons certainly ought to be prohibited and that it was only a question of time until it would be regarded as contrary to medical practice to perform the operation on any pretext.[106]

It may have been anticipated that these pleas for a more restrictive approach to the induction of abortion, bolstered by the ever-increasing safety of the Caesarian,[107] would have led to a decline in the operation. However, Lyle's views, like those of Radford before him, were heterodox. Notwithstanding the lack of medical consensus as to the conditions justifying therapeutic abortion, there developed well before 1938 a measure of agreement that it was warranted not merely to save or prolong the mother's life, but also to protect her health.

This trend was presaged as early as 1899, when a Dr McVie addressed the Edinburgh Obstetrical Society on the subject of the 'mother *v.* child' dilemma.[108] He urged that the value of the fetus was not actual but only potential and he described it as 'a parasite performing no function whatsoever'.[109] If, he added, the life expectancy of the mother were greatly shortened in comparison with that of the fetus the balance might tilt in favour of the latter, but the general practice was to prefer the mother's life even if her life expectancy were ten to fifteen years shorter.[110]

It is doubtful whether McVie's description of the fetus as a mere parasite would have enjoyed the approval of the profession as a whole. What is clear is that by 1938 the indications for therapeutic abortion were more consistent with his evaluation of fetal life than that advanced by Lyle, for it had become acceptable to preserve not only life but also health, both physical and mental.

This broadening of the indications is reflected in a collection of six papers on the induction of abortion delivered at the Annual Representative Meeting of the B.M.A. at Nottingham in 1926. The first was presented by Dr Watts Eden, consulting obstetric physician to the Charing Cross Hospital.[111] Indications, he explained, were either 'obstetric' or 'medical'. The latter included phthisis and heart disease.[112] The former, which were 'few and relatively unimportant' included missed abortion and toxaemic vomiting.[113] Provided there were good reasons for believing that the continuation of the pregnancy would endanger the mother's life, or prejudice her future health, abortion was justifiable.[114] He cited one case in which he had induced abortion on the ground that the woman had only recently given birth to a second child.[115] Of particular interest in his paper, however, is his sweeping language when referring to general considerations relating to the question of induction. At one point, he went so far as to say:

It is an ethical question of great interest to what extent we as doctors have the right to insist that a woman shall pass through an ordeal which she is unwilling to face, even if we do not think that she will sustain any permanent injury from so doing.[116]

Instead of a 'rigid' attitude to the question, he urged a sympathetic consideration of each case on its merits. He even appeared to contemplate induction in the absence of a pathological condition: 'it may at times be right to terminate pregnancy, even if the mother is not suffering from any condition which could, strictly speaking, be called disease'.[117]

According to Dr Louise McIlroy, Professor of Obstetrics at the University of London, Eden's paper was not only moderate and well-balanced but also epitomised the opinions of a large majority of the profession.[118] However, both from her own paper and from those of other contributors, it appears that Eden's views went, at least in some respects, beyond established medical opinion. McIlroy felt that induction was a confession of failure and should only be resorted to in cases of dire necessity. She declared that patients were too frequently sent to the obstetrician for the performance of the operation before other methods of treatment had been given a fair chance.[119] Echoing Lyle, she aired an expectation that scientific progress would relegate the procedure to virtual obsolescence. She continued that they were beginning to recognise that the ovum was only a temporary lodger and that its advent did not always have the malignant effect upon the mother that their predecessors had tended to believe.[120] Similarly, Dr Evers urged that obstetricians, whose most important function was the preservation of the ovum, should limit induction to the extremely few cases where it had demonstrated its worth, and he cautioned against 'speculative' indications.[121] Quoting Lyle, he maintained that induction should practically never be considered, not only because of the value of the fetus but also on account of the great improvements which had taken place in the treatment of the complications of pregnancy and because the original indications were mostly speculative and groundless.[122]

In the discussion which followed the presentation of the papers, Dr Eden was unrepentant. He advocated 'broad views' on the subject: the rigidity of professional opinion drove people to the abortion-mongers.[123] Broaching the question of eugenic abortion, he argued that the doctor could not divest himself of all responsibility for the welfare of the child which might be born diseased.[124] In his paper he had specifically mentioned the risk to the child as a factor worthy of consideration in the decision to abort. It was not, he said, to the advantage of the community that children should be born over whom there hung a risk of tuberculosis several times greater than that run by other children.[125]

A eugenic indication was not as yet, however, recognised by the profession as a whole. Still, the papers delivered at the B.M.A. meeting and subsequent evidence indicate that, if professional opinion was against a eugenic indication, it was nevertheless supportive of induction to preserve health, even if there was a certain amount of disagreement as to the nature and severity of the justificatory conditions.

This was recognised by Dr John Fairbairn, obstetric physician to St Thomas's Hospital. At a joint meeting of the Medico-Legal Society and the obstetrical section of the Royal Society of Medicine in 1927, he remarked that although there was general agreement that induction was warranted in cases of toxaemia of pregnancy, opinion was far from unanimous when pregnancy aggravated a pre-existing chronic disease from which the woman was suffering. He declared that in some diseases, such as chronic kidney disease and diabetes, there was general agreement that pregnancy should be interrupted but that in regard to such conditions as tuberculosis, grave malnutrition, and nervous and mental states there was room for wide variation in practice.[126] Moreover, whereas some doctors waited for evidence that pregnancy was aggravating the disease, many accepted unquestioningly the ill-effect they thought might arise and ended the pregnancy forthwith. [127] The principle which had originally guided the profession was that abortion was only lawful if the woman's life was in danger, but this had rightly been extended to the prevention of serious or permanent damage to her health, and there was something to be said for relieving a mother suffering from a serious disease from the physical and mental strain of bearing and rearing a child, even if statistics showed little gain from it.[128] In deciding upon the threat to health, the decision to abort had to be made largely on the basis of the balance of probabilities and there was room for much disagreement.[129] Referring to the B.M.A. meeting of the previous year he observed that many doctors even ventured into the realm of non-medical indications:

the principle of danger to life and health of the mother has . . . been jettisoned, and many in the profession go so far as to act on the supposition that it is not unlawful to take into consideration other than purely medical factors and to allow social, economic, eugenic, and other reasons to weigh in justifying the induction of abortion.[130]

He attacked this as a lowering of standards and urged that only purely medical considerations ought to weigh in the decision.[131] He warned that once non-medical factors were allowed to count, no line could be drawn between therapeutic and criminal abortion.[132] He was echoed by the next speaker, Lord Riddell, who said that the doctor should confine himself to the 'medical and surgical' aspects of the case.[133]

Subsequent papers and the ensuing discussion again reveal a certain diversity of opinion. Although there was agreement that induction was justifiable to preserve life and health, beyond this the consensus broke down. Dr Russell Andrews disagreed with Fairbairn that the traditional principle had been rejected[134] and in this he was supported by Professor Donald.[135] Dr McCann urged the meeting to adopt a restrictive ethical position since 'Once loopholes were created the whole position fell'.[136]

Both meetings suggest that the preservation of health had become a generally accepted indication for abortion and that even wider indications were accepted by a number of practitioners. The meetings also demonstrate that health was understood to embrace both physical and mental well-being. Dr Eden cited 'diseases of the nervous system' and 'psychopathic disturbances' as grounds for the operation.[137] An instance of the former was a case where a patient had been aborted because of her unshakable fear of death if she went to term. Eden wrote that there was absolutely no reason for the intervention apart from her mental condition.[138] His opinion that a morbid fear of death might justify induction was supported by Dr Robert Cole, lecturer in mental diseases at St Mary's Hospital, in a paper delivered at the 1926 meeting.[139] On the other hand, his paper, which was devoted entirely to the psychological grounds for induction, did not lend support to Eden's opinion that abortion was indicated by a history of insanity. Indeed, he concluded overall that in the treatment of mental conditions, induction was the exception rather than the rule.[140] This restrained conclusion was perhaps influenced by his fear that danger to mental health, which he considered to be problematical in many cases, was capable of being construed in an 'elastic' sense and of being applied to improper cases, thereby leading to abuse and consequent criticism of the privileged position of practitioners.[141]

At the 1927 meeting, Lord Riddell not only defended the validity of the mental health indication but went so far as to state that if the medical attendant concluded that the continuance of the pregnancy was likely to result in admission to a mental home, he was duty-bound to induce abortion.[142] In the same year, a paper was published which lent authoritative support to this indication.[143] Its author was J. R. Lord, President of the Royal Medico-Psychological Association. In his opinion, the only ethical grounds for induction were the preservation of life; the alleviation of serious illness, whether physical or mental; and the prevention of serious illness, again whether physical or mental and whether permanent or temporary.[144] Not only, therefore, did he regard induction as justifiable when employed as a curative measure but also when used as a prophylactic, even if the condition to be averted was only a temporary mental illness. Nor was he alone in subscribing to this opinion. He remarked that he was convinced that the modern practice of induction to prevent the recurrence of mental disorder was growing.[145] However, although condoning abortion in the interests of mental health, he felt its value was 'problematical'. He questioned the sufficiency of the evidence for the ability of the operation to alleviate mental disorder or to prevent its first attacks.[146]

His circumspect approach was echoed in the discussion which followed his paper.[147] For example, Dr Boyle remarked that induction was itself a disturbing event which often induced a 'definite mental conflict'.[148] Summing up the feeling of the Association, Lord declared that the weight of evidence told definitely against the growing practice of inducing abortion for the prevention of mental disorder and that those practitioners who favoured it might be unwittingly harming society. He added that fear of exposure, shame, depression and misery following the 'breaking of the moral law' should not be confused with the symptoms arising from the disordered mind, for such were the reactions of the normal mind and were, in fact, direct evidences of it.[149]

In a paper on the same subject Percy Smith, consulting physician to St Thomas's Hospital, catalogued seventeen cases drawn from twenty-seven years of practice in which induction had been considered on the ground of mental disorder.[150] In ten cases, abortion was induced either to prevent the occurrence of disorder or to defuse the threat of suicide.[151] Evidently, Smith also believed the operation to be of limited application in the context of mental health. Moreover, he expressly supported Fairbairn's view that when induction was under consideration, only medical factors should be allowed to weigh.[152]

A similarly restrictive approach to the mental health indication was evidenced in 1929 at the Medical Society of London.[153] Dr Hart divided mental illnesses into the psychoses, or 'definite insanities' and the psychoneuroses. He pointed out that induction was only of limited value in the former, unless the psychosis were recurrent.[154] However, as pregnancy might be a central factor in the production of psychoneurotic symptoms, induction might be justified to avert mental breakdown, though he stressed that the grounds were uncertain and that each case had to be judged on its merits.[155] Further, it was by no means easy to exclude non-medical factors from consideration: social and economic circumstances might react upon the patient's health in all sorts of ways and though a practitioner might decline to take them into account directly, they might force themselves upon him indirectly. There was, he said, no general rule and factors of many different types had to be considered.[156] Indeed, there was a danger that the practitioner might be unconsciously swayed by the demands of the patient or her relations as the grounds were so uncertain, and there was so much room for individual differences of opinion.[157] Finally, he said that it was generally agreed that, if the woman's suicide was not unlikely, her pregnancy should be terminated.[158]

An even more authoritative endorsement of the mental health indication came from the B.M.A. Committee on Medical Aspects of Abortion which reported just two years before the trial of Dr Bourne, who was one of the Committee's members.[159] A section of the report was devoted to 'Mental indications' and followed Hart's subdivison of these indications into psychoses, psychoneuroses and suicide threats.[160] The Committee agreed with Hart that psychoneurosis seldom warranted induction. Whether this was true of threatened suicide was left to the mental expert to decide on the merits of the case before him. With regard to psychosis, if pregnancy was a causal factor, abortion might be justified to prevent aggravation or relapse and, in other cases, to preserve life or to prevent the possible onset of mental disorder.[161] As for manic-depressive psychosis occurring during pregnancy, the woman usually recovered and there was no proof that abortion shortened the attack. In some cases, however, the psychosis might definitely be due to anxieties and conflicts associated with the pregnancy. In such cases, suicide was a distinct danger and justification for abortion was probably commoner in this class of case than in any other. Abortion might also be advisable in cases of schizophrenia, organic psychoses, or where the patient had previously suffered from psychosis.[162]

The Committee's report is significant not only because it represents official approval, by an authoritative body of eminent members of the medical establishment, of the mental health indication but also because it provided a comprehensive catalogue of the physical indications, ranging from cardiovascular to organic nervous conditions, which might justify induction.[163] Indeed, it went even further and considered sympathetically both 'eugenic' and 'humanitarian' indications. The report condoned induction for certain 'Miscellaneous conditions', one of which was 'Pregnancy following rape below age of consent'. It stated:

A valid medical reason based upon physical considerations can seldom be advanced on account of age alone, but whether the severe *mental* injury, caused by an experience so dreadful as childbirth at a tender age, should not be accounted an even greater indication than physical danger is a point to be considered very seriously.[164]

Following the Committee's reasoning, the indication would apply whether the girl had been raped or not, since the gist of the indication was the mental disturbance of childbirth at a young age.

Even more remarkable, however, is the Committee's express condonation of eugenic abortion. The report declared that induction should be considered when, in the light of modern medical knowledge, there was reasonable certainty that serious disease would be transmitted to the child.[165] This might be 'mental deficiency', when abortion would be allowable if, for example, both parents were certified mental defectives, or other hereditary conditions, such as certain blood disorders.[166]

The breadth of the discretion which the report conceded to the doctor is apparent not only from the number of indications which it recognised but in its acceptance that it was impossible to lay down hard and fast rules as to their interpretation and application in a given situation. Each case had to be judged on its merits.[167]

The report confirms that, before *Bourne*, increasingly broad indications for induction had gained recognition even within the upper echelons of the medical profession.[168] Moreover, evidence from other sources indicates not only that professional opinion had become more permissive, but that the actual practice of some members went even further, either because they did not share the ethical views of their colleagues or because, for reasons of self-interest or otherwise, they capitulated to the requests of their patients. Earl Russell declared that the practice of gynecologists had been extended to a degree that amounted to relieving their patients from a very inconvenient time, a practice which did not appear to be legally justified. This showed, he said, how doctors were the high priests of modern civilisation and above the law.[169] Similarly, Dr Roche Lynch said that certain obstetricians in recent years appeared to have practised abortion in cases where the mother's convenience and not her life were at stake.[170]

In 1927 Fairbairn noted that the pressures to abort were more acute in private than in hospital practice. Private patients paid the piper and demanded some say in calling the tune. The private practitioner was, therefore, much more influenced by his patients and his patients' relatives and his judgement was swayed by their wishes.[171] He warned that if the lax views of many doctors were espoused by the profession as a whole, unrestricted abortion-mongering would become a vested interest of those on the medical register, who would become merely the instruments of those who hired them for this purpose. He urged that medical indications alone should be considered and that they should be defined as those clearly involving danger to the life or health of the mother or damage to the pregnancy sufficient to interfere with its future development.[172] Lord Riddell also claimed that doctors were paying increasing attention to patients' wishes. He said that the increasing tendency of doctors to induce abortion seemed to be due to a growing desire on the part of medical men to please their patients: the 'pontifical' doctor was becoming a thing of the past.[173] Dr McIlroy made the observation that a country practitioner might not be able to afford to subscribe to pontifical ethics: complete ruin might follow a failure to comply with the wishes of an influential patient.[174]

An illustration of the type of situation in which the practitioner might find himself under pressure from his patient was provided by Dr Eden in 1926. He described a case in which he had been consulted by the wife of a barrister with a view to the termination of her pregnancy. The only reason she advanced for the desired abortion was that the pregnancy, her third, had followed shortly after the delivery of her second child and the couple therefore believed that it would materially affect her health. Shaken by this view, Eden referred them to a more experienced doctor who, to his surprise, took their side. The doctor felt that the couple's fears were exaggerated but that their medical attendants had no right to ignore them, and that repeated pregnancies often affected health badly. The pregnancy was, therefore, terminated. Within six months, however, the situation recurred. This time Eden flatly refused to intervene, but the couple found a more 'pliable' colleague.[175] Commenting on this case, Fairbairn said that it was the frequency of such cases that had served to weaken the profession's former reluctance to induce abortion save for grave danger to the woman.[176] Contemporary women enjoyed greater opportunities than their Victorian predecessors and wanted much more than a family life, but they were less able to endure strain and their reproductive capacity was inferior. Moreover, the induction of abortion had become safer, and public morality had fallen due to the Great War and the spread of contraceptive propaganda. It was not surprising, he concluded, that these changes in attitude should have influenced the profession, for the attitude of the public had to affect the profession which both served the public and was part of it.[177]

Changing practice in relation to the induction of abortion was examined more methodically by Eardley Holland, an eminent gynecologist. Addressing the Medical Society of London in 1929 he observed that the preservation of health was considered to be an acceptable indication, although there was a wide divergence of opinion as to what constituted avoiding injury to health.[178] Not only had medical indications been extended but non-medical considerations were now believed by many to be taken into account.[179] Interestingly, he produced statistical evidence to support the view that abortion was more commonly induced in private than in hospital practice and according to less rigid criteria. He divided indications into 'positive', 'debatable' and 'doubtful'.[180] The first consisted of medical states, such as heart disease, in which abortion was clearly indicated and which predominated in hospital practice: of 4000 admissions to the London Hospital's gynecological wards between 1924 and 1927 inclusive, thirty abortions were induced, twenty-three of which were for 'positive' indications.[181] He said that, in hospital,

there is much more of a tendency to restrict the induction of abortion to purely medical indications than in private practice, in which social and personal considerations are apt to obtrude themselves more.[182]

The second and third type of indication were more controversial. 'Debatable' indications included both medical and eugenic grounds.[183] 'Doubtful' indications consisted of a 'heterogeneous collection of combined medical, social and personal states' upon which the doctor's decision would depend not only on his knowledge of medicine but also on such factors as his ethical outlook and the degree of pressure from the patient and her relatives.[184] These more controversial indications predominated in private practice, where abortion was more commonly performed.[185] Between 1920 and 1928 inclusive, out of 3000 new private patients, he induced abortion on twenty-eight occasions, three for 'positive', twelve for 'debatable' and five for 'doubtful' indications.[186] He vividly summed up the change in professional practice in the space of a generation, and said that ethical standards in relation to induction were not as strict as they had been. In particular, he added,

social and eugenic reasons were allowed to add weight to a purely medical reason to an extent which would not have been tolerated by a former generation. Some of the older gynaecologists would have been horrified at the present standard, and it is probable that the present generation of gynaecologists will be just as horrified at the standard of their successors.[187]

Conclusion

This overview of therapeutic abortion from the late eighteenth century to the *Bourne* case reveals that, even in the absence of a therapeutic proviso in the anti-abortion legislation, the operation was performed throughout this period and that the indications for the procedure gradually expanded. (For major obstetrical texts published before 1938 which discussed the induction of labour both before and after viability, see Table 1.) Lord described this expansion (albeit simplistically), in five stages. The first was the performance of abortion to save life; the second, to prevent permanent physical illness; the third, to prevent even temporary illness; the fourth, to preserve mental as well as physical health; and, in the fifth, eugenic and economic indications were recognised.[188]

In spite of the apparent inflexibility of the law, medical men induced abortion according to criteria established by themselves. Moreover, provided practitioners abided by professional ethics, the risk of prosecution appears to have been negligible. There seems to have been no prosecution of a doctor who terminated a pregnancy in accordance with these standards before 1938. The prosecution of Dr Bourne in that year was not really an exception to this prosecutorial policy of non-intervention, for he actively courted the initiation of proceedings.[189]

The evidence of obstetrical sources indicates, therefore, that professional attitudes were an important factor in determining the indications for medical abortion before 1938; that when these attitudes changed (due possibly to such factors as a greater concern for the woman's health as well as her life; for prevention as well as cure; and for the wishes of the patient as well as the opinions of the doctor) abortion was induced for increasingly broad indications and decisions were no longer arrived at in the light of medical considerations alone.

The *Bourne* case of 1938 did not, therefore, liberate medical discretion from an uncompromising law. In fact, this was recognised by Bourne himself. Writing shortly after his trial he conceded that his aim had not been to reform the law but to ensure its declaration. He wrote that he decided to bring forward a test case in which there was no real danger to life, but in which great danger to health might be strongly suspected, and he added that he was also concerned to establish that mental health was just as important in the eyes of the law as physical health, and in certain cases perhaps more so. He stressed: 'I also wish to state once again that I did not bring the case forward as an attempt to alter the law by direct action, but to obtain a further definition of the present law'.[190] If this was Bourne's aim, he was clearly pushing at an open door.[191] Ironically, his actions may have actually closed the door to a degree, for Macnaghten J. imposed conditions on the performance of the operation and limited it to the preservation of the woman's life or, at most, the prevention of physical or mental breakdown.

Had Bourne defended his action in aborting his patient on the ground that he believed the pregnancy to be the result of rape, and that his motive was essentially humanitarian, then he would indeed have challenged the law. There is in fact some evidence that this may have been his original intention but that before the trial he shifted his defence on to the broader and safer ground of averting danger to health. In his evidence to the Inter-Departmental Committee on Abortion, the Director of Public Prosecutions pointed out that on 12 June 1938 information was received at Scotland Yard that the raped girl had been admitted to hospital for an abortion on 'humanitarian' grounds.[192] He and the Attorney-General decided to initiate proceedings lest inaction be construed as official sanction of a change in the law.[193] Had this line of defence been pursued and had the judge ruled it valid in law, then would the case have merited the significance which has hitherto been mistakenly attributed to it.

Table 1. List of virtually all major obstetrical texts published in England from 1794 to 1937, showing which directly or indirectly condoned the induction of labour (i) before and (ii) after viability

Text	(i)	(ii)
Thomas Denman, *An Intro. to the Practice of Midwifery* (2 vols.) (London: 1794)	—	II, 213–220
Alexander Hamilton, *Outlines of the Theory and Practice of Midwifery* (Edinburth: 5th edn, 1803)	173	—
John Power, *A Treatise on Midwifery* (London: 1819)	—	—
Wm. P. Dewees, *A Compendious System of Midwifery* (London: 1825)	607–608	606–607
David D. Davies, *The Principles and Practice of Obstetric Medicine* (2 vols.) (London: 1836)	—	II, 1149–1151
Henry Maunsell, *The Dublin Practice of Midwifery* (London: 1834)	—	140–141
Charles Severn, *First Lines of the Practice of Midwifery* (London: 1831)	—	83–84
The London Practice of Midwifery (London: 6th edn, 1833, ed. Geo. Jewel)	234–235	234–235
John Burns, *The Principles of Midwifery* (London: 9th edn, 1837)	507–508	408
James Blundell, *The Principles and Practice of Obstetrics* (London: 1840)	559–560	—
John Ramsbotham, *Practical Observations in Midwifery* (London: 2nd edn, 1842)	—	—
Wm. & Alex. D. Campbell, *Introduction to the Study of Midwifery* (Edinburgh: 2nd edn, 1843)	335; 336; 338	335–336
James Whitehead, *On the Causes and Treatment of Abortion and Sterility* (London: 1847)	254	—
Fleetwood Churchill, *On the Theory and Practice of Midwifery* (London: 2nd edn 1850)	—	236–248
Dr. Conquest's Outlines of Midwifery (London: 1854, ed. James M. Winn)	—	182–183
Charles Clay, *The Complete Handbook of Obstetric Surgery* (London: 1856)	8–9	144–145
W. Tyler Smith, *A Manual of Obstetrics* (London: 1858)	546–549	546–556

Text	(i)	(ii)
Charles Waller, *Elements of Practical Midwifery* (London: 4th edn, 1858)	139	138–139
Alfred Meadows, *Manual of Midwifery* (London: 1862)	—	143–146
Francis H. Ramsbotham, *The Principles & Practice of Obstetric Medicine and Surgery* (London: 5th edn, 1867)	306n; 337	329–337
Alexander Milne, *The Principles and Practice of Midwifery* (Edinburgh: 1871)	316	306–307
William Leishman, *A System of Midwifery* (Glasgow: 2nd edn, 1876)	621–628	622–623
W. S. Playfair, *A Treatise on the Science & Art of Midwifery* (2 vols.) (London: 5th edn, 1884)	I, 222–223; II, 82–85; 152–153	II, 152–154
Robert and Fancourt Barnes, *A System of Obstetric Medicine and Surgery* (2 vols.) (London: 1884)	I, 354; 489; II, 723	II, 724
William Thompson Lusk, *The Science and Art of Midwifery* (London: 3rd edn, 1885)	351	341–343
Alfred Lewis Galabin, *A Manual of Midwifery* (London: 1886)	538–539	529–530
A System of Obstetrics (2 vols.) (Edinburgh: 1888, ed. Barton Cooke Hirst)	II, 195–196	II, 197
Robert Reid Rentoul, *The Causes and Treatment of Abortion* (London: 1889)	250–251	137–138
W. A. Newman Dorland, *A Manual of Obstetrics* (London: 1896)	265–267	267–268
W. E. Fothergill, *Manual of Midwifery* (Edinburgh: 1896)	431	426–427
W. R. Dakin, *A Handbook of Midwifery* (London: 1897)	362–365	362–363
A. F. A. King, *A Manual of Obstetrics* (London: 8th edn, 1901)	425–442	425–426
David James Evans, *Obstetrics* (London: 1901)	371	373
Charles Jewett, *Essentials of Obstetrics* (London: 2nd edn, 1902)	337–338	330
A Textbook of Obstetrics (2 vols.) (London: 2nd edn, 1902, ed. Richard C. Norris & R. L. Dickerson)	II, 403	II, 403–404

continued

Table 1 — *continued*

Text	(i)	(ii)
Henry J. Garrigues, *A Text-Book of the Science and Art of Midwifery* (London: 1902)	269–270	272
J. Clifton Edgar, *The Practice of Obstetrics* (London: 1903)	916–917	916–917
Robert Jardine, *Clinical Obstetrics* (London: 1903)	182	537–539
J. Clarence Webster, *A Text-Book of Obstetrics* (London: 1903)	659–660	663–664
J. Whitridge Williams, *Obstetrics* (London: 1903)	338	341
J. W. Ballantyne, *Essentials of Obstetrics* (Edinburgh: 1904)	136	194–195
Henry Jellett, *A Manual of Midwifery* (London: 1905)	966–967	968–971
Adam H. Wright, *A Text-Book of Obstetrics* (London: 1905)	519	520
E. Hastings Tweedy and G. T. Wrench, *Rotunda Practical Midwifery* (London: 1908)	86; 168	99
Egbert H. Grandin & George W. Jarman, *A Text-Book on Practical Obstetrics* (Philadelphia: 4th edn, 1909)	354–361	367–378
Alfred Lewis Galabin and George Blacker, *The Practice of Midwifery* (London: 1910)	803–804	792–793
G. Balfour Marshall, *A Manual of Midwifery* (Glasgow: 1912)	334–335	335–337
Comyns Berkeley and Victor Bonney, *The Difficulties and Emergencies of Obstetric Practice* (London: 1913)	172	708–709
Frederick Elmer Leavitt, *The Operations of Obstetrics* (London: 1919)	49–67	49–67
Thomas Watts Eden, *A Manual of Midwifery* (London: 5th edn, 1919)	625–626	626
O. St J. Moses, *Manual of Obstetrics* (London: 1920)	202	203–204
Aleck W. Bourne, *Synopsis of Midwifery* (Bristol: 2nd edn, 1921)	190	190
Gibbon Fitzgibbon, *Practical Midwifery* (London: 1923)	457	457–458

Text	(i)	(ii)
Midwifery by Ten Teachers (London: 3rd edn, 1925, ed. H. Russell Andrews, J. S. Fairbairn and Comyns Berkeley)	724	733–735
John S. Fairbairn, *Obstetrics* (London: 1926)	170–173	170; 175–176
R. W. Johnstone, *A Text-Book of Midwifery* (London: 5th edn, 1926)	480–482	476–477
George Peaslee Shears, *Obstetrics Normal and Operative* (Philadelphia: 6th edn, 1929)	567	570
The Queen Charlotte's Practice of Obstetrics (London: 2nd edn, 1930, ed. J. Bright Banister and A. W. Bourne)	494–495	497–498
O'Donel Browne, *A Manual of Practical Obstetrics* (Bristol: 1936)	276–277	276–277
Glasgow Manual of Obstetrics (London: 2nd edn, 1936, ed. Samuel J. Cameron et al.)	521–522	529
J. M. Munro-Kerr, *Operative Obstetrics* (London: 4th edn, 1937)	547	277–278
Tweedy's Practical Obstetrics (London: 7th edn, 1937, ed. Bethel Solomons)	225	543

4

The medical profession and the enactment of the Abortion Act 1967

In the preceding chapter it was maintained that the O.A.P.A. 1861 did not explicitly permit therapeutic abortion but that this did not prevent the performance of the procedure by medical men: abortion was openly induced according to indications established not by the law but by the profession. When these indications expanded, so too did the performance of abortion, even though the law remained unchanged in its apparent restrictiveness. Only in 1938, after the law was challenged by a member of the medical establishment was legal theory unequivocally brought more into line with the realities of clinical practice. It is apparent, therefore, that medical men exerted a significant influence not only on the restriction of the law in the nineteenth century but also on its subsequent relaxation. Did the profession exert any significant influence on the more recent relaxation of the law by the Abortion Act 1967?

The Act came into force on 27 April 1968. It represented the culmination of a campaign led by the Abortion Law Reform Association (A.L.R.A.) to make abortion more widely available. The history of that campaign has been adequately documented elsewhere.[1] It is the aim of this chapter to consider, against this background, the views of the representative medical bodies on the reform of the law and their influence on the Act as it finally emerged from the legislative process.

The 1967 Act placed therapeutic abortion on a statutory footing. Previously, it had been regulated by case-law in the form of the summings-up in *R. v. Bourne* (1938), *R. v. Bergmann and Ferguson* (1948), and *R. v. Newton and Stungo* (1958).[2] However, it not only enshrined therapeutic abortion in statutory form but also extended the indications for the procedure beyond the preservation of the woman's life and health. Section 1(1) provides:

Subject to the provisions of this section, a person shall not be guilty of an offence under the law relating to abortion when a pregnancy is terminated by a registered medical practitioner if two registered medical practitioners are of the opinion, formed in good faith –

(a) that the continuance of the pregnancy would involve risk to the life of the pregnant woman , or of injury to the physical or mental health of the pregnant woman, or any existing children of her family, greater than if the pregnancy were terminated; or

(b) that there is a substantial risk that if the child were born it would suffer from such physical or mental abnormalities as to be seriously handicapped.

Subsection 2 reads:

In determining whether the continuance of a pregnancy would involve such risk of injury to health as is mentioned in paragraph (a) of subsection 1 of this section, account may be taken of the pregnant woman's actual or reasonably foreseeable environment.

Subsection 3 requires any treatment for the termination of pregnancy to be carried out in a hospital vested in the Minister of Health or the Secretary of State, or in a place approved by either for the purposes of the section. Subsection 4 provides that the restriction on the place of termination and the requirement of a second opinion shall not apply when a registered medical practitioner is of the opinion, formed in good faith, that termination is immediately necessary to save the life, or to prevent grave, permanent injury to the physical or mental health, of the pregnant woman.

Section 2 of the Act provides for the making of regulations by the Minister of Health, with respect to the certification of opinions, the notification of the operation, and the disclosure of information furnished pursuant to the regulations.[3]

Section 4 makes provision for conscientious objection to treatment authorised by the Act, except when the operation is necessary to save the woman's life or to prevent grave, permanent injury to her health.

To what extent did the opinion of the medical profession influence these provisions? One striking feature is their approximation not to the proposals of A.L.R.A., which inspired and organised the cause of reform, but to the recommendations of the medical bodies.

The Act originated in the Medical Termination of Pregnancy

Bill, a private member's measure introduced by Mr David Steel, M.P. for Roxburgh, Selkirk and Peebles. The circumstances in which the Bill proposed to render abortion lawful were in several respects more extensive than those specified in the Act. In particular, they were not confined to the physical or mental condition of the mother or child. The circumstances in relation to which two registered medical practitioners were required to certify their belief were set out in four paragraphs:

(a) that the continuance of the pregnancy would involve serious risk to the life or of grave injury to the health, whether physical or mental, of the pregnant woman whether before, at or after the birth of the child; or

(b) that there is a substantial risk that if the child were born it would suffer from such physical or mental abnormalities as to be seriously handicapped; or

(c) that the pregnant woman's capacity as a mother will be severely overstrained by the care of a child or of another child as the case may be; or

(d) that the pregnant woman is a defective or became pregnant while under the age of sixteen or became pregnant as a result of rape.[4]

In short, the Bill contained 'therapeutic', 'eugenic', 'social' and 'humanitarian' indications. It did not, however, contain a provision expressly allowing the doctor to take account of the woman's actual or reasonably foreseeable environment in arriving at his decision.

The Bill was similar, in respect of the indications it permitted, to an Abortion Bill which had been introduced into the House of Lords by Lord Silkin in November 1965 and again in April 1966,[5] and which had been dropped in favour of its successor in the Commons. Silkin had urged that Steel's Bill should reproduce his own, in the form eventually accepted by the Lords, on the ground that this would facilitate its passage through Parliament, but prominent A.L.R.A. members succeeded in persuading Steel to introduce a broader measure.[6] It was urged that it should be broader in four respects: any doctor, irrespective of status, should be allowed to terminate pregnancy; notification should not be required; rape should be included as a separate ground; and the concept of 'well-being' should be added to the 'therapeutic' ground. Steel was advised by a committee comprising his twelve parliamentary sponsors and A.L.R.A. representatives, but A.L.R.A.'s recommendations were accepted only in part; rape was reinstated as a ground, but the concept of 'well-being' was not imported and notification was still to be required for abortions performed other than in National Health Service (N.H.S.) hospitals. However, the Bill went further than Silkin's Bill by omitting to grant the Chief Medical Officer (C.M.O.) power to disclose notifications to a police officer and by specifically allowing abortions to be performed in registered nursing homes in addition to places approved by the Minister of Health or the Secretary of State. Hindell and Simms relate that, after two sessions of the committee, the Bill emerged much as A.L.R.A. wanted it.[7] Mr Peter Diggory, a consultant gynecologist who was to become Steel's medical advisor at the Committee stage of the Bill, felt the Bill was an improvement on Silkin's, which had started as a very good measure but ended up as a 'highly restrictive code of practice'.[8] The Bill received its first reading on 15 June 1966.[9] Although it met with A.L.R.A.'s approval, it was to undergo significant amendment before enactment, as is evident from the final form of s. 1. To what degree, if any, was the amendment of the Bill a response to medical opinion?

A survey of the opinions of the major medical bodies reveals that none opposed reform as such, although those whose task it was to perform abortions, the gynecologists, were less enthusiastic for reform than their colleagues in other areas of practice. The profession was, however, firmly opposed to any reform which compromised clinical freedom either by taking the final decision out of the hands of the medical attendant or by specifying the indications for abortion too exactly. One of the concerns underlying the latter objection was undoubtedly that too great a degree of precision might enable the pregnant woman to diagnose herself as qualifying for termination under the legislation and demand the procedure.

The views of the major professional bodies were not, however, identical. Some supported greater legal relaxation than others, and the degree of support varied inversely with the degree of involvement with the operation: whereas gynecologists favoured only limited reform, psychiatrists supported extensive change.

4.1 The Royal Medico-Psychological Association (R.M.-P.A.)

The psychiatrists' professional body produced a Memorandum on Therapeutic Abortion which was approved by its Council on 5 July

1966. It favoured legislation, complaining that many medical men were inhibited from advising or performing abortion through fear of the law. In reaching a decision on abortion, it added, in addition to the traditionally accepted medical and psychiatric criteria, all the social circumstances should be taken into account. If, the report stated, after considering all these factors, the psychiatrist formed the opinion that the mental health of the mother and the whole family would be promoted by termination then it should be lawful for him to recommend it.[10] Abortion ought not, however, to be lawful merely on the ground of inconvenience to one or both of the parents.[11] Still, even the remote effects of continuation of pregnancy on health and well-being ought to be taken into consideration. A greatly overburdened mother, for example, might need relief not only from the pregnancy itself but from the cares of looking after another infant in an already overlarge family.[12] Not only was therapeutic abortion in this broad sense supported, but so was eugenic abortion, as likely to be beneficial to society.[13] Again, severe emotional overstrain from the care of a child would provide an indication for termination. The report explained that this would embrace the young, unmarried girl; the rape victim; or the woman beset by very disturbing marital or family conflicts.[14] There was, moreover, a *prima facie* case for termination when a severely subnormal woman or one suffering from severe, chronic, mental illness became pregnant. Even when the condition was some lesser degree of subnormality, or psychopathic disorder, or other mental illness, abortion might still be indicated: such patients often made inadequate parents. Every child, both for its own sake and that of society, needed conscientious parents to give it care and affection. If parents were incapable in this respect their children tended to become unhappy, mentally disordered, and particularly prone to antisocial behaviour. The likelihood of serious parental inadequacy of this sort did, in the Association's view, constitute adequate grounds for termination.[15] As for safeguards such as notification or a board of consultants and social workers, they were rejected as an undesirable and unnecessary addition to the patient's stress. Provided two doctors agreed – normally the general practitioner and the consultant gynecologist but, where the grounds were social and psychiatric, a consultant psychiatrist – abortion should follow the same pattern as other medical procedures. Ultimately, the statement observed, the safeguard must lie in the integrity of members of the profession. It also warned against undue infringement of clinical freedom: 'doctors would not wish a situation to be created by law which would encroach upon their independence in matters requiring professional and ethical judgement'.[16] This might occur if the permissible indications were defined too closely:

Spelling out in detail when a doctor should or should not have the right to induce abortion, even if the legislation is cast in permissive terms, would have the effect of introducing an element of coercion in the sense that in each defined situation the patient might reasonably expect the doctor to acquiesce and the role of the surgeon or gynaecologist would be reduced to that of a technician carrying out an objectionable task.[17]

4.2 The British Medical Association (B.M.A.)

On 2 July 1966 there was the publication of the report of a Special Committee of the B.M.A. on Therapeutic Abortion. This Committee, which had been set up by Council on the instruction of the Representative Body of the Association[18] to update the report of the Committee on the Medical Aspects of Abortion which had reported in 1936, also expressed concern over the preservation of professional freedom. It stated that it was not usually possible to specify the maternal disorders which had to be present to warrant abortion, especially in view of the dynamic state of medical science. Whether a pregnancy should be terminated was a question which could only be decided in the circumstances of each particular case and should be left to the medical attendants concerned:

The ultimate decision to advise termination of pregnancy rests with the doctors in charge of the case and, subject to the conditions laid down to safeguard the security of the pre-viable fetus, the law should not seek to influence this decision by further defining the degree of risk which must be present before termination can be regarded as lawful.[19]

The Committee was of the opinion that the law needed reform, not only because the judicial directions on the lawfulness of abortion might be overruled, but also because the existing therapeutic exception was insufficiently extensive: it did not, for example, cover eugenic indications.[20] Since the report of the Inter-Departmental Committee on Abortion in 1939,[21] a considerable amount of knowledge about fetal abnormalities had accumulated and in certain cases prediction was now possible with some degree of certainty. Consequently, the Special Committee recommended that the law be amended to allow risk of serious fetal abnormality to be taken into account in deciding whether or not to advise abortion.[22] The assessment was, the Committee contended, essentially a medical one and solely for the practitioners involved. By contrast, the grounds contained in paragraph (d) did not justify abortion: 'From the medical point of view the fact that pregnancy resulted from a sexual encounter which was unlawful is not, in itself, an indication for terminating pregnancy'.[23] As for the most common of such cases encountered in medical practice – pregnancy in a girl under 16 – the Committee did not advise reform of the law. It stated that it did not consider any extension to the changes in the law already recommended in its report would be necessary to cover such cases and that specific provision to provide for such cases would be undesirable.[24] As such a provision might lead to pressure being brought to bear on the girl or her medical attendants, it was strongly disapproved.[25] With regard to pregnancy resulting from rape, incest or unlawful intercourse with a mentally subnormal woman, the Committee, although recognising that a considerable body of public opinion favoured abortion in such circumstances, took the view that considerable difficulties would arise in the administration of a law allowing abortion on such grounds and that complex problems of medical ethics would arise.[26]

The Committee also pointed out that medical opinion was agreed on the need for safeguards for a procedure which involved the destruction of 'potential life'. Three safeguards in particular were approved relating to consultation, the status of the operating doctor, and the place of termination. The normal process of consultation from general practitioner to consultant was envisaged, though the Committee did not want the approval of the family doctor to be made a statutory requirement as the woman might not have one or, if she did, she might not wish to involve him or he might have a conscientious objection. In some cases a consultant gynecologist would want to confer with another consultant but the Committee was again opposed to the enactment of a requirement to this effect, which would introduce complications in an emergency. Consequently, the Committee merely recommended that before termination was advised there should be agreement between two registered medical practitioners after both had examined the woman.[27] One of the concurring opinions should be that of the operating doctor, who would normally be an N.H.S. consultant gynecologist or obstetrician. However, non-N.H.S. consultants ought not to be prohibited from operating and the Minister could be empowered to approve such practitioners. As for the second opinion, a requirement of a minimum period of registration would, subject to consultation between the profession and the Minister, be acceptable.[28] A second safeguard would be provided by the status of the operating practitioner, who would normally be an N.H.S. consultant, though the Committee did not want a less senior member of the hospital staff, operating under his instructions, to be excluded. Thirdly, an abortion should only be lawful if performed in an N.H.S. hospital or premises approved for the purpose by the Minister. The Committee also recommended that the Ministry should be responsible for the inspection and approval of such premises, that the criteria be stringent, and approval subject to annual review. In a departure from its interim report, the Committee recommended that a doctor operating in an emergency should not incur liability for failure to comply with these safeguards.

The Committee also advised confidential notification by the operating practitioner to the C.M.O. within 14 days. This, however, was intended not as an additional safeguard but as an accurate source of statistical data. Accordingly, a given notification should only be disclosed to the police on the production of a court order.[29].

4.3 The Royal College of Obstetricians and Gynaecologists (R.C.O.G.)

The most conservative report from a medical body came from the R.C.O.G. Published in April when Silkin's Bill was still the focus of debate, the report – which represented the unanimous view of the College's Council – declared that the majority of gynecologists saw no urgent need for reform of the law: the flexibility of the existing law allowed them to terminate pregnancy after consultation whenever it was felt to be in the interests of the woman and her unborn child.[30] Nevertheless, the Council did accept that there was a case for making it positively clear that abortion was justified in the interests of the physical and mental health of the woman. It would, moreover, be wise to include as an indication a considerably increased risk that the child would be born seriously handicapped either physically or mentally.[31] This was advocated even though it would often, in practice, lead to the death of a potentially normal child.[32] The report stressed that the interpretation and application of any new Act would be largely the responsibility of obstetricians and gynecologists and that the legislature should be reasonably sure of their co-operation before deciding upon any alteration of the law.[33] It then listed a set of provisions under which the Council felt the majority of gynecologists could work. An abortion should only be legal if performed when there was a serious risk to the life or of grave injury to the health of the pregnant woman, either before or after the birth, or when there was a substantial risk that the child would suffer from such physical or mental abnormalities as to deprive it of any prospect of reasonable enjoyment of life. The law might also provide that the practitioner could take into account such circumstances, whether past, present or prospective as were in his opinion relevant to the physical or mental health of the woman or of the child if born. The law should also make provision for exceptional circumstances, though without altering the grounds for abortion, and should also require a written request for, and consent to, the operation.

The College also recommended safeguards. The need for abortion should be certified by two consultants, one the operating gynecologist and the second a doctor in any branch of medicine who was under contract to work in an N.H.S. hospital. The operation should be performed either by a consultant obstetrician or gynecologist under contract to work as such in an N.H.S. hospital or by a doctor also employed by the N.H.S. to whom the operation had been delegated by the consultant. Moreover, the procedure should be confined to N.H.S. hospitals and places approved for the purpose by the Minister and should be notified to the C.M.O. within 14 days with such particulars as might be prescribed by the Minister, provided that the rules of professional secrecy were not thereby infringed. Failure to comply with notification requirements, particularly if repeated, should be a serious and punishable offence. Similarly, any new Act should state that the attempted induction of abortion in circumstances other than those defined in the legislation was a serious offence carrying heavy penalties. To this end, the defence under the existing law should be repealed.

An important consideration which underlay the report was the preservation of professional autonomy. The Council enunciated five principles for legal reform, and professional autonomy under-pinned all five. The preservation of clinical freedom, it urged, militated against a precise legal statement of the conditions under which abortion might be induced. This was so, firstly, because medicine was advancing:

The indications for legal abortion should not be defined too exactly lest they impose restrictions which do not apply at present, and lest they militate against the flexibility which is necessary to ensure that practice keeps abreast of the ever-advancing medical knowledge and rapidly changing opinion.[34]

Similarly, the extent of the risk justifying abortion in cases of handicap should only be defined in general terms.

Secondly, the Council feared that patients might begin to demand treatment, and this danger was particularly acute when abortion was expressly sanctioned by the law after unlawful intercourse. It declared that reference to the age of 16 years could give rise to the idea that any girl who was younger could risk conceiving in the belief that she could demand abortion if the need arose and it added that this could encourage promiscuity.[35] In any event, age was a factor taken into consideration when the practitioner judged the impact of the continuation of pregnancy on maternal health. Similarly, in other cases of unlawful intercourse the circumstances under which conception occurred were, if the facts were 'reasonably established', taken into account in assessing the ill-effects of the continuance of the pregnancy.[36] One of the five principles focussed directly on the preservation of medical discretion:

Gynaecologists and other doctors concerned must retain their freedom of action and never be put in the position of being coerced by the terms of the Bill and the conditions of their employment into terminating a pregnancy if they have any ethical objections, and unless they themselves are con-vinced that it is in the best interests of a particular woman or her potential child. This situation could be safeguarded by ensuring that the gynae-cologist expected to undertake the operation is one of those certifying the need for the operation. For he will always be ultimately responsible for the operation and the care of the patient.[37]

It added that the gynecologist's responsibility should also extend to the choice of the other doctor certifying the need for the operation. He should not be the woman's family doctor, who might be subjected to pressure from the woman or her relatives, but a consultant on the staff of the hospital. Registrars had neither the experience nor the competence to make such an important decision and they too might be subjected to coercion.

The remaining three principles set out in the report also protected professional autonomy. One sought to ensure that the activities of those currently performing illegal abortions were curtailed by defining when, where and by whom abortion might be lawfully performed and by making abortion notifiable. A second urged that it should be made clear that abortions performed other than in the circumstances specified in the legislation were subject to severe penalties and that, if there were reason to doubt the necessity for an operation, the practitioner should have to justify his decision in court. Thirdly, the Council recommended deferral of any radical amendment of the indications for abortion until more information had been gathered. There was evidence that some foreign legislation had reduced professional autonomy: it was stated that gynecologists from countries where non-medical indications were lawful found themselves having to adopt an apologetic attitude towards colleagues from other countries and to explain that they were often under governmental pressure to abort against their better judgement.[38] There were, the Council therefore felt, compelling arguments for the establishment of an interdepartmental committee into the question.

The report as a whole reveals an overriding concern for the preservation of the clinical freedom of the consultant gynecologist. Abortion law reform was not, as such, opposed but only reform which threatened professional discretion. Legislation which, by a circumspect declaration and extension of the permissible indications, placed the decision to terminate and the operation itself firmly in the hands of the consultant gynecologist, thereby entrenching and extending his existing autonomy, was unobjectionable.

Steel's Bill was read for a second time on 22 July, the vote in favour of second reading being 223 to 29. In spite of this overwhelming support, however, Steel was subjected to pressure from several quarters later in the year to amend his Bill. Apart from A.L.R.A., the most influential of the pressure groups proved to be the medical bodies.[39]

4.4 The Medical Women's Federation (M.W.F.)

In October 1966 the M.W.F. approved the report of a subcommittee which had looked into the question of reform.[40] The report agreed that any new law should aim at the elimination of abortion by untrained and unskilled personnel. Notwithstanding this conclusion, the report recommended the removal of paragraphs (b), (c) and (d) of Steel's Bill. Echoing the reports of the three other medical bodies, the M.W.F. strongly opposed any rigid codification of the indications for abortion: each required individual assessment and the mother's total environment and circumstances had always to be carefully considered. With reference to paragraph (b), the report recommended that where there was a risk of fetal abnormality this should not be a categorical indication but expert counselling should be obtained. As for paragraph (c), it maintained that valid assessment of the woman's capacity to be a mother was impossible. Rejecting paragraph (d), it expressed the view that neither age nor (in view of the difficulties of proof) rape should be an absolute indication. One general clause was proposed to replace paragraph (a):

It shall be lawful to terminate a pregnancy in the interests of physical and mental health of the mother, taking into account her whole family situation and circumstances past, present, and future.[41]

The report also recommended safeguards along the lines of the B.M.A. report. First, the operation should be performed only by a registered medical practitioner under the direction of the head of an appropriate department in a recognised hospital or nursing home approved for the purpose and the operator should notify the abortion to the C.M.O. within forty-eight hours. Further, at least two practitioners should examine the woman, neither being related to her nor to each other nor in partnership. They should certify the need for the operation before it was done and one should actually perform the operation. Further, no woman should be urged to have an abortion against her wishes, and, in the case of a minor, written consent should be required. Neither abortions arising inevitably from emergency procedures to save life, nor accidental abortions secondary to other procedures, should be classed as criminal.[42] However, any abortion performed outside the limitations recommended in the report should remain punishable. Finally, no doctor or patient should be required to act against conscience in the matter of abortion.[43]

4.5 The Royal College of Obstetricians and Gynaecologists and the British Medical Association

December 1966 saw the publication of a joint report on the Bill by the R.C.O.G. and the B.M.A. Observing that cl. 1(1) permitted any doctor to terminate pregnancy, they recommended that it should be obligatory for the operation to be carried out by or under the supervision of a consultant in the N.H.S. or such other doctor of equivalent status and experience as the Minister should approve for the purposes of the Act. Both agreed it should be a consultant in gynecology and the R.C.O.G. wanted this written into the Act, but the B.M.A. felt it was preferable not to exclude other consultants lest the operation be unobtainable in areas where a consultant gynecologist was not readily available.[44]

On many occasions, the report continued, it would be necessary for more than two doctors to agree on the advisability of the operation, so it recommended a requirement of at least two concurring opinions. Turning to cl. 1(2), the report recommended the deletion of the reference to 'any' registered nursing home and the confinement of the operation to an N.H.S. hospital or a place approved by the Minister for the purposes of the Act. Provided the above safeguards were incorporated, it would be both unnecessary and undesirable to frame the indications for abortion too narrowly, as did the Bill in its existing form. The report added:

The requirements that the risk has to be *serious* and the injury to health *grave* in clause 1(1)(a) are capable of causing considerable difficulties in practice and may mean that terminations carried out on certain medical indications which are accepted under current medical practice would become questionable in future.[45]

The indications should be framed merely 'in the interests of the health of the mother or because of the (substantial) risk of serious abnormality of the foetus'. The B.M.A. even had reservations about the word 'substantial' in the light of the difficulties which had followed upon its inclusion in previous statutes qualifying medical opinion.[46] The report's criticism of paragraph (a) reveals that medical practice had already outstripped the very constraints the Bill sought to impose on the decision-making process.

As for paragraphs (c) and (d), the report objected to their inclusion on the ground that they specified indications which were not medical. This objection was also, however, clearly related to the concern for professional autonomy. The report stated that these paragraphs would give rise to serious difficulties in practice. It explained:

They might well lead to an excessive demand for termination on social grounds, and this would be unacceptable to the medical profession. Each case has to be assessed on its own merits, and express reference to the factors mentioned in (c) and (d), though only permissive, would inevitably lead the public to believe that termination would automatically be carried out in the instances mentioned.[47]

However, a subclause which provided that, in arriving at a decision, a practitioner could take account of the patient's total environment, both actual and reasonably foreseeable, would be desirable.

The report also made recommendations with regard to cl. 2 of the Bill, which allowed the Minister to make regulations relating to the certification of opinions, notification of the operation, and disclosure of the information so notified. It recommended that the Minister should be placed under a statutory duty, and not merely enjoy a discretion, to make regulations; that the operating practitioner ought to be able to certify the need for the operation; that all abortions, both inside and outside hospital, ought to be notified; that notifications ought to be disclosed to the police only on production of a court order; and that notification should be made not to the 'Ministry of Health' but rather to its C.M.O. on a doctor-to-doctor basis.[48]

Clearly, a recurring theme in all the reports of the medical bodies was the preservation of clinical freedom. The *British Medical Journal* commented that the emphasis in all of them was on the need to keep the medical attendant's judgement free to advise the patient in her best interests. It added that, as a corollary to preserving his independence of clinical judgement, the Act must not require him to decide matters outside his expert knowledge.[49]

A.L.R.A. made concerted attempts to persuade Steel to retain the social clause. At its annual general meeting in October 1966, it had amended its own statement of aims to include abortion on social grounds as it was increasingly clear that women sought abortion more for social than for other reasons.[50] On 15 December Steel was informed by A.L.R.A. that no fewer than 228 M.P.s had intimated support for the social clause.[51] Apparently, he was unimpressed by this claim and Dr Winstanley, one of his most influential parliamentary sponsors and a B.M.A. official, did not think paragraph (c) could be passed.[52] Both had met representatives of the B.M.A.'s Special Committee in November 1966,[53] and after the publication of the joint report, copies of which were sent to the Home Secretary, the Minister of Health, and the Bill's sponsors, Steel was again exposed to medical opinion at a meeting with Sir John Peel P.R.C.O.G. This proved to be the last meeting with the representative of an important body before he tabled his amendments.[54]

According to Hindell and Simms, Steel was influenced more by the views of the B.M.A. than by those of the R.C.O.G., since if the Bill were passed, G.P.s would be largely responsible for its implementation. He was, therefore, willing to accept some of its proposals to keep its support or at least to avoid its opposition.[55] They add that he was also greatly influenced by the Scottish gynecologist Sir Dugald Baird – more so than any individual doctor he met – and that it was not until he had discussed abortion with Baird in November 1966 that his aims crystallised. Baird urged strongly that social should not be separated from medical factors in reaching a decision on termination and that there was virtue in combining both in the same clause.[56]

On 21 December 1966, the same day that the Council of the B.M.A. approved the joint report, Steel tabled an amendment which met the medical profession's recommendation that the therapeutic indication ought not to be defined too closely. The new paragraph (a) required neither that the risk to life be serious nor that the risk of injury to health be grave, and it extended the indication to include risk to the woman's 'well-being'. Further, it expressly allowed the doctor, in deciding whether there was a risk of injury to the patient's health or well-being, to take into account her total environment, actual or reasonably foreseeable. Steel proposed to include the wider paragraph (a) at the expense of (c) and (d) and, as Hindell and Simms observe, his proposal 'seemed to accept the main arguments of the B.M.A. and R.C.O.G. and to sacrifice the heart of the Bill'.[57] In his statement accompanying the amendment, Steel acknowledged the influence of these bodies in framing his new paragraph. He explained that he thought his amendment would get the best of both worlds by satisfying both the profession and the reformers: both could interpret 'total environment' and 'well-being' to suit themselves.[58] In a letter to Vera Houghton, Chairman of A.L.R.A., who had objected that paragraph (c) was the only significant reform in the Bill, he wrote:

I believe (a) will be more acceptable than (c) or (d) and will make the difference between support or opposition from the B.M.A. I have already had a letter from Dr. Havard of the B.M.A. welcoming the amendment.[59]

Steel moved the amended paragraph at the third sitting of the Standing Committee, on 1 February 1967.[60] He stated that the debate concerned the question of how far provision was to be made for social considerations to be taken into account and observed that the R.M.-P.A. was in favour of taking all social considerations into account. He also quoted in his support an editorial from the *Medical Tribune* which remarked that most abortions, legal or illegal, were performed for social reasons; that it was time that the charade of fitting them into other categories was abandoned, and that the idea that medicine was not concerned with the social problems of patients died hard.[61] In addition, he invoked the views of the M.W.F. and also of the Law Society and the British Academy of Forensic Sciences, whose joint report favoured the legalisation of abortion either when two doctors decided that the continuation of pregnancy was likely to damage the physical or mental health of the woman or the 'future well-being of herself or the child', or when there was a substantial risk that the child would be born with such serious physical or mental abnormalities as to be seriously handi-capped.[62] He declared that it was wrong to give the impression that social and medical indications were distinct, which some, such as the B.M.A. and Baird, regarded paragraph (c) as doing, and he urged that it was the whole thesis of his argument that social considerations were not separate but had to be part and parcel of a correct medical judgement.[63] The words 'total environment' and 'well-being' in the amendments would give a clear guide to doctors that they could take such considerations into account. He stressed that it was not possible to draw a sharp dividing line between health and social well-being.[64] 'Well-being' he could only define as 'a positive state of good health and a lack of strain, and so on'.[65] He also revealed that the words 'serious' and 'grave' had disappeared as a result of a meeting with the B.M.A.[66]

The reaction of the medical bodies to the addition of the concept of well-being was not, however, wholly favourable. Although the B.M.A. approved, the President of the R.C.O.G. did not. Sir Bernard Braine, M.P. for Essex Southeast, who was closely involved with the medical bodies throughout the passage of the Bill, disclosed that Sir John Peel had written to him enquiring how the word differed from 'health' and intimating that the College would prefer its deletion.[67] Braine also reminded the Committee that the B.M.A. was opposed to paragraph (c). He had been advised that it would lead to repeated problems of interpretation and that very few gynecologists would be prepared to operate in such ill-defined and non-medical circumstances.[68] The ground of maternal inadequacy was, the B.M.A. added, repugnant to the majority of the profession and it stressed:

The ultimate decision to advise termination must be a medical matter and should be reached on medical grounds in the light of all relevant circumstances. We feel deeply that the law should not be framed in a way unacceptable to our professional ethics.[69]

Paragraph (c) was dropped by Steel, even though the A.L.R.A. fought hard for its retention, just as it had done earlier during the passage of Silkin's Bill through the House of Lords.[70] Braine then moved to omit paragraph (d). He reminded the committee that the B.M.A. was also opposed to this paragraph and had expressed the view that the specification of an age was too rigid, since girls varied in maturity.[71] Steel replied that he had included paragraph (d) out of tradition and that, since second reading, the joint report of the R.C.O.G. and B.M.A. had cautioned that it might mislead women into thinking that abortion would be automatically granted in the circumstances it specified. He added that the grounds mentioned in paragraph (d) were already catered for in the Bill as amended and that there was simply 'a difference in terms of relaying this Bill to the public'.[72]

Indeed, before paragraphs (c) and (d) were dropped, not only had Steel's revised paragraph (a) been accepted but it had been accepted after an amendment which widened its scope even further. Mr Edward Lyons had moved that it should refer to the risk of injury to the 'physical or mental health of the pregnant woman or the future well-being of herself and/or the child or her other children'.[73] Braine opposed the amendment, pointing out that it went against the recommendations of the R.C.O.G. and B.M.A., but Steel adopted the new wording as it catered for woman's existing children.[74] Another recommendation of the joint report – that relating to the status of the certifying and operating practitioners – was also overridden. Two amendments were moved which were designed to incorporate the recommendation, but neither was passed. The first, moved by Braine, proposed that one of the certifying practitioners should be a consultant gynecologist holding an appointment as such under a hospital board or a doctor of 'equivalent status' who had been approved by the Minister or the Secretary of State for the purposes of the section.[75] Braine said that he had been influenced by the weight of medical opinion which counselled caution and that he was attempting to make the Bill more welcome to those who would have to operate it. The clause as it stood allowed any two newly qualified doctors to recommend abortion and was therefore open to 'grave abuse'.[76] Moreover, women were entitled to the best possible advice.[77]

The amendment was heavily criticised. Steel maintained that it introduced a new principle into medical practice, that the Bill already restricted the law by requiring a second opinion, and that this and the other two safeguards it contained would prevent two irresponsible doctors from setting themselves up to perform abortions.[78] He added that he had found considerable opposition among doctors to the principle of differentiation.[79] Dr Winstanley pointed out that even the B.M.A. itself had reservations about Braine's amendment. It was, he said, extremely reluctant to accept the view that the Royal College should have such a monopoly.[80] The Parliamentary Secretary to the Ministry of Health, Mr Julian Snow, expressed the Government's opposition to the amendment. The ordinary practitioner was, he declared, quite capable of certifying the advisability of abortion.[81] However, pointing to the concern of the B.M.A. and the R.C.O.G. over the status of the operator, he said that there was much to be said for an amendment restricting the performance of the operation, rather than its certification, to practitioners of a certain status.[82]

With the defeat of Braine's motion by twenty votes to seven, just such an amendment was moved by Mr Abse. He proposed that the operation only be performed,

by a person who is or has been a consultant holding an appointment under a hospital board involving the practice of gynaecology or by a practitioner who holds such an appointment and is nominated either generally or for the purposes of the treatment in question by such a person. . . .[83]

He pointed out that the proposal conformed to N.H.S. practice.[84] Moreover, as the Bill did not give the Minister power to regulate those operating in approved places, it would ensure that the operator was at least engaged in part-time hospital work.[85] They were, he urged, under a duty to prevent unscrupulous practitioners from exploiting patients.[86] Steel opposed the amendment. He repeated the objection of practitioners to the principle of differentiation and quoted an editorial in *Medical World* which objected to the removal of abortion from the normal relationship between doctor and patient.[87] Moreover, medical advances would render the proposed restriction redundant.[88] Notification of operations and approval of premises would, he felt, be sufficient to prevent exploitation.[89] Other committee members also spoke against the amendment. Mr Sharples pointed out that the amendment would restrict the existing law.[90] Dr Miller argued that the amendment exaggerated the dangers of the operation, which was no more hazardous than other forms of surgery, that it interfered with the doctor–patient relationship, and that the principle might be extended to other operations.[91] Dr Winstanley objected that the amendment would wipe out the responsible part of the private sector and make abortions and advice about abortion more difficult to obtain.[92] By contrast, the Parliamentary Secretary supported the amendment. He maintained that Steel was mistaken to assume that notification would provide a safeguard against doctors who were not well qualified operating in approved places or that the exercise of the Minister's powers could ensure the woman's safety or prevent racketeering. The Ministry took the view that the amendment would protect her health and discourage racketeers.[93] Steel replied that he did not believe that the Minister could not withdraw approval in cases of suspected abuse, as the criteria for approval were a matter for his own judgement,[94] and the amendment was defeated by thirteen votes to eleven.

However, other amendments which had been recommended by the medical bodies met with greater success. Further provision was made for abortion in emergency,[95] and the Minister's discretion to make regulations was transformed into a duty.[96] Moreover, Steel successfully moved amendments requiring even hospital abortions to be notified,[97] specifying that all notifications were to be sent to the C.M.O.[98] and, even though he felt it unnecessary, making provision for the protection of conscientious objection to participation in treatment for abortion.[99] The protection of conscientious objection was supported not only by the B.M.A. and R.C.O.G. but also, as Braine pointed out, by the Royal College of Nursing and the National Council of Nursing.[100] Steel conferred with Mr St John-Stevas, M.P. for Chelmsford, and they produced a clause which was agreed to by the Committee.[101]

Even after the amendments made in Committee, however, the major medical bodies were not satisfied. A joint delegation of the B.M.A. and R.C.O.G. asked Steel in May 1967 to confine the operation to doctors of consultant or equivalent status.[102] They also criticised the words 'future well-being', even though the B.M.A. had supported their insertion during the committee stage, as opening the door to 'purely social indications of convenience'.[103] Steel conceded this part of the Bill but resisted the pressure to limit the operation to consultants or doctors approved by the Minister of Health. As Hindell and Simms point out: 'Both A.L.R.A. and Steel recognized that they must resist the introduction of this clause or risk emasculation of the whole Bill'.[104] Indeed, it would not only have restricted the Bill but would even have limited the existing law.

Before the report stage, Steel tabled an amendment dropping the reference to 'future well-being' but left the reference to the woman's existing children and did not restrict the status of either the certifying or operating practitioners.[105]

In spite of the fact that Steel did not concede all the demands of the major medical bodies, the importance of medical opinion persisted throughout the report stage, where it helps to explain both why amendments were moved and their outcome.

The Bill was reported to the House on 2 June 1967 and several amendments, aimed at its restriction, were moved. Braine, emulating Abse's attempt in committee to restrict the status of the operating practitioner, proposed that the operation should only be performed by or under the supervision of a registered medical practitioner holding an appointment as a consultant in the N.H.S. or a registered medical practitioner approved by the Minister or the Secretary of State.[106] He reminded the House that the restriction of the operation to consultants was supported by both the B.M.A. and the R.C.O.G. and repeated that it would provide a safeguard against two newly qualified doctors abusing the law.[107] The amendment had, moreover, recently been suggested by the leaders of the profession in a letter to *The Times*.[108] It would ensure that the patient received the best possible care in respect of both the decision to terminate and the operation itself.[109] Anticipating the objection that the amendment introduced a new principle of discrimination between practitioners, he maintained that the principle had already been broached in other areas of practice such as compulsory admission to hospital under the Mental Health Act 1959, which required a recommendation from a doctor with special experience in the diagnosis and treatment of mental disorder. Abortion was, he urged, not like any other operation for it involved the destruction of a life and offered a lucrative income to any two doctors who chose to specialise in it in the private sector.[110]

Steel again opposed the amendment. He countered Braine's reliance on the B.M.A. and R.C.O.G. by invoking the support of the R.M.-P.A., over 200 G.P.s who had written to him specifically on this issue, and the views of the doctors on the Standing Committee. He disputed that the operation was exceptional – the Caesarian involved the lives of both child and mother and was highly dangerous – and stated:

I think that we can leave it to medical practitioners to decide when they are or are not qualified to carry out this operation and to advise whether the operation should be carried out.[111]

He added that the evidence suggested that the racketeers actually had the highest qualifications and he reassured the House that the three safeguards provided in the Bill – consultation, notification and location – were adequate.[112] A further blow was dealt to the amendment when the Minister of Health, Mr Kenneth Robinson, declared that the B.M.A. was not as enthusiastic about the amendment as the R.C.O.G., and urged the House not to require him to make invidious distinctions between doctors – a responsibility he would find quite unacceptable.[113] The amendment was defeated.

A series of amendments attempting to define more precisely the grounds for abortion in cl. 1(1)(a) was also defeated. One amendment, for example, moved by Sir John Hobson, attempted to require the risk referred to in the paragraph to be 'medically unacceptable'.[114] Steel successfully resisted the amendment, pointing out that the medical profession had not requested the risk to be qualified. He remarked:

We are leaving to the medical profession what members of that profession consider and have represented to us that they, and they alone, have every right and qualification to determine and that it is not for Parliament to tie their hands.[115]

In line with the recommendation of the B.M.A. and R.C.O.G., he successfully moved the deletion of the reference to 'well-being'. Mrs Knight claimed this as a 'very great triumph' for those who opposed abortion on social as distinct from medical grounds.[116] Steel, however, replied that the word was being dropped because it was incapable of precise definition and because the application of the concept of well-being to the child was 'a little absurd'. Moreover, he disagreed that the omission of the word made a dramatic difference to the substance of the Bill and he drew the House's attention to the World Health Organization's definition of 'health' as a state of 'complete mental, physical and social well-being, and not merely the absence of disease or infirmity'. Further, social factors were adequately covered by cl. 1(1)(a)(ii), which allowed doctors to take the woman's environment, both actual and reasonably foreseeable, into account. Finally, his amendment did not delete the reference to the woman's existing children, which was, he said, supported by the leaders of the medical profession.[117] His amendment was passed by 140 votes to 77.[118]

One recommendation of the medical bodies was not, however, conceded. This was that notifications should only be disclosed on production of a court order. Braine moved an amendment to give effect to this recommendation but was unsuccessful. He argued that the profession was anxious to ensure strictly limited disclosure of the information notified and that the reason for their concern was the welfare of the woman. Any apprehension, especially in the delicate matter of abortion, that confidence would not be respected could result in women being reluctant to consult their doctor, or resorting to criminal abortion.[119] Steel objected that the amendment went too far. It was sufficient to leave the Minister to make regulations relating to disclosure, regulations which would no doubt be drafted after consultation with the B.M.A.[120] Robinson remarked that it would be undesirable to specify in the Act who would be allowed access and he assured the House that the course the Government was recommending had been found to be acceptable by the Chairman of the B.M.A.'s Special Committee, who appreciated that it would be necessary for the police to have access to the information notified.[121] He added that there would be the fullest consultation with the profession before drafting the regulations and that it was certainly not envisaged that there would be anything like a routine police inspection of the records or that inspection would be possible without specific grounds.[122] The amendment was defeated by 125 votes to 51.[123] On 13 July the Bill, as amended, received its third reading.

Medical opinion as a whole was still behind the Bill. A delegation from the R.M.-P.A. visited the Home Office after the report stage to confirm the Association's support for reform.[124] The Council of the B.M.A. stressed in its annual report that, although during the committee stage of the Bill the views of individual doctors had received very considerable publicity, with the result that a misleading impression was given that the profession was widely divided, the Council had never doubted that the profession as a whole was strongly in favour of the views expressed in the report of the Special Committee.[125] This was borne out at the Association's Annual Representative Meeting (A.R.M.) in July 1967, where a motion to request Parliament not to approve the Bill until an independent body, such as a Royal Commission, had scrutinised all the relevant facts was defeated by 274 votes to 98.[126] Dr Doris Odlum, a member of the Special Committee, was one of its opponents. She pointed out that the Committee had succeeded in securing a number of modifications to the Bill. There was no question of any kind of abortion on demand and discretion lay in the hands of the profession. The Committee was still unhappy about the reference to existing children, which it felt both undesirable and otiose, and the absence of a requirement of consultation with a practitioner of specialised knowledge. Nevertheless, it was probably the best Bill they would ever get, and she added: 'We cannot see that the medical profession can have any objection to this Bill subject to one or two slight amendments'.[127] The Chairman of Council, Dr Ronald Gibson, suggested that to pass the motion would show a lack of responsibility and he hoped that, having set up the Special Committee, the Association would not begin to vacillate by calling on Parliament to delay the Bill.[128]

The Bill was read for a second time in the House of Lords on 19 July 1967, and the majority in favour of the second reading motion, which was moved by Lord Silkin, was 127 votes to 21. All the medical peers who voted, together with Viscount Dilhorne, who had been a prominent and dogged critic of the previous Bills on the subject which Silkin had introduced, voted in favour. During the committee stage, however, Dilhorne secured two crucial amendments on matters which, as Dr Odlum had pointed out at the

B.M.A.'s meeting, still concerned the Special Committee. The first related to the status of the certifying practitioners. Dilhorne's amendment required one of these practitioners to be employed in the N.H.S. as a consultant or to be approved by the Minister or the Secretary of State. Without this amendment, he maintained, the Bill would allow any rackets to become more widespread.[129] Lord Beswick, for the Government, advised against the amendment. He said that it was too broad in allowing any consultants, whether in gynecology or not, to certify and too narrow in excluding those of lesser status but with gynecological experience, and also former N.H.S. consultants. It would have been better to require the operating practitioner to be of consultant status.[130] Lord Stonham, Under-Secretary of State at the Home Office, repeated Robinson's objection to the foisting of a responsibility to discriminate between practitioners upon a government department.[131] Dilhorne, however, pressed his amendment to a division and it was passed by 116 votes to 67.[132]

The second amendment which he secured was the removal of the reference to existing children. He said that it was difficult to envisage how the health of an existing child could be affected by the birth of another but that, even if it could, it did not justify the termination of a potential life.[133] The medical peers were divided. Lords Waverley and Brock supported the deletion. The latter said that the words departed from the medical considerations of abortion so far as they affected the woman and introduced social reasons.[134] On the other hand, Baroness Summerskill urged that the words covered the case of the poor family living in overcrowded conditions which ought to be protected from the demands of another unwanted member.[135] Lord Platt stated that the doctor had a duty to regard abortion as something affecting the whole family: the words were almost the only ones in the Bill which went towards the goal of making the law more permissive, though they still constituted a medical and not a social provision.[136] The amendment was passed by a majority of one.[137]

The success of these amendments was, however, short lived. At the report stage, which began on 23 October 1967, Lady Stocks moved the deletion of the 'consultant clause'. The clause would not, she argued, prevent collusion between a general practitioner and a consultant. Parliament should, moreover, trust any two doctors to act in good faith. There were only 740 suitable consultants available, and many of these would be unwilling to implement the law because of conscientious objection and the Ministry of Health would be unwilling to approve substitutes.[138] Further, it was undesirable in principle to distinguish between practitioners employed in the N.H.S. and in private practice and the clause would also drive women to criminal abortionists and wreck the Bill.[139] Dilhorne defended the clause: it would reduce the risk of 'Harley St.' rackets and it had the support of both the B.M.A. and the R.C.O.G.[140] Nevertheless, the clause was deleted. Yet again the medical peers were divided: Lady Summerskill and Lord Amulree voted for its deletion; Lords Brock, Waverley and Segal against.

Dilhorne's second amendment was also reversed. Silkin successfully moved an amendment reinstating the reference to the pregnant woman's existing children. He maintained that it did not represent a 'social clause' but covered those cases, perhaps few, where the health of the existing children would be adversely affected by the continuance of a pregnancy.[141] The medical peers, with the exception of Lady Summerskill, followed the policy of the medical bodies and opposed Silkin's amendment.

Other, less controversial, amendments were passed before the Bill was returned to the Commons. One related to the degree of risk which would justify abortion and was moved by Dilhorne on behalf of Lord Chief Justice Parker. It required the two practitioners to consider whether the continuance of pregnancy would involve greater risk to the woman's life or to her or her children's health than its termination.[142] Another amendment allowed a third practitioner to perform the operation.[143]

The amendments made in the Lords were considered by the Commons on 25 October 1967 and were agreed to.[144] The Bill received the Royal Assent on 27 October and came into force on 27 April 1968.[145]

Conclusion

This chapter indicates that although the campaign for the relaxation of the law was ignited and fuelled by the Abortion Law Reform Association, the medical profession exerted a significant influence on both the enactment of the Abortion Act and on the scope of its provisions. It succeeded not only in entrenching its traditional autonomy over the recommendation and performance of abortion, but also in extending it. This influence was exerted chiefly through the major professional bodies, who actively represented the views of their members to Parliament, and also by individual practitioners who were consulted by the sponsor of the Bill and by other M.P.s. Significantly, the opinions expressed were not confined to strictly medical questions, such as the methods and dangers of abortion, but included recommendations on the desirability of reform, the appropriate scope of the Bill, and the wording of particular provisions. Equally significantly, the bulk of these recommendations were accepted. One aspect of the profession's successful defence of its autonomy was the recommendation that doctors should not be required to make judgements on matters beyond their expertise; that the indications for abortion should be 'medical', not 'social'. One aim of the next chapter is to consider whether this distinction has been preserved in the operation, as distinct from the creation, of the Act.

5

The Abortion Act 1967 and the performance of abortion by the medical profession 1968–1982

The last chapter dealt with the influence of the medical profession on the enactment of the Abortion Act 1967. This chapter considers how extensively the Act has been interpreted by some practitioners and the effectiveness of some of the checks on the exercise of medical discretion in relation to abortion.

5.1 Medical abortion: 1968–1982

According to Sir Roger Ormrod, although the Abortion Act 1967 seems a modest extension of the law, in practice the result has been very different:

Abortion has become generally available, if not yet quite on demand, but subject only to the attitude of the surgeon concerned or of the clinic to which the woman is referred.[1]

Is there any evidence to support this assertion? Some evidence which does provide some support takes the form of contributions on abortion to the medical press from 1967 to 1982, to which reference will be made in this section.[2] This evidence, together with that from other sources, such as abortion statistics, suggests that, since the enactment of the legislation, the number of medical abortions has increased and that a significant number have been performed at the request of the woman and for social reasons.

The exercise of medical discretion
Numerically, abortions notified to the Chief Medical Officer (C.M.O.) in accordance with the Act rose steadily from 22 256 in the first eight months of the Act's operation to a peak of 169 362 in 1973. They dipped to 129 673 in 1976 but have gradually increased since then, totalling 163 045 in 1982. The abortion rate per 1000

residents aged fifteen to forty-four rose from 3.46 in the first eight months to 11.39 in 1973, dipped to 10.46 in 1976 but rose again to 12.32 in 1982. The number of abortions performed in non-N.H.S. premises represented about 40% of the total in the first eight months of the Act's operation but rose to a peak of 67% in 1973, fell to about 60% in 1976 and remained at about the same level until 1982.[3]

Abortion 'on demand'. Sir Roger Ormrod refers to abortion 'on demand'. Others refer to abortion 'on request'. Although it is possible to distinguish between these two phrases, to refer respectively to the right of the woman to an abortion (and the correlative duty of the physician to provide it) and to the provision of abortion by the physician for no other reason than the wish of the woman, in most cases they seem to be used interchangeably to mean the latter (a usage which will be followed here). Notwithstanding the lack of precision, is there any evidence from within the medical profession itself that Sir Roger's assessment of the operation of the Act is accurate?

At a symposium on the working of the Act, held at the Royal College of Obstetricians and Gynaecologists (R.C.O.G.) in February 1969, several speakers expressed concern at the way the Act was being applied. One of its least desirable effects, said Professor Keith Simpson, was the protection it gave to 'professional abortionists' to whom 'floods of patients' from both home and abroad were paying up to £250 each, and he observed that some clinics and nursing homes were flourishing on the new 'abortion trade'.[4] He added that the Act was being used to legitimise termination, whether performed in good faith or not.[5] Dr Tredgold remarked that the increased demand for abortion in the wake of the Act had reduced gynecologists to the status of 'tradesmen' and he suggested as a possible solution that the gynecologist confine himself to the proper task of advising the patient on the balance of risks involved and leave the final decision to her.[6] The significance of non-medical factors in the decision-making process is evident from the remarks of Dr P. H. Tooley, who said that the degree of sympathy for the patient often determined the doctor's decision.[7] He added that among the indications which should be taken into account were 'social stresses beyond the patient's ability to cope . . . .'.[8]

Concern at the extensive interpretation of the Act was also expressed at the British Medical Association's Annual Representative Meeting (B.M.A.'s A.R.M.) in July 1969, where a motion associating the meeting with disquiet over the operation of the Act was passed.[9] One speaker said that the profession and public were showing increasing concern over abortion on demand.[10] Another declared that private abortions were creating a smear on the profession.[11] In the same year Mr T. L. T. Lewis, a gynecologist, wrote that his colleagues were doing many more abortions, not to mention the 'large numbers of pregnancies that are being terminated in registered nursing homes for reasons of convenience and financial gain, masquerading as legal operations under the new Act'.[12] In October 1970 the B.M.A. decided to appoint a special panel under its Board of Science and Education to investigate the subject of abortion. The panel's recommendations were published the following May and its observations confirmed the belief that the Act was not being uniformly implemented by the profession. It noted:

There is ambiguity in regard to the distinction between medical and socio-medical indications (Section 1, subsections (1) and (2) of the Act), leading to discrepancies in practice. The Act is regarded as abortion on demand at one extreme, whereas stricter interpretation is applied at the other.

The public, it remarked, expected 'abortion on demand', but the panel felt that this was not the intention of Parliament and that the discrepancy should be examined.[13]

This expectation of the public, and the variation in interpretation of the Act by doctors, also emerged in an R.C.O.G. survey carried out between 1969 and 1970.[14] The report was based on a questionnaire which had been sent to all consultant obstetricians and gynecologists employed in the N.H.S. in England and Wales and 80% of those eligible to reply had done so. The overall picture which emerged from the report was that about 10% induced abortion freely – a few even 'on demand'.[15] Asked whether they favoured abortion on demand, 16 (4%) had replied that they did.[16] The report stated that it was clear that some gynecologists were modifying their attitudes and were to some extent moving with changing medical and public opinion.[17] The findings revealed a good deal of variation of opinion about the wording of the Act and its implementation.[18] Commenting on the report, the *British Medical*

Journal observed that those providing abortion on demand did not necessarily do so on principle, but because the brevity of their decision allowed proper time for the treatment of other patients and the teaching of staff and students.[19]

In 1970 Dr Bender, a consultant gynecologist, wrote that since 1967 the gynecologist had become increasingly harassed and disgruntled. He was seeing more patients who had legal indications and who before the reform of the law had thought it futile to apply, but, for every such patient, there were several who did not have an indication within the terms of the Act as he interpreted it. Nevertheless, these patients and/or their doctors interpreted the Act as very nearly allowing abortion 'on demand'.[20]

Similarly, in their paper on the effect of the Act on their gynecology unit in the N.H.S., Rawlings and Khan commented in 1971 that most doctors were aware that, in the private sector, abortion was available 'on demand' for those who could pay. They concluded:

We believe the time has come to get rid of this hypocritical attitude and either have abortion on *medical* need only (and thus reduce overnight the number of terminations to 1% of the present total) or be honest and have abortion on demand for *all*.[21]

Further, it seems that the professional bodies were also aware both of the variation in interpretation of the Act by practitioners and of the readier availability of abortion in the private sector. In 1972, a working party of the R.C.O.G. pointed out that the variation followed the distinction between N.H.S. and private facilities. Of 2575 referrals to both types of facilities, 20% of the 200 referrals to the former were refused abortion, but only 1% of the 2375 referred to the latter.[22] The report stated that whereas the law was, by and large, very strictly interpreted in the N.H.S., the available statistics showed that in many of the private clinics an 'abortion on demand' service was being provided. It also observed: 'Those doctors who feel that abortion on demand is correct are able to apply that belief to their practice'. The circumstances mentioned in the Act could be interpreted widely or narrowly and the inevitable consequence was that there was, and would continue to be, a very wide range of interpretation and consequently a very wide difference in practice.[23]

Similarly, in its submission to the Lane Committee, which was set up by the Secretary of State in 1971 to examine the working of the Act, the B.M.A. stated that the existing law was far from clear and that very many, though not the Association, believed that abortion 'on demand' was the law. Inevitable differences in interpretation led, it added, to gross inequity and the main factors which resulted in this uneven provision of abortion were differences in philosophy and clinical judgement among both family doctors and consultants. Decisions were swayed by moral, conscientious and religious considerations and also by other factors such as the personal objections of nursing and junior hospital medical staff. The inconsistency in the working of the Act was, it continued, exacerbated by the fact that those able to afford private consultation were always able to obtain abortion, especially if prepared to travel away from their home area. The Association therefore recommended that an attempt be made to make the meaning of the Act clearer both to the general public and to the profession and in particular to emphasise that abortion on demand was not the law. The Act was, it added, a welcome piece of legislation, but it had fallen into some disrepute, largely because of its use in the private sector, particularly to accommodate the large number of foreign women arriving specifically for abortion.[24]

Lane concluded: 'in some parts of the commercial private sector the provisions of the Act have been flouted and abortion on request has been the rule'.[25] It did not, however, recommend any change in the criteria for abortion but concluded that the problems in the operation of the Act, though considerable, should be resolved by better education of the public and administrative and professional action.[26] These views were welcomed by the *British Medical Journal* which observed that abortion for a wide range of indications had become an established part of conventional medical practice. Turning to Lane's view that no woman should have to seek abortion outside the N.H.S., it observed that there would always be some who, refused an N.H.S. abortion, would resort to the private sector, for the principle which obtained in the private sector, where abortion was always available, was very near to abortion 'on request'.[27]

The 'social clause'. References to abortions performed under the 'social clause' are far from uncommon in the medical press.[28] However, it is often unclear to which section of the Act reference is being made. In some cases, it is that part of s. 1(1)(a) which allows abortion in the interests of the woman's health; in others, that part which allows abortion in the interests of the health of existing children; and in still others, it is s. 1(2), which allows the woman's actual or reasonably foreseeable environment to be taken into account in deciding whether abortion would be safer than the continuance of the pregnancy. It is the last two usages of the phrase which are of interest, in that they lend support to the view that, since the Act came into operation, abortion has been performed for indications which would not previously have been condoned by the profession.

In April 1968, the same month that the Act came into effect, the annual report of the B.M.A. Council reiterated the opposition of both the Association's Special Committee on Therapeutic Abortion and its Central Ethical Committee to the legalisation of abortion in the interests of the health of existing children. Having reconsidered its views, the Council saw no reason to depart from its interpretation of the Declaration of Geneva as permitting abortion only in the interests of the mother's health or where there was a risk of serious fetal abnormality.[29] The ethical code of the Association has not, however, prevented the performing of abortions on this ground. In the first eight months of the Act's operation, 957 were performed on this ground alone, with a further 3228 on this ground in combination with others.[30] By 1973, the figures had climbed to 3672 and 29 731 respectively,[31] though by 1980 – the last year for which figures in this form are available – they had dipped to 1961 and 15 703, respectively.[32] Clearly, therefore, this is one area in which medical attitudes and practice in relation to abortion appear to have changed significantly since the Act came into force.

Although such abortions are sometimes described as having been performed under the 'social clause', they clearly fall within s. 1(1)(a) of the Act as they are performed in the interests of health, albeit that of existing children. This is not so, however, with all abortions which are said to have been performed 'under the social clause', for the phrase is sometimes used to refer not to s. 1(1)(a), but to s. 1(2). As s. 1(2) merely allows a woman's environment to be taken into account in determining whether the continuance of her pregnancy would involve greater risk than its termination, it does not permit abortions on social grounds alone. However, Lane reported that very many within the profession regarded this subsection as allowing abortion for purely environmental reasons.[33] Moreover, in some reported series of abortions, there is not even any reference to the subsection, but merely a bare reference to the indication for given numbers of abortions as 'social'. In 1970 a paper published in the *British Medical Journal* described a series of 400 abortions performed by vacuum aspiration. The indications for these operations were classified according to the main indication and not the categories on the notification form, and read as follows:[34]

Obstetric 4 (1%)
'At risk' fetus 11 (2.75%)
Medical 15 (3.75%)
Psychiatric 56 (14%)
Psychiatric–Social 150 (37.5%)
Social 164 (41%)

Similarly, the following year, a larger series consisting of 1000 terminations performed by this method was presented. The authors noted that in the months since the advent of the Abortion Act, referral of patients was becoming more common 'for less well defined – that is, social – reasons'. This was reflected in the indications cited for the abortions performed, which ran as follows:[35]

Obstetric 10 (1%)
Medical 21 (2.1%)
'At risk' fetus 14 (1.4%)
Psychiatric 85 (8.5%)
Psychiatric–Social 297 (29.7%)
Social 573 (57.3%)

The penultimate category contained patients who had, 'in addition to social factors, minor psychiatric problems in the past or in whom these were present at the time of interview'. The last category, however, consisted of patients 'in whom only social factors were operative . . .'. In 1972, another series of abortions was published which again indicated the significance of social indications. Of 477 patients referred, 440 were recommended for abortion. The same five-fold classification revealed that 135 were performed for 'social–psychiatric' and 279 for 'social' indications.[36] In these series, it appears that the 'social' indication refers to operations performed not on account of the patient's existing children but because, possibly for environmental or personal reasons, the pregnancy was unwanted. If these reasons, and not the health of either the woman or her existing children, were the grounds for these abortions, then the operations were unlawful. Moreover, if representative, these series suggest that a sizeable proportion of abortions performed, even in the N.H.S., are illegal.

More detailed evidence relating to the significance of such social grounds is provided in a study published in 1973 discussing the provision of therapeutic abortion in Aberdeen.[37] Part of this comprehensive survey consisted of the analysis of 1671 case records of women referred for abortion between 1963 and 1969. The analysis was undertaken by two gynecologists, Macgillivray and Dennis.[38] Having examined one hundred cases, they decided upon five main categories: 'medical', 'eugenic', 'medico-psychiatric', 'socio-psychiatric', and 'social'. However, as there proved to be social factors present in a 'large proportion of cases other than those where the main indication seemed to be the social circumstances of the woman and her family . . .', three further mixed categories – 'medical/social', 'socio-psychiatric/social', 'medico-psychiatric/social' – seemed appropriate.[39] The analysis revealed that the significance attributed to social factors increased over the period studied:

about three-quarters of the referrals for the years 1963–9 fell into either the category 'social' or one of the three combined categories in which there was a strong social component. The proportion in these categories increased from 57 per cent in the earlier to 79 per cent in the last year of the series. At the same time the proportion classified as primarily medical declined although absolute numbers remained fairly stable.[40]

The authors reiterated these conclusions in their elaboration upon 'medical' and 'social' indications. They regarded the indication as 'medical' when the patient suffered from a recognised medical condition which was likely to deteriorate during pregnancy and/or to be aggravated by the care of a child. Examples were heart disease, nephritis, and debility through frequent and complicated child-bearing. A decreasing proportion each year had presented with solely medical indications, 4% in 1969 as compared with 11% in 1963–1964.[41] The bulk of indications were either purely or partly 'social'. The authors described 'social' indications as follows:

Where the external environment, both economic and cultural, is considered to be seriously prejudicial to continuation of the pregnancy. The woman's reaction to the pregnancy is thought to be in proportion to the effects of the unfavourable environment and there is no evidence of abnormality in the patient's previous personality. Social indications cover a wide range of environmental factors.[42]

A quarter of the women who had been referred had no grounds other than their social difficulties for requesting abortion. By 1969, their numbers had doubled. In 1963–1964 few of these pregnancies were illegitimate but by 1969 women with illegitimate pregnancies applying for abortion for social reasons outnumbered women with legitimate pregnancies by two to one. Although acceptances for abortion were lower in this category than in any of the others, no fewer than 38% were terminated.[43] Two case histories were given to illustrate the type of patient who fell into this category. Both reveal the absence of a medical condition indicating abortion. The first read as follows:

A first-year student, aged 18, pregnant to a student in the second year of a four-year course. The couple had discussed contraception with the doctor and had asked to be referred to the family planning clinic, but she had already fallen pregnant. The doctor was impressed by them and thought they were a sensible, responsible pair who had a stable relationship. He felt that termination would be the most satisfactory solution to their immediate problem and probably the least damaging to their relationship in the long term. The gynaecologist thought she was an immature person and that the putative father was not prepared to support her if she had the baby. Accordingly she had a suction termination of an 8 weeks pregnancy. When seen for follow-up eight months later she was very well and was on an oral contraceptive.[44]

The second case history ran:

A woman of 34, married for eleven years to a man who had recently set up his own business but had found that the business was encumbered with debts. He was trying to pay these off and she had to manage on £6 per week. They had three children aged between 10 and 20 months and lived in a three-roomed flat up three flights of stairs, at a rent of £9 per month. She was worried and tired and did not feel able to cope with another baby. A hysterotomy and sterilisation was performed on a 16 weeks pregnancy and when seen for follow-up eight months later she was very well.[45]

The authors caution that their categorisation of indications was retrospective and that, therefore, it does not follow that each of the cases placed by them in a particular category was so categorised by the referring practitioner or the consultant.[46] They also pointed out the difficulty of categorising patients according to indications.[47]

Nevertheless, the study does reveal the degree to which social indications were considered to justify abortion, and the increasing proportion of operations performed for such indications. This increase is not wholly attributable to the Act, however, for the study indicates that reliance on social indications was increasing even before it came into effect.[48]

In addition to the above evidence which suggests the availability of abortion at the request of the woman, at least in the private sector, and the increasing provision of abortion for 'social' indications, there is the evidence of surveys of practitioners' attitudes to abortion since 1967. These surveys disclose a corresponding increase in the number of practitioners – both family doctors, consultant gynecologists and psychiatrists – willing to terminate or recommend termination at the woman's request and for social reasons.

Changing medical attitudes
Between 1967 and 1982 several surveys have been carried out into the attitudes of medical practitioners in relation to abortion.[49] They lend some support to the view that, since the passage of the Abortion Act, abortion has been available on request and for social reasons.

General practitioners. Four studies have thrown light on the attitude of G.P.s to abortion. In 1967 Cartwright asked 1726 subjects for the name of their G.P. A total of 702 names was given, of whom 531 (76%) were either interviewed or filled in a postal questionnaire.[50] In late 1970, Cartwright and Waite, of the Institute for Social Studies in Medical Care (I.S.S.M.C.), sent postal questionnaires to 900 G.P.s in 52 randomly selected areas of England and Wales: 601 (68%) replied.[51] The questionnaire asked if the doctor would, generally speaking, recommend termination on request, and in six sets of circumstances, if the woman had given serious consideration to alternatives. The circumstances and the percentages of those replying affirmatively are shown in Table 2. The replies reveal a significant proportion of G.P.s willing to recommend abortion on request – no fewer than 34% of male doctors and 35% of female doctors – and for non-medical reasons. Only 3% of respondents said they would never recommend abortion. The results also suggest a significant relaxation in attitudes since 1967. Whereas, for

Table 2. Those who declared that they would, generally speaking, recommend/perform abortion if request made before ten weeks and serious consideration had been given to alternatives

	For whoever requested it (%)	For an unmarried girl aged 14 or under (%)	For an unmarried university student in her final year (%)	For a woman with severe kidney disease (%)	For a woman who contracted rubella during first trimester (%)	For a married woman with 6 children (%)	For an unmarried, poorly paid working-girl (%)
G.P.s (I.S.S.M.C., 1971)[a]	34	86	60	87	84	69	63
Consultant psychiatrists (Waite, 1974)[b]	35	84	56	79	82	70	55
Consultant gynecologists (Waite, 1974)[c]	19	87	53	92	91	72	56
(Wessex, 1978)[d]	—	81[e]	81	88	88	72[f]	69

[a] See Chapter 5, n. 51.
[b] See Chapter 5, n. 87.
[c] See Chapter 5, n. 68.
[d] See Chapter 5, n. 90. The period of gestation in this study was twelve rather than ten weeks.
[e] For a girl aged under sixteen years.
[f] For a married woman with four children.

example, 22% of Cartwright's sample gave an unqualified 'Yes' when asked if they would recommend abortion for a woman with several children and an unwanted pregnancy, the figure in the I.S.S.M.C. survey was 69%. Cartwright and Waite conclude: 'Clearly there has been a substantial change. The Abortion Act, which came into force between the two surveys, has apparently either encouraged doctors to express their attitudes more freely or has led to a change in their views'.[52]

A more recent study, carried out by Gallup on behalf of the medical newspaper *Doctor* in 1974,[53] reveals a similar trend. A stratified sample of 600 G.P.s from all parts of Britain was asked to complete a questionnaire and 70% did so. Questions were also asked of a representative sample of over 1000 people in the general population. The survey revealed that 75% of doctors approved of abortion on 'social' grounds, a higher proportion than in the general population. The 'social' grounds specified in the survey were, first, a schoolgirl of 16 who had planned a career before marriage and, secondly, a married woman of limited financial resources with four children. The percentage of practitioners approving abortion in these circumstances contrasts markedly with the 37% in Cartwright's sample who said that abortion was never justified on social grounds.[54]

Further and more in-depth evidence of a more relaxed attitude to the provision of abortion is provided by Aitken-Swann's survey, conducted in the mid 1970s, of medical attitudes and practice in relation to fertility control in north-east Scotland.[55] Some 130 G.P.s were interviewed, only one of those selected for interview being unwilling to participate. The interviews lasted an average of forty-five minutes and in order to encourage free discussion the sixteen questions were generally phrased.[56] Five questions related to abortion. One asked whether the practitioner had any objections to abortion on principle: 100 (77%) replied that they had not, and many of the twenty-seven who did voice an objection were concerned less with principle than with the undesirability of too much abortion.[57] Most were prepared to compromise and not to let their principles stand in the patient's way.[58] The practitioners were also asked whether their attitude to abortion had changed in any way over the years:[59] forty-two replied that their attitude had not changed but had always been liberal.[60] Nevertheless, forty-eight replied that their attitude had become more liberal.[61] Aitken-Swann comments that although after the passage of the Act and the increasing demand for abortion many doctors became concerned at the social ramifications of more frequent termination, by the time of her survey attitudes had again changed and become more relaxed: her respondents spoke of having been 'brainwashed' and their standards as having 'slipped' or been 'eroded'.[62] Moreover, whereas before the Act G.P.s referred carefully selected patients, the survey found that practice had changed to such an extent that if the patient persisted in wanting an abortion the doctor would almost always refer her for a second opinion:

In very few instances . . . would the doctor fail to refer her if she were determined on it. The degree of determination she brings to bear on him and the amount of pressure from family and friends is all-important.[63]

A few even felt that the decision was for her to make once the implications of abortion were explained to her.[64] Occasionally a doctor mentioned that 'if he considered the grounds for the request inadequate he would offer the woman the opportunity of having the abortion as a private patient . . .'.[65] G.P.s had, therefore, followed public opinion, and had become less selective in referring women for a second opinion, thereby shifting most of the decision making to the gynecologists.[66]

Consultant gynecologists. Four major surveys of the attitudes and practice of consultant gynecologists have been carried out since 1967. The first was conducted in 1969–1970 by the R.C.O.G. and has already been mentioned.[67] The second was carried out by Waite in 1971.[68]

Waite sent postal questionnaires to 399 consultant gynecologists of whom 332 (83%) replied. Only 7% declared a conscientious objection and all but two of these described circumstances in which they would recommend abortion.[69] They were all asked their opinion in the six sets of circumstances mentioned in the I.S.S.M.C. survey of G.P.s, and their replies, which reveal a majority in favour of abortion in each situation, are set out in Table 2. Those in favour of abortion on request before the tenth week of pregnancy totalled 19%,[70] a smaller proportion than the 34% of G.P.s who expressed the same view, but nevertheless a marked increase on the 4% who, only the previous year, had informed the R.C.O.G. that they were willing to perform termination in such circumstances. Waite cautions that the differences in the phraseology of the question in the two studies probably influenced the results to a certain extent, the words 'abortion on request' being more acceptable than 'abortion on demand'.[71] Nevertheless, she concluded that the difference between the two years was substantial – a twentieth compared to a fifth answering affirmatively – and that it is possible that there was a shift of opinion in favour of abortion 'on request'.[72] A further indication of the shift to more relaxed attitudes was the finding that more consultants (34%) saw themselves as more likely than their colleagues to grant abortion requests than had been the case in the R.C.O.G. survey (19%),[73] though again the wording of the questions might have influenced the replies. Whereas the earlier survey asked whether the respondent considered himself more 'permissive' than average, the later survey merely asked whether he thought he would be more or less likely to grant abortion requests than consultants generally.[74] Waite concluded her study by observing that, although it appeared that consultants performing abortions had turned down more than 30 000 requests in 1970, they had, since 1969, apparently shifted to a more 'liberal' position on abortion.[75]

Aitken-Swann's survey in the mid 1970s also detected a shift towards more relaxed attitudes. She interviewed all thirteen consultants and senior registrars in gynecology in Aberdeen. The interviews lasted thirty minutes on average and fifteen questions were asked, ten of which related to abortion.[76] The study provided an opportunity to test the findings of previous research in Aberdeen and elsewhere. Research by Farmer in 1968–1969 among nearly all the same consultants had shown that with the increase in referrals after the Act all the consultants saw themselves as becoming more conservative towards operations which they found psychically wearing and technically unstimulating.[77] Subsequent research, however, had revealed that in the light of the increasing belief that women seeking abortion were not psychologically at risk from abortion, fewer abortion requests were being refused: the emphasis seemed to have changed from justifying the performance of abortion to justifying refusal.[78] Aitken-Swann's research confirmed this trend towards a more relaxed approach. Asked whether they had any objections to abortion in principle, the thirteen respondents were almost unanimous (one described his attitude as contradictory) in saying they had not.[79] Aitken-Swann remarks:

The choice between a doctor's moral principles and his humanitarian instincts may be hard to make and most of the gynaecologists, and certainly many of the general practitioners in the survey, had solved it . . . by opting out of moral problems. . . . Not long ago birth control was considered a moral problem . . . but it has now come to be widely accepted as an essential of civilised living. The study suggests that attitudes to abortion have already begun to undergo the process of change.[80]

Another question asked whether they thought abortion should be available 'on demand' in the sense of a woman having the right to decide after the doctor has explained the medical aspects and risks. Six thought it should. Seven disagreed, though one did not rule it out in the earliest stages of pregnancy. Of the six who agreed, four did so conditionally, the main qualifications relating to the absence of contraindications and the stage of gestation.[81] Of the seven who disagreed, three were moved by the risks of the procedure and four by the threat to clinical freedom.[82] The proportion in favour is markedly greater than the 4% in the R.C.O.G. survey of 1969 and even the 19% in Waite's, conducted in 1971. Had the question been phrased in terms of 'request' rather than 'demand', it seems likely that the proportion would have been even larger, particularly in view of the number of dissenters who were concerned primarily with a threat to clinical freedom.

Had their attitude to abortion changed over the years? Aitken-Swann observed that although Farmer had found that the increased demand from patients during the first year of the Act's operation had made the consultants regard themselves as more conservative, he had nevertheless found that some were less conservative than others: refusal rates varied from 37% to only 18% of referrals. Moreover, by the time of Aitken-Swann's own survey in 1974, fewer than 10% of referrals were refused. She remarked that there had clearly been a 'marked liberalisation' of practice in the group as a whole.[83] Eight of the respondents stated that they were now more 'liberal' than they had been, another three that they had always been 'liberal'.[84] The relaxation in the attitudes of some could be traced to the fact that they had been trained in places (such as most Scottish medical schools) where students had been taught that abortion could not be performed legally, or had worked in places where the law was restrictive and had adopted a 'liberal' approach only when they had come to Aberdeen, where the liberal performance of abortion undermined their earlier teaching. Some had changed because of the difficulties of objective decision making in the light of such factors as the ability of the patient to present her case well.[85] Aitken-Swann noted:

It is difficult enough to adjudicate among patients requesting early abortion on socio-economic grounds even if decision-making were as reasonable and objective a process as it is supposed to be. But when it is influenced by so many extraneous factors thoughtful gynaecologists must ask themselves . . . how they can justify anything but a liberal policy in such cases.[86]

In short, she observed, the attitudes of consultants to abortion had become 'noticeably more relaxed' since Farmer's study in the first year of the Act's operation.[87]

A further question asked whether there were any reasons for wanting abortion to which the consultants would be unsympathetic. Several felt the word 'unsympathetic' inappropriate but agreed that they were more doubtful about some reasons than others, and high on the list were those classified as social convenience'.[88] Examples were the woman's impending wedding or holiday. Nevertheless, it would appear that even in these circumstances abortion was not always ruled out, for, as some consultants acknowledged, abortion was already available on demand in early cases.[89]

More recent research, in the form of the Wessex Abortion Studies, conducted in 1978–1979, confirms some of the conclusions of the earlier studies. In the first of the Wessex Studies, 197 Wessex women who left the region over an eight-week period to have private abortions in Brighton and 111 who had N.H.S. abortions within the region at Southampton General Hospital were interviewed. The table of their reasons (see Table 3) reveals that the women themselves regarded the reasons as predominantly social and not medical.[90] The producer of the report, Ashton, states that the reasons women gave were many and often multiple, but that only 12 (10.8%) of the Southampton patients and 3 (1.5%) of the Brighton patients gave reasons directly related to mental or physical health.[91]

The second of the studies[92] focussed on the attitudes of consultant gynecologists to the provision of abortion and concluded that, although they referred to the same criteria in deciding whether to abort, the application of these criteria was more individualistic,

Table 3. Reasons given for termination by location of operation in Wessex survey

	Location of operation			
	Brighton		Southampton	
Reason	Numbers	Rank order	Numbers	Rank order
Unstable personal life	52	1	19	2
Material	42	2	21	1
Age/immaturity	37	3	16	3
Family complete	31	4	16	3
Career	22	5	10	5
Other	11	6	6	7
Not husband's child	4	7	3	8
Mental health	2	8	2	9
Physical health	1	[9]	10	5

Source: see Chapter 5, n. 90.

which partly explained the interdistrict variation in provision of abortion revealed in the first study. The results of the study were based on interviews with thirty-two of the thirty-four consultant gynecologists serving the Wessex Regional Health Authority conducted between July and September 1978. The study focussed on how the consultant assessed the woman's eligibility for abortion; how this assessment was affected by his judgement of the risks of operating at certain stages of gestation, given the medical and social conditions of the patient and the availability of resources; and how he assessed the adequacy of resources to do this part of his work, in relation to other pressures and priorities.

The consultants were asked to state whether they would agree to abort in the six sets of circumstances referred to by Cartwright in 1967 and by Waite in 1971. Their replies are recorded in Table 2 (p. 120) and confirm the willingness of the majority to perform abortion even in the absence of a medical condition. This is underlined by their replies to another question asking what they considered to be appropriate medical and non-medical, 'that is, socioeconomic', grounds for abortion.[93] Their answers to this question are given in Table 4.

Table 4. Main examples of conditions considered appropriate grounds for abortion

Medical grounds		Non-medical grounds	
Main examples	Frequency mentioned	Main examples	Frequency mentioned
Fetal abnormality	14	Age – very old or very	12
Heart disease	13	young	
Woman's life/health threatened	9	Poverty or accommo- dation problems	10
Hypertension	6	Marital status (single,	8
Rubella	6	separated, divorced)	
Renal disease	6	Unwanted pregnancy	8
Carcinoma	3	Grand multipara	5
Other examples[a]	30	status	
		Mental illness	7
		Other examples[b]	18

[a] Other examples included respiratory disease, severe debilitating illness, pelvic malignancy, and some diabetes.
[b] Other examples included rape, failed contraception, and inability to rear children.
Source: [1980] 1 *Lancet* 140, 141, Table 1.

Consultant psychiatrists. The most thorough survey of psychiatrists' attitudes towards abortion was carried out in 1971 by Waite.[94] Postal questionnaires were sent to a random national sample of 476 consultant psychiatrists and 388 (82%) replied. The study showed that, on average, each psychiatrist in 1970 saw twenty-six patients with reference to abortion, of whom nineteen were recommended and eighteen aborted or at least not refused by the gynecologist.[95] Only half the respondents felt abortion referrals had increased since the Act.[96] Attitudes to abortion were, however, relaxed. A full 35% said they would recommend termination for any woman who requested it before the tenth week if she had seriously considered the alternatives, and only 3% declared a conscientious objection.[97] Asked their opinion in the six sets of circumstances given in previous studies, a majority would have recommended abortion in each case (see Table 2, p. 120). The survey reveals an attitude to the provision of abortion comparable to that of the other groups of practitioners surveyed. A similar percentage of G.P.s in the 1971 study favoured abortion 'on request', and the recommendations of the psychiatrists in the six hypothetical situations were similar to those of the gynecologists in the study of the same year.[98]

Apart from demonstrating that a significant proportion of psychiatrists would recommend abortion on request in early pregnancy, the study also adumbrated the extent to which practitioners generally relied on social grounds. Asked whether they felt that their involvement in the decision-making process was useful and appropriate, a fifth of psychiatrists replied that patients were frequently referred unnecessarily for a psychiatric opinion and over a third that this happened sometimes.[99] They were asked the main reasons why psychiatric assessments were requested. The study reveals that a third gave reasons which could be labelled, at least in part, 'social' such as: 'the absence of a clear physical indication together with good social reasons'.[100]

5.2 The safeguards against excessively permissive interpretation of s. 1 and their effectiveness

Section 5(2) of the Abortion Act and the 'statistical argument'
Section 5(2) of the Abortion Act 1967 provides that anything done with intent to procure miscarriage is unlawfully done unless the conditions set out in s. 1 of the Abortion Act 1967 are satisfied. If the protection of the Act is not secured by compliance with these conditions, the operator leaves himself open to a charge under s. 58 of the Offences Against the Person Act (O.A.P.A.) 1861. Does the practice of abortion simply at the request of the woman fall within the ambit of s. 1 of the Act? Or is such practice outside its terms, prohibited by s. 5(2) of the Act and punishable under s. 58 of the O.A.P.A. 1861?

It will be recalled that Sir Roger Ormrod said that the Act seems a modest extension of the law,[101] and it is certainly the case that the Act's sponsor did not concede that it would allow abortion on request. During the second reading debate on his Bill he said: 'We want to stamp out the back-street abortions, but it is not the intention of the Promoters of the Bill to leave a wide open door for abortion on request'.[102] However, there is an argument to the effect that the Act allows just this. The argument runs that, as the risk to the woman's life is, statistically, greater if she goes to term than if she has her pregnancy terminated before the fourteenth week, the Act always allows abortion before that time. Glanville Williams states that a doctor can adopt this 'statistical argument' provided that it is not rendered inapplicable in an individual case by either the risk of morbidity or the patient's condition.[103] It is submitted that this is an accurate statement of the law. Consequently, the Act is not, as has been claimed, 'very precise and restrictive'[104] but is, as Lane concluded, 'imprecise and can be widely interpreted'.[105]

To what extent is the exercise of this broad, though not unlimited, discretion supervised by the courts? Hitherto, the courts have shown a marked reluctance to interfere. In *R. v. Smith* (1974), Scarman L.J. in the Court of Appeal observed that the Act placed 'a great social responsibility' on the shoulders of the medical profession, though he did point out that, if a case was brought to trial which concerned the good faith of a doctor, the decision rested with the jury and not with the medical profession.[106] This comment must, however, be read in the light of the court's ruling that a verdict against a doctor will often be likely to be unsafe in the absence of evidence as to professional practice and medical probabilities.

An even greater judicial reluctance to interfere with clinical freedom was evident in *Paton v. Trustees of B.P.A.S. and another* (1978), where a husband unsuccessfully sought an injunction to prevent his wife from having an abortion without his consent.[107] Counsel for the plaintiff contended that if the two doctors did not hold their certified opinions, or had reached them in bad faith, his client might be granted an injunction. This was disputed by counsel for the trustees of the nursing-home involved, and the judge declined to decide the question. Nevertheless, he did indicate the reluctance of the courts to question the exercise of medical discretion. Citing Scarman L.J.'s dictum that the law placed the great social responsibility on the medical profession, Baker P. said it would be quite impossible in his view for the courts to supervise its operation. He observed that in the case before him the two doctors had given a certificate, and he went on to remark: 'It is not and cannot be suggested that the certificate was given in other than good faith and it seems to me that there is the end of the matter in English law'.[108] Although this statement should be viewed in the light of Baker P.'s earlier refusal to decide the question, his comments as a whole betray an unwillingness to interfere with the exercise of medical discretion in relation to an abortion performed, at least ostensibly, in compliance with the terms of the 1967 Act.

Moreover, when deciding what those terms are, the courts have interpreted the Act liberally. In *Royal College of Nursing of the United Kingdom* v. *Department of Health and Social Security* (1981), the House of Lords held, by a majority, that the Act was to be interpreted in the light of its policy. This was, to broaden the grounds on which abortions might be lawfully obtained and to ensure that they were carried out with proper skill in hygienic conditions in ordinary hospitals and as part of ordinary medical care, in accordance with ordinary medical practice in which tasks forming part of the treatment were entrusted to nurses under the instructions of the doctor in charge of the treatment. Accordingly, the majority held, provided a doctor prescribed the treatment for abortion, remained in charge and accepted responsibility throughout, and provided that the treatment was carried out in accordance with his directions, the pregnancy was 'terminated by' a registered medical practitioner within s. 1 of the Act, even though the treatment was carried out by a nurse.[109] The majority's 'purposive' interpretation of the Act is illustrated by the following words of Lord Keith, stating that the court's ruling was,

fully in accordance with that part of the policy and purpose of the Act which was directed to securing that socially acceptable abortions should be carried out under the safest conditions attainable.[110]

Certification, notification, and the approval of premises
During the Parliamentary debates on his Bill, Mr Steel said that it was necessary for such a measure as his to contain 'safeguards' against abuse, and he pointed to three 'essential and new' safeguards in his Bill: the requirements of certification of opinions, notification of abortions, and approval of premises where the operations were to be performed.[111] To what extent have these safeguards, which he said would prevent abuse of the Act,[112] operated as a check on excessively permissive interpretation of s. 1?

The Abortion Regulations 1968–1980. The Abortion Regulations 1968[113] came into effect on the same day as the Abortion Act in discharge of the statutory duty placed on the Minister by s. 2(1) of the Act. Section 3 of the Regulations deals with the certification of the practitioner's opinions. Section 3(2) requires the two opinions to be certified on 'Certificate A' before treatment is begun.

This regulation undoubtedly represents a restriction on the practitioner's freedom in that it introduces a formality which he must observe, on pain of a fine. However, certification hardly restricts the exercise of medical discretion, for although it ensures a second opinion it requires neither the second practitioner to be of a particular status nor limits the number of practitioners who may be approached for a second opinion. It does not even require the second practitioner to see the patient. Indeed, it was concern at the failure of some doctors to do just this that led to the amendment of the Regulations, at the recommendation of Lane, to require the certifying practitioners to state whether they had seen or examined the patient.[114] However, the Regulations as amended do not require either of the practitioners to see the patient and it is difficult to see how they might do so without being *ultra vires*.

As a safeguard against abuse of medical discretion, therefore, certification is only of limited effectiveness.[115] Its main virtue is in ensuring a second opinion, but this had been standard practice well before the enactment of the Regulations, among both reputable and disreputable practitioners. Although the ostensible function of certification is the protection of the patient, it also serves the interests of the practitioner by helping to protect him from suspicion of impropriety.

If certification is only a limited safeguard against abuse of the Act, what of notification? This safeguard was built into the Act in the form of s. 2(1)(b), and its requirements are specified in s. 4 of the Regulations. Section 4(1) requires the operating practitioner to notify the abortion to the C.M.O. within seven days, including in the notification form such information as is specified in Schedule 2 to the Regulations.[116]

Unlike certification, notification did represent a significant innovation in this area of medical practice, for whereas it had long been usual to obtain a second opinion, practitioners had not previously reported the operation to a third party. Moreover, failure to notify might, like failure to certify, involve the practitioner in liability under s. 2(3) of the Act, and also in suspicion of illegal abortion.[117]

However, the effectiveness of notification as a safeguard is also limited, for, just as a practitioner could certify an illegal abortion as falling within the terms of the Act, so too could he notify such an operation as having been performed within the Act, and it would be extremely difficult to prove the absence of good faith. Moreover, if a practitioner fails to notify, his offence will be difficult to detect for, *ex hypothesi*, the C.M.O. will not have been informed that an abortion has been performed.

There is, in fact, no way of knowing how many abortions have not been notified since 1968, but the available evidence suggests that the number is substantial. It would appear that, shortly after the Act's introduction, this was even the view of the Ministry of Health. In 1970 Mr Richard Crossman, former Secretary of State, wrote that there was more than a strong suspicion at the Health Ministry that the number of abortions far exceeded the number of notifications.[118]

It is also noteworthy that as notification is made to the C.M.O. on a doctor-to-doctor basis rather than to, say, the police, any suspicion of criminality which might arise from the form is less likely to be followed up. Further, the forms enjoy that confidentiality which normally attaches to communications between doctors, and s. 5 of the Regulations, which covers disclosure of notified information, is narrowly drawn. In an attempt to improve the efficacy of notification as a safeguard, s. 5 was amended in 1976, again pursuant to a recommendation by Lane, to allow information to be disclosed at the request of the President of the General Medical Council (G.M.C.), either to himself or to a member of his staff authorised by him, for the purpose of investigating whether there has been serious professional misconduct by a registered medical practitioner.[119] The strictness of s. 5 is understandable in the light of professional concern for the preservation of confidentiality.

It is noteworthy that the major professional bodies recommended a requirement of notification, provided confidentiality was preserved. The R.C.O.G., for example, urged that notification within fourteen days of the operation should be required, provided that the information remained confidential and the rules of professional secrecy were not infringed.[120] The B.M.A. Special Committee also favoured notification but stressed, significantly, that the Association did not regard it as part of the safeguarding procedure at all. It said that the purpose of notification was to provide an accurate source of facts and figures which would be of statistical use and that all notifications should be confidential and made by one medical

medical practitioner to another.[121] The concern of the medical bodies over confidentiality was made clear while the Regulations were being framed. In February 1968, representatives of both the R.C.O.G. and the B.M.A. met with the C.M.O., Sir George Godber, and representatives of the Ministry of Health and the Home Office to discuss draft Regulations relating to notification. The medical representatives stressed that the confidentiality of all information relating to the patients must be preserved to the utmost or the whole object of the Act might be defeated.[122]

The number of prosecutions for failure to comply with the requirement of notification is small, though the Department has returned forms which have not been completed to its satisfaction.[123] This was highlighted recently when the notification form was amended.[124] The Department of Health and Social Security (D.H.S.S.) maintained that the new form – H.S.A. 4 – was designed to provide more information about aspects of abortion which had attracted public and professional concern since the introduction of the Act, such as the period of gestation, and to reduce the amount of personal data required.[125] Some practitioners, however, failed to complete that part of the form – Q.3 – which dealt with the grounds for termination. The practitioner was required to tick the ground on which pregnancy had been terminated and, if the ground was risk either to the woman's life or health, to state the 'main medical condition(s)' involved. This contrasted with the corresponding question – Q.11 – on the previous form which had asked the practitioner to state the 'medical condition of woman' but had also allowed him to declare 'non-medical grounds' for termination. In the view of some doctors and M.P.s, the omission of the reference to 'non-medical grounds' in the revised form amounted to an attempt to restrict the Act so as to allow only medical grounds for abortion. A report of the incident in the *British Medical Journal* states that the Minister of State for Health, Dr Vaughan, explained that the new form omitted the reference to non-medical grounds because they were not part of the parent Act.[126] The report continues that on 1 May 1981, two months after the introduction of the new form, Dr Vaughan was informed by the C.M.O., Sir Henry Yellowlees, that a few doctors had not completed it properly and that they were returned, on the suggestion of the latter, in July. Most were then sent in properly completed.

Between thirty and forty practitioners asked for further clarification, which they received. A small number declined to complete the form, and the C.M.O. referred their names to the Director of Public Prosecutions for a legal ruling.[127] In the event, the Director did not prosecute those doctors whose names had been referred to him. The Attorney-General explained that police investigations had not disclosed any evidence to show that the abortions in question had been performed for social reasons. In each case, he said, the doctors had claimed there were medical grounds for abortion.[128] However, Mr Huntingford, one of the gynecologists whose names were referred to the Director, maintains that there was no medical indication for the abortion he performed which was the subject of investigation; that against the section on the notification form requiring the medical condition to be stated he wrote 'None'; and that, in spite of a written request from the C.M.O. and encouragement from the police to do so, at no time did he alter his view that there was no medical indication for the operation. In fact, the available evidence, and in particular his interview with the police,[129] reveals that he did in fact claim that there was a medical ground for the abortion, namely, that abortion was safer than delivery. In other words, the medical condition justifying termination was the pregnancy itself. This, therefore, rather than any pathological condition, would appear to be the medical ground to which the Attorney-General was referring.

The incident underlines the discretion enjoyed by practitioners under both the Act and the Regulations (and the reaction to the incident from some doctors confirms that they believe the Act to allow abortion for social reasons). It would appear that even if a doctor fails to record a medical condition on the notification form, this will not prevent him from successfully contending that there were nevertheless medical grounds for the abortion such as to bring it within the terms of the Act, even if it is the mere fact of pregnancy itself.

Finally, the fact that the form merely requires the operator to tick the ground of the Act under which the abortion was performed means that, provided a doctor satisfies this requirement, he can *ex hypothesi* only notify a legal abortion. The only cases in which abuse will appear on the face of the form are, therefore, such unlikely eventualities as a doctor stating an excessive gestational age or that the operation was performed in unapproved premises.

Approval of premises: s. 1(3) of the Act. If, then, certification and notification are only of limited value as safeguards against abuse of the Act, what of the third safeguard, namely, the restriction of operations under the Act to hospitals vested in the Minister and to places approved by him?

This restriction, found in s. 1(3) of the Act, places a restriction on the practitioner's freedom in that it confines abortions to N.H.S. hospitals and to places recognised by the D.H.S.S. as meeting certain standards. No longer, therefore, can a G.P. lawfully perform an abortion in his surgery – a practice not unknown before the Act. Moreover, the granting of approval to premises for the purposes of the Act has, since the Act came into operation, been subject to increasingly strict requirements.[130] Nevertheless, these requirements do not appear to impinge to any significant degree on the exercise of medical discretion.

This was particularly evident during the early years of the Act's operation. Asked in April 1969 whether he felt his powers under the Act were adequate, the Secretary of State for Social Services, Mr Crossman, replied that his powers were adequate to deal with matters with which the Minister was instructed to deal, which related to the physical conditions in the home. He added that the Minister's job was not to tell the doctor how to do his job, but to see that the job was done in adequate physical conditions.[131] Later in the same year he said that he had no reason to believe the Act was not working well throughout the N.H.S., though he did concede that things were taking place in a very small segment of the private sector, concentrated in London, of which neither he nor the medical profession approved. However, he expressed the view that he had no control over such matters: if things were taking place inside that sector which conflicted with the spirit of the law, it was not a matter for him but for the doctor's own conscience and the medical profession's own disciplinary authorities.[132]

It is apparent, however, that although additional conditions have been attached to the granting of a licence, such as an undertaking to accept patients referred only by pregnancy advisory bureaux approved by the Department, it has impinged only peripherally on the freedom of the individual practitioner to perform abortions at his discretion. As with certification and notification, therefore, the power of approval has proved to be incapable of preventing the performance of abortion on request or for social reasons.

The General Medical Council

The view that the G.M.C. is the appropriate body to deal with abuse of discretion in relation to the Act has been voiced by influential figures both outside and inside the profession. In 1969, Mr Steel, speaking against a Bill introduced by Mr St John-Stevas which proposed that one of the two opinions be that of a consultant, urged that the G.M.C. both could and should be taking action in cases of abuse, as one of its definitions of infamous conduct was the 'abuse of financial opportunities offered by medical practice'.[133] Similarly, the *Lancet*, objecting to the same proposed restriction of the law, stated that those acting outside the spirit of the law should be restrained not by the House of Commons but by the G.M.C. It added that one of the Council's functions was to demonstrate that the code of medical ethics was 'something outside and, in a sense, more powerful than the Law'.[134] In 1975, however, the same journal criticised the failure of the 'timid' G.M.C. to prevent the biggest abuse: profiteering in the private sector.[135]

An examination of the minutes of the G.M.C. between 1968 and 1982 reveals that very few practitioners have in fact been disciplined by the Council for illegal abortion. Indeed, over that period, only seven doctors have been disciplined for performing an unlawful termination of pregnancy in the U.K. and, in all seven cases, proceedings followed conviction by a criminal court.[136] Six practitioners were erased from the Medical Register and one suffered suspension. The names of four of those erased had, however, been restored to the Register by 1982.[137]

The reason for the failure of the Council to act as an effective check on the abuse of discretion in relation to abortion is not hard to find: it has no power to initiate proceedings and must await the filing of a complaint. Matters which might result in disciplinary action against a practitioner are brought to the Council's attention by, for example, the notification to the Registrar of the Council of the conviction of a registered medical practitioner.[138] Its disciplinary function is, therefore, essentially reactive and not apt for searching out possible abuses of medical discretion.[139] This inevitably renders it incapable of exercising an effective supervisory function in relation to the implementation of the Abortion Act.

Conclusion

The previous chapter suggested that the profession exerted a significant influence on the framing of the Abortion Act 1967, ensuring in
particular that the decision whether to recommend abortion remained firmly in the hands of two registered medical practitioners.
This chapter maintains that there is evidence from practitioners
themselves, in the form of contributions to the medical press and
sociological surveys of practitioners' attitudes, which lends support
to the view that, since the Act came into operation, the discretion it
conferred has been exercised variably and extensively, even to the
extent of an apparently significant number of abortions being
performed at the request of the woman and for social reasons. The
chapter also suggested that one explanation for this is that safeguards which were built into the Act to prevent abortion on request
have not achieved their objective – essentially because, like the Act
as a whole, they are built on the premise of non-interference with
clinical freedom. The failure of the profession's own disciplinary
authority to achieve the same objective can largely be attributed to
its inability to investigate suspected abuse, though it would not be
unreasonable to surmise that, again, respect for clinical freedom has
helped to confine disciplinary action to those cases where the
criminal justice system has already dealt with illegal abortion.

6

The reaction of the medical profession to proposed restriction of the law 1969–1979

Chapter 5 suggested that the discretion which the Abortion Act 1967 afforded to medical practitioners has been exercised in an extensive way to such a degree that, in medical practice if not in legal theory, abortion has been available 'on request' and for social reasons both in the private sector and, to a somewhat lesser degree, in the National Health Service (N.H.S.), and that the safeguards which were incorporated into the Act ostensibly to curb such practices have proved largely ineffective. Further evidence to support these suggestions will be provided in this chapter, which outlines the major legislative attempts made between 1969 and 1979 to curb perceived abuses of the law by amending the Act restrictively, and which focusses on the profession's reaction to such proposals.

6.1 The St John-Stevas Bill (1969)

After the Act had been in operation for only fifteen months, Mr St John-Stevas introduced a 'ten minute rule' Bill entitled, 'A Bill to improve the law governing abortion and the status and rights of the medical profession in relation thereto'.[1] Clause 1 of the Bill sought to provide that one of the two opinions required by the Act was given by a consultant gynecologist holding office under the N.H.S. (or a doctor of equivalent status approved by the Minister of Health) and that the operation was performed by him or under his supervision. The declared aims of the Bill were to check racketeering, which the Act's safeguards had been unable to prevent, and to ensure that the operation was performed under the best possible conditions.[2] St John-Stevas quoted the Secretary of State, who had conceded: 'There is no doubt that the way the Act is working, in particular in the private sector, is giving grave alarm even to those who were keen supporters of it'.[3] He also invoked the support of the

British Medical Association (B.M.A.) and the Royal College of Obstetricians and Gynaecologists (R.C.O.G.) for his Bill, which had been introduced after discussions with their representatives.[4] Mr Steel spoke against the Bill and said that although one or two doctors were putting financial interests before their patients' welfare, the Secretary of State had power to introduce new regulations and could require more information on the notification form, and the G.M.C. could also take action in cases of abuse.[5] He urged that the growth of the private centres of abortion in London had been stimulated by the restrictive interpretation of the Act by some doctors elsewhere, such as in Birmingham.[6] The narrow defeat of the Bill by 210 votes to 199 suggests the concern felt in Parliament at the operation of the Act.

6.2 The Irvine Bill (1970)

Concern over the Act was again evident the following year, when Mr Godman Irvine introduced a similar Bill. In moving its second reading, he explained he had chosen to introduce the Bill because of the support of the medical bodies for its proposals.[7] He pointed out that the principle behind his Bill had been approved by the B.M.A. at its Annual Representative Meeting (A.R.M.) in July 1967 and in every subsequent year.[8] Opposing the Bill, however, Steel questioned whether medical opinion was fully behind the proposals, and cited the dissentient voice of the *Lancet* and *Medical News-Tribune*.[9] Similarly, Mrs Short produced an N.O.P. poll which revealed that 66% of G.P.s in the U.K. felt that the Act should be left as it was or amended to make abortions easier to obtain, and only 28% that the Act should be restrictively amended.[10] Fearing defeat, the Bill's supporters 'talked it out'. In spite of the fact that it had enjoyed the support of the two main medical bodies, the Bill's chances of progress could only have been prejudiced by the evidence that G.P.s, probably concerned to preserve their autonomy in relation to abortion, were unenthusiastic about granting consultants a monopoly over the final decision in each case.

6.3 The Grylls Bills (1973–1974)

Between 1973 and 1974, Mr Michael Grylls made two unsuccessful attempts to prohibit the giving of advice or information about abortion for reward, except by registered medical practitioners or persons approved by the Secretary of State. His first Bill fell because of the dissolution of Parliament.[11] Moving for leave to reintroduce his measure in May 1974, he explained that he had been motivated by the scandals surrounding some referral agencies, through which a few unscrupulous operators were flourishing. Taxi-drivers touted at airports and fringe doctors advertised abroad. 'This nasty trade', he said, 'is the unacceptable face of the Abortion Act'.[12] The Bill reached the Standing Committee stage, but several members of the Committee criticised it for not going far enough to curb the abuses which had grown up under the Act. Mrs Knight, for example, maintained that ministerial discretion had already proved ineffective.[13] Even the Bill's sponsor conceded that it was a 'very modest measure'.[14] The Bill fell when four committee members walked out, leaving the Committee inquorate.[15]

Grylls had based his Bills on a recommendation of the Lane Committee, which reported in April 1974. The Committee, it will be recalled, had been appointed in June 1971 by the then Secretary of State for Social Services, Sir Keith Joseph, to examine the operation of the Act.[16] The Committee's report on the working of the Act was generally favourable and, straining its terms of reference, recommended that the grounds for abortion should be left unamended.[17] However, the report did concede that some practitioners performed abortion 'on request'[18] and others for purely social indications.[19] The evidence submitted to the Committee by the medical bodies also laid emphasis on the variation in interpretation of the Act, though these bodies did not go so far as to recommend restriction of the grounds for abortion. The B.M.A., it will be recalled, merely criticised aspects of its implementation, such as the marked variation in the provision of abortion.[20] Similarly, the Royal College of General Practitioners, far from calling for the restriction of the Act, urged the provision of more resources to ensure its smooth implementation.[21] The fact that Lane recommended no change in the criteria for abortion was welcomed by the *British Medical Journal*, which regarded the Committee's approach to the problem as humanitarian. It also expressed the hope that the 'shrill and emotional' argument for change would die away, and it observed that abortion for a wide range of indications had become an established part of conventional medical practice.[22] Again, in July 1974 Sir Stanley Clayton P.R.C.O.G. revealed that most of his College's members supported the recommendations that the Committee has made, although a minority was opposed to abortion on socio-economic grounds.[23]

6.4 The White Bill (1975)

The profession's support for the 1967 Act was even more evident when further restrictive Bills were introduced. In 1975 Mr James White introduced a measure which was more far reaching than any of the previous Bills.[24] It fell into three parts. Part I sought not only to regulate the activities of referral agencies, as had Grylls, but also to restrict the conditions under which abortion could be performed. Clause 1(a) required the risk to the woman's life to be 'grave' and the injury to health 'serious', and one of the two certifying practitioners (who could not normally be in practice together) to have been registered for at least five years. Clause 7 prohibited abortions after twenty weeks (except when an N.H.S. consultant was reasonably satisfied that the child would be born with a major disability, in which case the limit was twenty-four weeks). Clause 2 prohibited abortion (except in emergency) unless the operator was reasonably satisfied that the patient had been resident in the U.K. for the previous twenty weeks, and cl. 3 required him (with the woman's consent) to notify the patient's regular doctor. Part II of the Bill prohibited experiments on the fetus or fetal material resulting from abortion otherwise than in accordance with conditions listed in Schedule 2 to the Bill. Part III contained several miscellaneous provisions, one of which – cl. 11 – placed the burden of proof that the requirements of the Act had been satisfied on the defendant in a criminal prosecution.

White moved that his Bill be read a second time on 7 February 1975. He said that he took no hard line on abortion and supported the 1967 Act in principle.[25] However, public opinion was concerned at abuses in its operation, against which his Bill was directed.[26] The abuses were concentrated in the private sector and involved an influx of foreign women who obtained abortion on request for cash. The number of abortions on foreign women totalled 56 000 in 1973 and was increasing, though the figure represented only half the real total, since many went unnotified.[27] But, he said, it was vain to attempt to ensure the safety of women until the serious enforcement difficulties surrounding the existing law were remedied, which his Bill sought to do.[28] He welcomed the offer which the Government had made to set up a Select Committee to investigate the problem of abortion but sought a clear undertaking that the Government would re-establish such a committee in the next session of Parliament.[29]

Mr Steel was not hostile to the idea of a Select Committee.[30] However, he opposed the Bill. He felt that the House could be proud of the overall working of the Act: maternal mortality and morbidity from abortion had fallen and criminal abortion had been virtually eliminated.[31] Problems could, as Lane had recommended, be dealt with by administrative and professional changes. To restrict the grounds for abortion would drive women back to criminal abortionists.[32] Moreover, the combined effect of cl. 1 and 11 would be to create uncertainty among the medical profession and this would result in a substantial reduction in N.H.S. abortions.[33]

The Minister of State at the D.H.S.S., Dr Owen, promised that the Government would re-establish the Select Committee if it did not complete its work in that session.[34] As for the working of the Act, he accepted Lane's finding that there was inequality of provision due to both shortage of resources and differences in interpretation of the Act by doctors. He conceded that in the private sector a small number of doctors had used the Act to make large profits and that there had been instances of gross irresponsibility in medical practice.[35] He said:

The Bill's essential provision is to prevent the abuses which we all know have existed in the private sector. . . . I profoundly wish that my own profession had put its house in order. I wish that, immediately following the passage of the Act, when the abuses were at their height, successive Governments had used administrative measures to prevent abuse.[36]

The Government supported legislation to control pregnancy advisory bureaux, but favoured the flexibility of existing administrative regulation in relation to abortion clinics.[37] Dr Owen reminded the House, moreover, that Lane had opposed restriction of the grounds for abortion[38] and the banning of foreign patients, which would require the doctor to apply a residency test and would conflict with his duty to his patient.[39] Further, the number of foreign women had fallen, in line with the relaxation of abortion laws abroad, and he added that he had no evidence that the number of notifications was an underestimate.[40] Other speakers maintained that private clinics flourished only because of inadequate provision in the N.H.S. It was absurd, said Dr Cronin, that twice as many N.H.S. abortions should be performed in Newcastle than in Birmingham, and it was monstrous that some hospitals were flouting the intention of the 1967 Act by performing abortions only rarely.[41] Winding-up the debate for the sponsors of the Bill, Sir Bernard Braine reminded the House that the Bill aimed to put a stop to abuses in the private sector. He said that some doctors interpreted the Act to allow abortion in every case.[42] Administrative action alone could not remedy the abuses: safeguards had to be written into the law.[43] In spite of White's attempt to withdraw the Bill in the light of Government assurances, it was given a second reading by 203 votes to 88, and referred to a Select Committee without a vote.[44]

A year later, a motion to re-appoint the Select Committee was debated. Braine urged that there was a pressing need for the Committee to be re-appointed to continue its unfinished work: although it had made interim recommendations for administrative action to curb abuse, which had been accepted by the Secretary of State,[45] there were other matters which required consideration, such as the provision of abortion on demand by some doctors.[46] However, Dr Owen felt that what was needed was not further investigation of the operation of the Act by the Committee, but a period of time to see how the recommendations which it had made to the Secretary of State worked out in practice.[47] He doubted whether it would be able to reach a substantial measure of agreement on the more controversial aspects of the Act which it proposed to consider.[48] The motion was, however, carried.

How did the medical profession react to the White Bill? The opposition of the B.M.A. was apparent during the proceedings of its Council in June 1975.[49] The Chairman allowed a deputation of doctors and medical students to address the Council. One member of the delegation declared that the Bill was a dangerous piece of legislation which would jeopardise the health and lives of women and their families if they were forced to continue with unwanted pregnancies, and asked the Association to support the aims of a demonstration organised for later that month by the National Abortion Campaign and to publicise widely the Council's decision.[50] Dr J. H. Marks pointed out that the General Medical Services Committee had passed a motion opposing the Bill, in the following terms:

That this Committee, respresentative of all family doctors in the N.H.S., opposes the attempt in Clause 1 of the Abortion (Amendment) Bill to put the law on abortion back by a generation. It also opposes the concept, enumerated in Clause 11, of a doctor being guilty of an offence until proved innocent, and alerts the profession and the public to the dangers of the Bill.[51]

The Committee felt that the Bill would prove unduly repressive of the rights of women and of the position of any doctor recommending or performing abortion. Similarly, Sir John Peel, presenting the commentary on the Bill by the Board of Science and Education, of which he was Chairman, and moving that it be approved for submission to the Select Committee, observed that the Bill would restrict the intentions of the 1967 Act and that many of its proposals were unworkable.

The mood of the meeting is reflected by the fact that not a single Council member expressed support for the Bill. The President-elect, Sir John Stallworthy, congratulated the Board on its report. Dr J. S. Happel suggested that the Council should revise both its view that the 'social clause' was too wide and would lead to abortion 'on demand', and its support for a 'consultant clause'. The Council approved the commentary on the Bill and its submission to the Select Committee was confirmed. It also decided that in the light of the opinions of members of Council, the Association should take steps to communicate its opposition to the Bill to both M.P.s and the public.[52]

At the A.R.M. in Leeds the following month, Dr Kathleen Frith moved that the meeting take note of Council's approval of the evidence for the Select Committee and said that current abuses could be controlled by a simple change in the Regulations.[53] Dr Marks, supporting the motion, said that he had presented the evidence to the Committee – evidence which had demolished the Bill clause by clause. He also pointed out that the Local Medical Committee conference had opposed the Bill by 360 votes to 4. He was as keen as anyone to catch 'abortion sharks' but without harm to ordinary, decent doctors and women. He said that the Royal Colleges of Pathologists and of Psychiatrists and the Association of Anaesthetists had all agreed that changes in the Act were unnecessary, and that 'legal jargon would not stop rogue doctors: only the profession could do that'. The Council had suggested to the Select Committee that the Regulations should be changed to require the certifying doctors to state whether the woman had been examined and to allow the C.M.O., in certain defined circumstances, to disclose notified information to the President of the G.M.C., either to substantiate a formal complaint to that body or, with the agreement of a medical advisory committee, when apparent abuses justified investigation by the profession. He said that this power could be added to Regulation 5 and could stop abuse almost overnight.[54]

One doctor opposed the words 'grave' and 'serious', objecting that they were not words for a doctor to interpret but were emotive and unscientific: medical decisions had to be made by doctors and not by lawyers.[55] Clinical freedom was also defended by other speakers. One practitioner protested that the Bill would place every doctor in peril.[56] The Bill was not, however, totally devoid of support. One doctor, for example, urged that abortion 'on request', which had never been intended by Parliament, had brought some doctors in the private sector into disrepute and, if the Bill meant that current excesses would be stopped, he hoped the Representative Body would oppose the motion.[57] The motion was, nevertheless, carried.

Indeed, at the next A.R.M., held in London in 1976, Dr Frith proposed an even more sweeping motion: 'That abortion on demand should not be against official B.M.A. policy'.[58] That meeting was, she pointed out, the only one since 1967 at which there had been only one motion on the subject of abortion. Turning to the Act, she remarked that there was a wide divergence of interpretation:

It was a woolly Act which could be differently interpreted by individual doctors. Some would have nothing to do with abortion. Others believed that the woman was the best judge, after discussing the problem with an experienced medical counsellor – often her own G.P. – and in some parts of the country abortion on demand was practised, whereas in others only in cases of severe abnormality could a woman secure a termination.[59]

Abortion 'on demand' was, she remarked, provocative, and perhaps abortion 'on request' or 'after discussion' was preferable. The motion was, however, heavily criticised. Dr J. A. Hicklin, a member of Council, opposed any treatment on demand in principle and asked how it could ever be B.M.A. policy to countenance any form of treatment involving the participation of a doctor without allowing him to exercise either his clinical judgment or some other form of choice based on his conscience?[60]

Again, the Chairman of the Central Ethical Committee, Dr Happel, said that the B.M.A. supported the Act and the Lane Report, and would continue to support abortion on proper medical grounds. The motion was heavily defeated.

It is apparent that a central factor influencing both the Association's opposition to an overt acceptance of abortion on demand and to the provisions of the White Bill was again concern for the preservation of clinical freedom. This is evident in the opposition to the Bill voiced by the *British Medical Journal*:

These provisions represent a serious threat to the professional freedom of doctors. In assessing an individual case the question would no longer be what was best for the patient: the legal test would be whether or not a court would regard the risk to life or health as 'grave' or 'serious'.[61]

Lane had stated that to refuse abortion after a woman had made a request after heart-searching was, in most cases, both 'unfeeling and ineffectual', and had recommended improved N.H.S. facilities as an answer to abuse. The journal agreed that 'repressive legislation' was not the answer, adding: 'The sordid racketeers will go out of business when women no longer need to go to them; and a determined effort by the Department of Health could achieve that objective'.[62]

There appeared in the same journal the results of a survey on the abortion law among 600 doctors who had replied to a questionnaire: 60% felt that the Act was a reasonable compromise and 22% that it was a major social advance. Only 14% were of the opinion that it had been a tragic mistake.[63]

6.5 The Benyon Bill (1977)

The profession as a whole was also opposed to the restriction of the Act proposed in February 1977 by William Benyon, M.P. for Buckinghamshire, in the light of the recommendations of the Select Committee. He moved the second reading of his Bill on 25 February and maintained that there was mounting disquiet in the House about the operation of the Act – disquiet reflected in the large vote in favour of the re-establishment of the Select Committee.[64] He denied that the withdrawal of some Committee members had rendered its report biassed and declared that his Bill sought to implement the Committee's proposals.[65] He also disputed the Secretary of State's opinion that abuses in the private sector had been largely eradicated; questioned whether abortion counselling could truly be impartial when the counsellor had an interest in the outcome and whether the 'conscience clause' was operating satisfactorily, and observed that the abortion rate was not falling.[66] He also expressed grave doubts as to whether administrative measures alone were capable of dealing with these abuses.[67] The essence of his Bill was, he said,

to remove the worst exploitation of women in the private sector, to afford greater protection to doctors and nurses in the performance of their tasks and to strengthen the law in certain other respects.[68]

The Bill did not, however, seek to amend the grounds for abortion: the Select Committee had concluded that a decision on this matter should be left up to the individual consciences of M.P.s.[69] Clause 1 limited the performance of abortions to the twentieth week, or such time as the Secretary of State might determine. Clause 2 required the second opinion to be given by a doctor of at least five years' experience who could not be a partner or employee of the doctor giving the first opinion, and prohibited certification if both practitioners were able to obtain financial benefit from a place approved for the purposes of cl. 1 or cl. 7 (which related to the performance of and referral for abortion respectively). Benyon said that abuses of the law would be less likely the more the scope for profit-making was reduced.[70] Clause 3 of the Bill required the operating practitioner to notify the woman's regular doctor, if he obtained her consent to do so. Clause 4 extended the period within which proceedings for an offence under s. 2(3) of the Act could be brought, from six months after the commission of an offence to three years. Clause 5 strengthened s. 4 of the Act by allowing a conscientious objection to be based on 'religious, ethical or other' grounds, and Benyon revealed that he had received more representations on this point than on any other.[71] However, he considered the most important part of his Bill to be clauses 6 and 7. The former proposed to make it an offence to use certain premises for certain purposes without a licence from the Secretary of State. These purposes were specified in cl. 6(7) as providing, for payment, consultation with a doctor prepared to certify the need for, and subsequently to perform, abortion; an advisory service about abortion; and a pregnancy testing service. Clause 6(8) exempted from the licensing requirement premises used by a practitioner for the purposes of his general practice; a hospital vested in the Secretary of State under the National Health Service Acts; and a place approved under s. 1(3) of the 1967 Act. Clause 6(4) set out certain conditions the existence of which would require the Secretary of State to refuse a licence, one of which was the existence of a financial arrangement or other agreement with a place approved under s. 1(3). Benyon noted the criticism that this would inhibit the work of agencies in the 'charitable' sector but remarked that it was impossible to distinguish between different parts of the private sector.[72] He also observed that the prospect of legislation to regulate referral and advisory services had been welcomed by the D.H.S.S. in its evidence to the Select Committee.[73] Clause 7 required the Secretary of State to make regulations in relation to the use of premises licensed under the previous clause, and it set out the matters which such regulations would have to cover.

The declared aim of clauses 8 and 9 was to improve the enforceability of the law. The former protected the anonymity of any female witness who had either had or been advised about an abortion which was the subject of proceedings. Clause 9 provided that senior police officers investigating offences under the Act, as amended by the Bill, could apply to a Crown Court judge to inspect and take copies of any entries in registers or other books kept by approved clinics or agencies.[74] Benyon urged: 'If the House accepts – this is the crunch – that the effective enforcement of the law is desirable, these two clauses are vitally necessary'.[75]

The Minister of State at the D.H.S.S., Mr Roland Moyle, showed little enthusiasm for the Bill. He pointed out that the number of foreign women entering the country for abortion had been halved since 1974, that the number of abortions on residents had also fallen, and that abuses had been reduced as his Department had progressively brought the private sector under control. Moreover, Lane's recommendations on examination of the patient, certification, and disclosure of notifications at the request of the president of the G.M.C., had all been implemented by amending regulations in 1976.[76] Although Lane had also recommended a statutory system for licensing pregnancy advisory bureaux, the

Department had recently introduced a register of approved referral agencies and he felt that this non-statutory system should be given an opportunity to prove itself.[77]

Turning to late abortions, he informed the House that abortions after twenty weeks were only allowed in hospitals or approved places with resuscitation equipment and staff trained to operate it. The number of such abortions, however, represented less than 1% of the total.[78] As for conscientious objection, he said that there was no evidence that recruitment to the specialities had been adversely affected or that anyone's career had been jeopardised and he added that there was no general desire to change the existing situation.[79] The House should also consider, he continued, the effect of the Bill on the resources of his Department, for in addition to the work which would be involved in replacing the existing administrative procedures with statutory regulation, there were the extra responsibilities which the Bill sought to impose, and the extra burden would lead to less effective surveillance of those parts of the private sector most vulnerable to abuse.[80] Another consideration was the inhibiting effect of the Bill on the 'charitable' sector which had contributed, through reasonable standards of care and moderate fees, to improvements in the private sector and which was already as closely supervised as other parts of the private sector.[81] He concluded that the existing administrative arrangements were more likely to be effective, because of their flexibility, than any 'cumbersome and rather rigid regulations' in a situation which had changed remarkably in the previous decade. Regulations, he added, could only be amended by further legislation whereas administrative control could be adjusted quickly to suit changing circumstances.[82] In the light of the administrative measures which had been taken, neither he nor the Secretary of State saw the need for further legislation.[83]

The Bill was also opposed by Mrs Short. She quoted a letter, signed by no fewer than 1200 doctors, which had been sent to the Prime Minister and which expressed disapproval of the Bill; the need for improved N.H.S. facilities; and concern for clinical freedom. It read:

Those abuses which occurred shortly after the inception of the Bill have now largely been overcome. Nevertheless we recognise that there are still problems within the working of the Act that require attention. The most important of these concerns the question of regional variations in the availability of abortion facilities within the Health Service. . . .[84]

The letter continued: 'Gynaecologists and other doctors would find themselves increasingly harassed and clinical freedom would be threatened'.[85] Mrs Short maintained that the Bill displayed a complete mistrust of the medical profession and was based on an unbalanced report from an unbalanced Select Committee. The Bill did nothing to remedy the abuse of the Act, referred to in the letter, which was the regional variation in the provision of abortion due to the refusal of 'reactionary consultants' to help women with grounds for abortion under the Act, and even facilitated this abuse.[86] Moreover, a range of important medical bodies, from the R.C.O.G. to the Royal College of Midwives, supported the Act and had opposed White's Bill.[87]

There was, indeed, little support for Benyon's Bill from the profession. The Council of the B.M.A. opposed legislation. It expressed particular concern at the proposals to license premises and to allow the inspection of clinic registers upon the production of a court order, and also made plain its preference for existing administrative controls over the statutory regulation proposed in the Bill. The *British Medical Journal* reported the Council's opinion as follows:

In view of the very close scrutiny which has been given to the working of the 1967 Act over the last six years by the Lane Committee and the Select Committee on Abortion, the improvements which have already been made in the operation of the Act as a result of such reviews, and the steady decline over the last three years in the number of abortions performed in this country, the Council believed that legislation was not required at the present time to amend the Act. Time should be allowed to assess the effects of the changes already introduced; any further changes which might subsequently seem desirable could best be effected by the more flexible system of administrative control, rather than by further legislation.[88]

Opposition to legislation was also expressed by groups of doctors with a particular interest in fertility control. One, The Doctors and Overpopulation Group, maintained that restriction would lead to more late abortions and a consequent increase in maternal mortality and morbidity.[89] Similarly, the *Lancet* pointed out that the 2000-strong Doctors in Defence of the 1967 Abortion Act had written to the Secretary of State, Mr Ennals, who replied that he agreed with the view of the Joint Consultants' Committee that the Bill was 'attempting to deal with a problem that has ceased to exist'.[90] The journal added its voice to the chorus of medical opposition to the

Bill. Pointing out that not one of the thirteen medical organisations consulted by the D.H.S.S. had supported the Bill as a whole, it urged that it would cripple the charitable agencies and introduce 'a mass of restrictive bureaucratic and punitive legislation which would deter doctors in the National Health Service from implementing the 1967 Abortion Act'.[91] Its main criticism of the working of the Act was regional variation in the provision of abortion, but it observed that the medical profession was against restrictive legislation and it noted the change in opinion since 1967:

many of the doctors now most energetic in defence of the Act were amongst the majority who originally expressed strong reservations: nine years' experience of the working of the Abortion Act has convinced them that this measure relieves their patients of much suffering.[92]

It added: 'The medical profession, which very largely opposed the original 1967 Abortion Act, now speaks with an almost united voice in its defence'.[93] Benyon's Bill was considered by a Standing Committee, but failed to progress further due to lack of time.[94]

6.6 The Braine Bill (1978)

In spite of the failure of the Benyon Bill, pressure for restriction of the Act was far from spent. In February 1978, Sir Bernard Braine moved to introduce a Bill which proposed to reduce the presumption of viability to twenty weeks, strengthen s. 4 of the Act, and require the licensing of pregnancy advisory bureaux. He explained that one purpose of his Bill was to give the House a chance to reassert its will to amend the Act.[95] He stressed, however, that the Bill did not interfere in any way with the criteria for abortion set out in the Act.[96] However, Sir George Sinclair objected that the Bill would pave the way for restriction of the Act and stated that it was opposed by the medical profession.[97]

Nevertheless, the Bill was given a second reading by 181 votes to 175. It did not proceed further, again due to lack of time. The prospects of the Bill receiving the Royal Assent could not have been enhanced by the opposition of medical opinion. The Council of the B.M.A., criticising the Bill, noted that conscientious objection was already protected by s. 4 of the Act, that an upper limit of twenty weeks was already 'generally observed' and that it was undesirable to sever pregnancy advisory bureaux from abortion clinics. It stated that no action should be taken to restrict further the availability of existing facilities to women who have grounds for an abortion under the terms of the 1967 Act which might well result from the severance of pregnancy advisory bureaux from abortion clinics.[98]

The Council added that the number of abortions had fallen considerably since June 1973 and that the introduction of a free family planning service in 1974 had possibly begun to reduce the number of unwanted pregnancies. It reiterated the view that the Act had been subjected to close scrutiny since its inception and that the Association welcomed the action which the D.H.S.S. had taken on the recommendations of the Lane Committee for controlling abuse, and it reaffirmed the Association's view that any difficulties could be remedied by appropriate changes in the Regulations. The Secretary of State and medical M.P.s had been reminded of this policy, and the Council resolved to continue to watch the position closely.[99]

At the Association's A.R.M. that year, several motions opposing the Bill were proposed. One, which was passed, declared: 'That this meeting deplores the persistent attacks on the 1967 Abortion Act and reaffirms its belief that it is a practical and humane piece of legislation'.[100]

6.7 The Corrie Bill (1979)

In spite of medical opposition to restriction of the Act, a further attempt was made in 1979. On 13 July Mr John Corrie, M.P. for Bute and North Ayrshire, moved that his Abortion (Amendment) Bill be read a second time.[101] The issue of abortion would not go away, he said, until some of the existing anomalies had been removed. One abuse was the use of the 'statistical argument' to allow abortion on request. As early as 1971, he remarked, Professor Peter Huntingford had said: 'I have no qualms about this at all, and I am quite certain that it does not contravene the Abortion Act'.[102] Huntingford, invoking the 'statistical argument' to justify his practice, also expressed his confidence that no legal or disciplinary action would follow and stated that his hospital governors did not object to his policy.[103] Moreover, a working party of the R.C.O.G., which had reported in 1972, had admitted: 'Those doctors who feel that abortion on demand is correct are able to apply that belief to their practice'.[104] Consequently, cl. 1 of his Bill sought to qualify the degree of risk required before abortion could be lawfully performed. The risk to life would have to be 'grave' and there would have to be 'substantial risk of serious injury' to health. This clause, he pointed out, followed the recommendation of the Select Committee that the House should be given an opportunity to decide on the critieria for abortion. In fact, the Bill as a whole was based on the Committee's recommendations, though it was not designed to incorporate them all. Absent, for example, were the provisions requiring the woman's regular doctor to be informed of her abortion, or ensuring the anonymity of complaints. A clause requiring the licensing of referral agencies was, however, included, as the Bill's sponsor said he was extremely worried about some of the reports of abuse he had heard.[105] Another clause attempted to ensure impartial counselling. Abortion, Corrie felt, should be a last and not a first resort, and he expressed sadness that the British Pregnancy Advisory Service and the Pregnancy Advisory Service referred almost all the women who consulted them. It seemed to him that pregnancy advice had disappeared and that these agencies had simply become referral agencies for those wanting abortions.[106] The central issue of the Bill, he said, was the proposed lowering of the 'upper limit' to twenty weeks, a figure which allowed for mistakes of two to three weeks in calculating the duration of gestation.[107] Another major issue was the amendment of s. 4 of the Act: many doctors, midwives and nurses had written to him claiming that their chances of promotion in gynecological work were nil because of their beliefs.[108]

The Bill was opposed by the ex-Secretary of State, Mr Ennals. He pointed out that the B.M.A. also opposed it and that the Act had reduced both mortality from abortion and the number of septic abortions.[109] He also maintained that administrative action taken by the D.H.S.S. had tackled the most serious issues which had existed.[110] The Minister, Dr Vaughan, was, however, less hostile. He suggested that the House was not discussing the merits of legal abortion, which had been settled in 1967, but a Bill aimed at reducing abuses which some sincerely believed still existed.[111] Turning to the clauses of the Bill, he pointed out that the grounds for abortion which it sought to qualify accounted for around 85% of all terminations and he advised the House to proceed carefully before restricting the criteria, a course which had not been proposed by the medical profession.[112] By contrast, he expressed sympathy with the proposal to extend s. 4 of the Act: it was common sense that those with strong ethical or moral objections and who were part of a profession which had a special sensitivity to the preservation of life should be able to opt out of abortion without jeopardising their careers.[113] However, he announced that the Government would be reluctant to endorse clauses 4 and 5 of the Bill, which dealt with the licensing of, and regulations for, specified premises, as they would increase the cost of administration and the complexity of the legislation.[114] He added that he had not yet heard any arguments for believing that a statutory procedure would result in stricter control of the private sector than was already exercised by voluntary procedures.[115] He concluded by reiterating his personal sympathy for the strengthening of s. 4 of the Act and the reduction of the 'upper limit', the two clauses which he saw as the nub of the Bill, and he expressed his intention to support the second reading motion. This was carried by 242 votes to 98.[116] The Bill was considered by a Standing Committee[117] and reached the report stage,[118] but suffered the same fate as previous Bills by running out of time.

Again, as with previous Bills, the opposition of the medical bodies was unmistakable. In August 1979, the C.M.O. wrote to several medical organisations, including the B.M.A., asking for comments on various aspects of Corrie's measure. The B.M.A. sent its comments to each member of the Standing Committee and made its opposition to the Bill as a whole plain. As for the proposed reduction of the 'upper limit', it reiterated that, although it had informed Lane that it should be considered normal practice for a gynecologist to refuse abortion after the twentieth week, and supported the opinion that twenty weeks should be considered the minimum time of viability, a five month limit was already generally observed: fewer than 1% of terminations were performed after that time and then only in places where resuscitation facilities were available.[119] It therefore opposed the reduction of the presumption of viability, unless the accepted maternal indications for termination after a new limit (whether it be 20, 22 or 24 weeks) were specifically protected.[120]

The Association also rejected the restriction of the criteria for abortion proposed by cl. 1 on the ground that this would not merely put the clock back to before 1967, but much further. The Association agreed with Lane that the criteria should not be altered. The words 'grave' and 'substantial' risk gave rise, in the absence of any close legal definition, to difficult problems for the profession. The decision to abort was, moreover, a clinical one for the doctors concerned and the existing law had not caused any difficulty in this respect. It should be enough, concluded the B.M.A., that doctors were required to act in good faith in the interests of the mother's health.[121]

Nor did the Association support the proposed strengthening of s. 4: a doctor's first obligation was to the health of his patient and if practitioners wanted to claim conscientious objection where their objection was contrary to the interests of the woman's health, the onus should be on them to prove it.

Clause 4 was criticised as a potential cause of considerable difficulty: it should be amended to ensure that premises used by registered medical practitioners for the purposes of general or specialist practice would not require a licence.

The Association had no objection to clauses 5 to 9, though it did object to the requirement in cl. 7 that an opinion that a child would be born seriously handicapped be based on the results of tests.[122]

The Association's journal was an outspoken critic of the Bill. It pointed out that none of the major medical organisations was supporting Corrie's proposals and that, at two of the last three annual meetings, the Representative Body had stated unambiguously that it saw no need for reform. It explained:

Doctors take this view because they know that in general the Act is working well: individual tragedies occur mostly as a result of delays and deficiencies in the overstretched NHS gynaecological services.[123]

A great deal of the indignation felt by the Bill's supporters, it added, arose from reports of dubious practices in the private sector, but there was little the law could do to stop abuses without hindering respectable practice:

since so much depends on medical judgment taken 'in good faith' these activities are not susceptible to legal control without crippling restrictions on bona fide clinical decisions.[124]

In particular, to limit abortions to less than twenty weeks of gestation would only further complicate decisions which were already difficult and sometimes harrowing. Moreover, in view of the 'legal vindictiveness' of extreme anti-abortionists, charges might be levelled against an N.H.S. obstetrician for a technical offence despite his having acted in his patient's interests. The journal argued that early abortion was more in need of legal clarification and went so far as to suggest that the law should move with technological advances and confine itself to the restriction of late terminations. It declared:

Most doctors in practice today can remember when suicide, attempted or completed, was a criminal offence – yet now such a concept seems barbaric. The same incredulity will, surely, soon apply to attempts by the criminal law to control termination of pregnancy in its early weeks. Legal regulation is reasonable later in pregnancy (on the grounds of the duty of the law to respect concepts such as the sanctity of life) but it must be flexible enough to take account of the rapid pace of development in antenatal diagnosis of genetic and developmental disorders. An ideal law should surely reflect clinical realities, and requires that the criteria for termination should become progressively more stringent with the length of pregnancy.[125]

Corrie's Bill, it concluded, was ill researched and ill conceived and should be rejected. The *British Medical Journal* was joined by the *Lancet*, which objected that the inclusion of the 'vague' words 'serious' and 'substantial' could limit doctors' freedom to deal with each patient in the light of her particular needs.[126] Moreover, it stated that the licensing proposals could work injustice, that a twenty-week limit would deny abortion to women with severe social, medical and psychological reasons and, with the uncertainty surrounding the exact duration of pregnancy, could inhibit many doctors from recommending abortion after sixteen to eighteen weeks for fear of breaking the law. It concluded that many practitioners wanted to see the issue of abortion resolved but not at the expense of the health and well-being of their patients.[127] The journal also carried a letter, signed by some seventy eminent doctors, including Baird, Barnes, Clayton, Black, Godber, Doll and MacGillivray, who claimed to represent a broad band of medical opinion and who wrote expressing their concern at 'a most swingeing attack' on the Act, which would cut the number of abortions by two-thirds and 'destroy the charities'. They felt that the Act had succeeded in reducing human suffering and that abuses of the Act had been eliminated. The one glaring failure was the regional variation in the provision of abortion within the N.H.S., but this proposal did nothing to remedy the problem. On the contrary, it would deny legal abortion to many women and there was, the letter warned, a real danger that it would lead to a resurgence of septic abortion.[128] The *Lancet* agreed that the Bill distracted attention from the two major failings in the Act: variation in provision and the sluggish adoption of day-care treatment. Of twenty-two Area Health Authorities offering day-care gynecology in 1977, only thirteen had a day-care abortion unit and the two charitable agencies were performing three times as many day-care abortions as the N.H.S.[129]

A second editorial in the *British Medical Journal* emphasised the profession's opposition to the Bill. It stressed that the authoritative medical bodies were unanimously against reform, adding: 'Twelve years' experience with the 1967 Act . . . has convinced doctors that it works satisfactorily in practice both for them and for their patients'.[130] It suggested that M.P.s need not concern themselves with the details of gestation and viability and of the balancing of risks, matters which had been discussed at length during the Committee stage of Corrie's Bill. Rather, it continued:

The single, crucial question is whether they believe that Parliament should seek to control the exercise of clinical judgment by doctors. For – whatever the intention of the legislators may have been – in practice nowadays most doctors faced with a pregnant woman who wants an abortion try to decide whether termination of the pregnancy seems in her best interest, judging each individual case on its merits.[131]

If the grounds for abortion were restricted, it added, some doctors would allow the law to override their clinical judgement, but others would not. They would continue to put their patients' interests first and hope that 'legalistic ingenuity' would find a way to circumvent the new Act. Society would, it felt, be unlikely to benefit from either approach. Re-emphasising the importance of respect for clinical freedom, it continued:

For the law does not seek to dictate other clinical decisions that, like recommending abortion, have moral and ethical overtones. Doctors are left free to make the best judgments they can when considering such difficult choices as whether or not to give active treatment to severely handicapped babies, or to patients with incurable terminal disease.[132]

Restrictive legislation would be a retrograde step, for abortion was increasingly regarded by doctors as a method of fertility control. 'Throughout the world', declared the *British Medical Journal*, medical termination of pregnancy has become accepted as a part of any logical approach to family planning. Most doctors believe that early termination of pregnancy is usually justifiable in cases of contraceptive failure.[133]

The Bill was, it added, allegedly designed to curb abuse in the private sector and to restrict the charities, but it warned that if the number of private abortions were reduced, the inevitable result would be a return to 'back-street' abortion, as the N.H.S. did not have the capacity to treat more patients. Before voting to change the law, therefore, M.P.s should look at the likely consequences in fact rather than in theory: 'History suggests that legislation designed to affect human behaviour rarely has the effects intended by the legislators'.[134]

Conclusion

Chapter 4 indicated the support of the medical profession as a whole for reform of the law in 1967 and its concern to preserve professional autonomy. This chapter provides some evidence that this concern has also been of central importance in relation to the profession's opposition to restriction of the Abortion Act. Chapter 5 noted the extensive exercise by some practitioners of the discretion which the Act granted to the medical profession and the apparent willingness of a substantial number of doctors to recommend or perform abortion even in the absence of a medical indication. This chapter tends to support the suggestion made in Chapter 5 that there has been a shift in attitude in the profession as a whole toward a greater acceptance of abortion, and it provides some evidence that it is regarded by some practitioners as an integral part of fertility control, with contraceptive failure in itself regarded as an indication for the procedure.

7

A theoretical overview

This final chapter outlines some of the general conclusions of the book and suggests a possible perspective from which to view the aspects of the development and operation of the law relating to abortion which it has considered.

Chapters 1 and 2 suggested that the emerging medical profession exerted an influence upon the gradual statutory restriction of the law against abortion between 1803 and 1861. Chapter 4 traced its support for, and shaping of, the Abortion Act 1967, and Chapter 6 its persistent defence from subsequent legislative restriction of the broad medical discretion afforded by the Act to doctors.

It appears that a central (though not exclusive) concern of the profession in both the restriction of the law in the nineteenth century and its relaxation in 1967 has been self-interest. As the *British Medical Journal* has noted, two central concerns of the profession are freedom from control and the prevention of encroachment upon its sphere of influence by the medically unqualified.[1] This book provides some evidence that both of these concerns have been prominent in the development and operation of the laws relating to abortion from 1803 to 1982. In 1967, the profession supported the passage of an Act whose central declared aim was the abolition of 'back-street' abortion – an aim which was to be achieved by granting registered medical practitioners a legal monopoly on the induction of abortion. It also supported the restriction of the abortion law in the nineteenth century – a reform which may also have served the interests of the profession by penalising the performance of abortion by irregular practitioners.

If the account of the professionalisation of medicine given by sociologists such as Elliott is accurate,[2] then this process was paralleled by the restriction of the law against abortion from 1803 to 1861. He states that in pre-industrial England medical practitioners suffered from internal divisions. On the one hand were the menial surgeons and apothecaries, who tended to the medical needs of the middle classes. On the other were the physicians, who enjoyed the patronage of the wealthier classes. Their higher social status was not, however, matched by professional competence: their expertise was limited to writing complicated prescriptions and they depended on their cultured gentility and patrons' ignorance to build up a practice. What little medical education for the practitioner there was in the late eighteenth century was unsystematic and the examinations which were set by the Royal College of Physicians were designed not so much to test medical knowledge as to ensure the admission of only those candidates with the appropriate social background.

However, continues Elliott, the first half of the last century witnessed the declining significance of social status and the increasing importance of medical expertise, together with the unification of the three branches of the profession – physicians, surgeons and apothecaries. These trends appear to have been encouraged by the spread of scientific knowledge from the Continent and, in the wake of the Industrial Revolution with its population growth and urban development, a burgeoning demand for medical services from the rising middle classes and the urban poor. The demand was met by the apothecaries and the growing number of surgeon–apothecaries – the original 'general practitioners'.

The Apothecaries Act 1815 reflected the readiness of this branch of the profession to improve its professional training, and although it did not meet the regulars' demand for the proscription of unqualified practice, marked the elevation of the apothecary from tradesman to practitioner. The Act empowered the Society of Apothecaries to supervise apprenticeship, examine apothecaries, and license practitioners throughout England and Wales. The Society required a period of apprenticeship, attendance at lectures, and experience in hospital, and its licence became a popular qualification in the first half of the century.

Just as medical education throughout this period was becoming more systematic, so too was professional organisation. In 1823 the medical reformer Thomas Wakley founded the *Lancet* and in 1832 the Provincial Medical and Surgical Association was established with the dual aims of representing the interests of 'general practitioners' and of providing a forum for study and debate. This was to become the British Medical Association in 1855. The Medical Act 1858 placed all the licensing bodies under the control of the forerunner of the General Medical Council, which was also charged to maintain a register of practitioners, admission to which was to be obtained through the existing licensing bodies. The licensing system now tested expertise – social status was no longer sufficient – and testified to the transition from a profession based on status to one based on skill. Moreover, Elliott continues, scientific advances were reinforcing this transition by enabling practitioners to meet more successfully than previously the demands for medical attention which were increasingly being made upon them: a 'status' profession could survive without expertise and rely simply on patronage, but a 'consulting' profession needed to attract and maintain a clientele if it was to survive.

If the above account of medical professionalisation is accurate, then it may well provide a useful conceptual framework in which to interpret the contemporaneous restriction of the law against abortion. Campaigning for the restriction of the law could well have furthered the emerging profession's interests by penalising the practice of abortion by their irregular competitors; asserting the probity of the regulars over their competitors in the public eye, and adding to the sense of cohesion among regulars themselves. The latest research into the history of the profession lends support to the suggestion that the process of professionalisation was related to the restriction of the law.

In his recent book, Loudon argues that the period 1800 to 1858 was one of enormous upheaval as far as the professional status of medical men was concerned. Their struggle for status and power generated conflict among regulars themselves, between the new majority – the 'general practitioners' – and the old corporations of physicians and surgeons.[3] Conflict was also generated between regulars and irregulars. The G.P., upwardly mobile and craving respectability, was concerned that, although he had spent about £1000 on his training, the public nevertheless failed to distinguish between him and his midwife and druggist competitors. He had, therefore, a keen interest in distancing himself as much as possible from irregulars and accusing them of abortion would be one way of branding them as disreputable while simultaneously parading his own rectitude.[4]

The professional status of practitioners may also help to explain certain aspects of the enactment, shape and operation of the Abortion Act 1967. It may be surmised that the significant influence which Chapter 4 suggested was exerted by the profession on the Act was due in no small measure to its social and expert status which has been enhanced since the nineteenth century, due perhaps to its perceived conquest of infectious diseases, mastery of technological medicine and improved professional organisation. Freidson has asserted:

> If we consider the profession of medicine today, it is clear that its major characteristic is preeminence. Such preeminence is not merely that of prestige but also that of expert authority. This is to say, medicine's knowledge about illness and its treatment is considered to be authoritative and definitive. . . . Medicine's official position is akin to that of state religions yesterday – it has an officially approved monopoly of the right to define health and illness and to treat illness.[5]

This may help to account for the success of the medical bodies in ensuring that the decision to abort remained firmly in the hands of doctors; that the discretion thereby conferred was virtually immune from legal challenge, and that the terms of the Act should not be restricted.

The influence of the profession on the law has not (as is normally the case with pressure groups) been confined to the enactment of legislation – be it legislation largely advancing their interests, as in 1861, or largely defending them, as in 1967 – for it has also, as Chapter 3 indicated, historically been allowed a broad discretion in determining what constitutes 'therapeutic' abortion and in acting upon that determination. The absence of any reported prosecution of a practitioner for the performance of the operation, according to professionally approved criteria, from the late eighteenth century to 1938, suggests the tacit approval of this discretion by the state. Throughout this period, abortion was induced according to criteria determined by the profession. The extent of medical discretion in this regard is underlined by the fact that, in the nineteenth century, abortion was induced by regular practitioners even though they were simultaneously calling for its stricter prohibition by the legislature. It could be suggested that they were acting as 'moral entrepreneurs'[6] both by pressing for certain forms of conduct (abortion by irregulars and irregular practice generally) to be defined by the state as deviant and to be punished by the courts, and by themselves defining the abortions they performed not as crimes but as medical treatments. In the light of the regulars' organisation and social status, it is perhaps not surprising that they should succeed in having their definition of when abortion was a crime and when 'therapeutic' imposed on their irregular competitors, to the latter's detriment. It could be said, therefore, that the influence of the regulars extended both to the criminalisation of abortion by statute and to its medicalisation in the context of their everyday practice. The freedom to define the circumstances in which abortion constituted a proper medical treatment rather than a crime may (like, for example, the freedom to prescribe even at great cost) be explicable in terms of their professional status. Interestingly, Freidson has said, 'the only truly important and uniform criterion for distinguishing professions from other occupations is the fact of autonomy – a position of legitimate control over work'.[7]

The profession's historical control over the definition and performance of therapeutic abortion gained formal recognition in the Abortion Act 1967. As Chapter 4 pointed out, the profession, although far from unanimous about the desirability of reform, appears to have exercised a significant influence in ensuring that the practitioner's autonomy was respected. Macintyre has gone so far as to assert that both the supporters and the opponents of legislation appear to have been concerned with professional freedom and differed merely on the likely effects on this of an Act.[8] Chapter 5 indicated that the Abortion Act 1967 not only respected medical discretion but, by rendering its exercise virtually unchallengeable, has allowed its variable and extensive exercise. The only restrictions imposed by the Act on the practitioner are compliance with certain formalities, which do not impinge directly upon the criteria which the practitioner applies in deciding whether to recommend or to perform abortion.

It would appear from the available sociological evidence and the views expressed by practitioners in medical journals that, just as the profession influenced the passage and shape of the Act, so too has the Act been a factor in influencing the performance of abortion by the profession. Clearly, the effects of the Act on medical practice are multiple, but the evidence relating to the indications for abortion suggests that wider indications for the operation have gained acceptance since 1968, and it appears that a significant minority of doctors – roughly one-third – are prepared to recommend abortion at the request of the woman, at least if the pregnancy has not advanced beyond the tenth week and she has seriously considered the alternatives.[9]

It is tempting to regard the evident increase in abortion since 1968, both numerically and conceptually, as evidence of a 'gap' between the letter of the law and the law in action. Certainly, the Act's sponsor would appear to be concerned at its current implementation for he was recently reported as saying, 'Abortion is, I am afraid, being used as a contraceptive. The present level is too high'.[10] On the other hand, it is by no means clear that the broad terms of the Act do not allow just this, for it conceded the profession's central demand for autonomy to decide when abortion is 'therapeutic'. It could be argued that it formally transferred the determination of what constituted therapeutic abortion from the courts to the medical profession, for it is difficult to envisage circumstances in which a doctor could not claim that the abortion he recommended was indicated in the interests of the patient's health, particularly if 'health' is given the sweeping definition in the World Health Organization's constitution as 'a state of complete physical, mental and social well-being and not merely the absence of disease or infirmity'.[11] Ingram has maintained that the wording of the Act is so vague as to be meaningless and that both the scrupulous and the cynical doctor are able to interpret it as they wish.[12] Though there may well, therefore, be a divergence between how the legislature intended the Act to operate and how it actually is operating, it is more difficult to establish that there is a similar divergence between its operation and its wording, as the discussion of the 'statistical argument' in Chapter 5 showed.

It is possible that the legislature anticipated a greater degree of self-regulation by the profession, but it is noteworthy that Freidson has argued in relation to the United States that self-regulation by the profession is far from effective.[13] (The evidence suggests that this is also true of at least the main formal disciplinary mechanism in Britain, the General Medical Council.) Interestingly, Freidson has argued that the profession's implicit assurance of self-regulation is essentially rhetoric designed to convince the state to grant and to maintain professional status.

Another of his observations may be relevant to the granting of extensive discretion by the Abortion Act to the profession. He asserts:

Disapproved behaviour is more and more coming to be given the meaning of illness requiring treatment rather than of crime requiring punishment, victimization requiring compensation, or sin requiring patience and grace.[14]

This analysis would certainly appear to have some application to recent developments in the law of abortion. The Abortion Act 1967 allowed doctors to expand the label of 'therapeutic' abortion to include cases which would previously have been defined as 'criminal'. Further, it conclusively assimilated abortion to other medical procedures in that the criterion for the procedure is a balancing of risks to the patient. In so doing, the Act categorised the fetus as a part of the woman's body.

It is arguable that the statutory transfer of abortion from the court to the consulting-room by the Act could only have been facilitated by the ease with which the problem lends itself to medicalisation. Medical control of pregnancy and childbirth has been long established, as has the termination of pregnancies which threaten life or health. It may well have seemed natural to entrust the doctor with the decision to terminate not only unhealthy but also unwanted pregnancies[15] especially at a time when the profession was developing the safer abortion technique of vacuum aspiration.

Why was abortion medicalised? Perhaps the explanation lies in a perceived failure of the criminal justice system to control a 'victimless' crime; perhaps it seemed to offer a compromise between restriction and permissiveness; or perhaps it was felt to be more humane to channel women who would otherwise be stigmatised as criminals to the care of doctors, particularly if it was felt that more middle-class women were resorting to abortion.[16] Perhaps it was due to a combination of such reasons.

Whatever the full explanation, a case can certainly be made that in medicalising abortion the State is, in return for ensuring that the decision to abort remains in medical hands, employing doctors as agents of social control, as 'gatekeepers', to allow the 'deserving' to have abortions and to keep the State notified of the numbers aborted.

The medicalisation of abortion raises several profound questions which are often overlooked, such as whether it really does eradicate stigma; whether social problems which underlie requests for abortion come to be classified as individual medical problems and are thereby politically defused; whether it does not encourage the surrender of personal responsibility to medical experts; and whether these experts are really qualified to make decisions about abortion.[17] Szasz, for example, stresses that the fact that the procedure of abortion is surgical no more makes it a medical problem than the use of the electric chair makes capital punishment a problem of electrical engineering. The question is, he stresses, what is abortion – the killing of a fetus or the removal of a piece of tissue from a woman's body?[18]

The Act may, therefore, be seen as a medicalisation of deviance and perhaps also as part of a broader process of such medicalisation. It is interesting to note, therefore, that Freidson has concluded that the role of the profession in this process is not that of a passive recipient of additional responsibilities but rather that it actively seeks them out.[19] This observation may well be applicable to the profession's role in relation to the Abortion Act 1967 where its political involvement, far from being passive, appears to have been both marked and influential. In the light of the profession's opposition to illegal abortion, with its resultant mortality and morbidity and the lucrative trade it offered to unqualified practitioners, its active involvement in ensuring professional control over abortion is understandable. Moreover, it may have appeared natural for the profession to be granted such control for, according to Freidson:

It is part of being a profession to be given the official power to define and therefore create the shape of problematic segments of social behaviour; the judge determines what is legal and who is guilty, the priest what is holy and who is profane, the physician what is normal and who is sick.[20]

The present author suggests that, in relation to the problematic area of abortion, medical men have long exerted an important influence on the determination of when abortion is 'criminal' and when it is 'therapeutic'. This influence has been exerted on two levels: first, the political level, where the profession supported legislation from 1803 to 1861 (which would perhaps help establish its professional status) and in 1967 (which would further its professional interests); and second, the practical level, where the practitioner exercises his extensive autonomy in deciding whether a given abortion would be 'therapeutic'. In conclusion, the professionalisation of medicine and the professional status of the doctor may help to explain the aspects of the development and operation of the law relating to abortion between 1803 and 1982 which have been considered in this book.

Appendices

Offences Against the Person Act 1861

S. 58 provides:
Every woman being with child, who, with intent to procure her own miscarriage, shall unlawfully administer to herself any poison or other noxious thing, or shall unlawfully use any instrument or other means whatsoever with the like intent, and whosoever, with intent to procure the miscarriage of any woman, whether she be or be not with child, shall unlawfully administer to her or cause to be taken by her any poison or other noxious thing, or shall unlawfully use any instrument or other means whatsoever with the like intent, shall be guilty of felony and being convicted thereof shall be liable, [at the discretion of the court],[1] to be kept in penal servitude for life,[2] or for any term not less than three years,[3] [or to be imprisoned][1] for any term not exceeding two years, with or without hard labour, and[3] [with or without solitary confinement.][1]

S. 59 provides:
Whosoever shall unlawfully supply or procure any poison or other noxious thing, or any instrument or thing whatsoever, knowing that the same is intended to be unlawfully used or employed with intent to procure the miscarriage of any woman, whether she be or be not with child, shall be guilty of a misdemeanor and being convicted thereof shall be liable, at the discretion of the court,[3] to be kept in penal servitude[2] for the term of three years, or to be imprisoned for any term not exceeding two years, with or without hard labour.[3]

Notes
[1] The bracketed words were removed by s. 1 of the Statute Law Revision (No. 2) Act 1893 (56 & 57 Vict. c. 54).
[2] Section 1(1) of the Penal Servitude Act 1891 (54 & 55 Vict. c. 69) confined sentences of penal servitude to a minimum of three and a maximum of five years, or any greater period authorised by the relevant enactment. Penal servitude was replaced by imprisonment by virtue of s. 1(1) of the Criminal Justice Act 1948 (11 & 12 Geo. VI c. 58). Section 1(2) abolished hard labour.
[3] The underlined words were removed by s. 1 of the Statute Law Revision Act 1892 (55 & 56 Vict. c. 19).

Abortion Act 1967

1967 CHAPTER 87

An Act to amend and clarify the law relating to termination of pregnancy by registered medical practitioners.

[27th October 1967]

BE IT ENACTED by the Queen's most Excellent Majesty, by and with the advice and consent of the Lords Spiritual and Temporal, and Commons, in this present Parliament assembled, and by the authority of the same, as follows:—

Medical termination of pregnancy.

1.—(1) Subject to the provisions of this section, a person shall not be guilty of an offence under the law relating to abortion when a pregnancy is terminated by a registered medical practitioner if two registered medical practitioners are of the opinion, formed in good faith—

(*a*) that the continuance of the pregnancy would involve risk to the life of the pregnant woman, or of injury to the physical or mental health of the pregnant woman or any existing children of her family, greater than if the pregnancy were terminated; or

(*b*) that there is a substantial risk that if the child were born it would suffer from such physical or mental abnormalities as to be seriously handicapped.

(2) In determining whether the continuance of a pregnancy would involve such risk of injury to health as is mentioned in paragraph (*a*) of subsection (1) of this section, account may be taken of the pregnant woman's actual or reasonably foreseeable environment.

(3) Except as provided by subsection (4) of this section, any treatment for the termination of pregnancy must be carried out in a hospital vested in the Minister of Health or the Secretary of State under the National Health Service Acts, or in a place for the time being approved for the purposes of this section by the said Minister or the Secretary of State.

(4) Subsection (3) of this section, and so much of subsection (1) as relates to the opinion of two registered medical practitioners, shall not apply to the termination of a pregnancy by a registered medical practitioner in a case where he is of the opinion, formed in good faith, that the termination is immediately necessary to save the life or to prevent grave permanent injury to the physical or mental health of the pregnant woman.

2. — (1) The Minister of Health in respect of England and Wales, Notification. and the Secretary of State in respect of Scotland, shall by statutory instrument make regulations to provide —

(a) for requiring any such opinion as is referred to in section 1 of this Act to be certified by the practitioners or practitioner concerned in such form and at such time as may be prescribed by the regulations, and for requiring the preservation and disposal of certificates made for the purposes of the regulations;

(b) for requiring any registered medical practitioner who terminates a pregnancy to give notice of the termination and such other information relating to the termination as may be so prescribed;

(c) for prohibiting the disclosure, except to such persons or for such purposes as may be so prescribed, of notices given or information furnished pursuant to the regulations.

(2) The information furnished in pursuance of regulations made by virtue of paragraph (b) of subsection (1) of this section shall be notified solely to the [Chief Medical Officer of the Department of Health and Social Security, or of the Welsh Office, or of the Scottish Home and Health Department].

(3) Any person who wilfully contravenes or wilfully fails to comply with the requirements of regulations under subsection (1) of this section shall be liable on summary conviction to a fine not exceeding [level 5 on the standard scale].

(4) Any statutory instrument made by virtue of this section shall be subject to annulment in pursuance of a resolution of either House of Parliament.

Annotations:
Sub-s (2): amended by the Transfer of Functions (Wales) Order 1969, SI 1969 No 388.
Sub-s (3): maximum fine increased by the Criminal Law Act 1977, s 31, Sch 6, and converted to a level on the standard scale by the Criminal Justice Act 1982, ss 37, 46.

3.[— Application of Act to visiting forces.]

Conscientious objection to participation in treatment.

4. — (1) Subject to subsection (2) of this section, no person shall be under any duty, whether by contract or by any statutory or other legal requirement, to participate in any treatment authorised by this Act to which he has a conscientious objection:

Provided that in any legal proceedings the burden of proof of conscientious objection shall rest on the person claiming to rely on it.

(2) Nothing in subsection (1) of this section shall affect any duty to participate in treatment which is necessary to save the life or to prevent grave permanent injury to the physical or mental health of a pregnant woman.

(3) In any proceedings before a court in Scotland, a statement on oath by any person to the effect that he has a conscientious objection to participating in any treatment authorised by this Act shall be sufficient evidence for the purpose of discharging the burden of proof imposed upon him by subsection (1) of this section.

Supplementary provisions.
1929 c. 34.

5. — (1) Nothing in this Act shall affect the provisions of the Infant Life (Preservation) Act 1929 (protecting the life of the viable foetus).

(2) For the purposes of the law relating to abortion, anything done with intent to procure the miscarriage of a woman is unlawfully done unless authorised by section 1 of this Act.

Interpretation.

1861 c. 100.

6. In this Act, the following expressions have meanings hereby assigned to them:

> "the law relating to abortion" means sections 58 and 59 of the Offences against the Person Act 1861, and any rule of law relating to the procurement of abortion;
>
> "the National Health Service Acts" means the National Health Service Acts 1946 to 1966 or the National Health Service (Scotland) Acts 1947 to 1966.

Annotations:
Words underlined prospectively repealed by the Health Services Act 1980, Sch 7, as from a day to be appointed.

Short title, commencement and extent.

7. — (1) This Act may be cited as the Abortion Act 1967.

(2) This Act shall come into force on the expiration of the period of six months beginning with the date on which it is passed.

(3) This Act does not extend to Northern Ireland.

Notes

Introduction

1 This book adopts the definition of abortion given by Professor Glanville Williams:
'For legal purposes, abortion means feticide: the *intentional* destruction of the fetus
in the womb, or any untimely delivery brought about with intent to cause the
death of the fetus' (*Textbook of Criminal Law* (London: 2nd edn, 1983) 290).
(Emphasis in original.)

2 See e.g. *Abortion and the Law* (Cleveland: 1967, ed. David T. Smith); Germain G.
Grisez, *Abortion: The Myths, the Realities and the Arguments* (New York: 1970);
Daniel Callahan, *Abortion: Law, Choice and Morality* (New York: 1970); Betty
Sarvis and Hyman Rodman, *The Abortion Controversy* (New York: 2nd edn, 1974);
Carl E. Schneider and Maris A. Vinovskis, *The Law and Politics of Abortion*
(Lexington: 1980).

3 See e.g. Bernard M. Dickens, *Abortion and the Law* (London: 1966); Keith Hindell
and Madeleine Simms, *Abortion Law Reformed* (London: 1971); L. J. F. Smith, The
abortion controversy 1936–1977: a case study in emergence of law (Ph.D. thesis,
University of Edinburgh, 1979); Barbara L. Brookes, Abortion in England,
1919–1939: legal theory and social practice (Ph.D. thesis, Bryn Mawr College,
Pennsylvania, 1982); Victoria Greenwood and Jock Young, *Abortion in Demand*
(London: 1976); David Marsh and Joanna Chambers, *Abortion Politics* (London:
1981); Colin Francome, *Abortion Freedom: A Worldwide Movement* (London: 1984).

4 See e.g. The Law Commission, *Report on Injuries to Unborn Children*, Cmnd 5709
(London: 1974); *C* v. *S* [1987] 1 All E.R. 1241 (C.A.).

5 See e.g. *Re P* (a minor) (1982) 80 L.G.R. 301 (Butler-Sloss J.); P. T. O'Neill and
Isobel Watson, 'The father and the unborn child' (1975) 38 *Mod. L.R.* 1974; D. C.
Bradley 'A woman's right to choose' (1978) 41 *Mod. L.R.* 365; *R.* v. *Salford Health
Authority ex parte Janaway*, The Times 5 January 1988 (C.A.).

Chapter 1

1 Cyril C. Means Jr, 'The phoenix of abortional freedom: is a penumbral or
ninth-amendment right about to arise from the nineteenth-century legislative
ashes of a fourteenth-century common-law liberty?' (1971) 17 *NY L.F.* 335, 373.
Cited hereinafter as 'Means 2'.

2 See generally Eugene Quay, 'Justifiable abortion – medical and legal foundations'
(1961) 49 *Georgetown L.J.* 395, 426–431; *Report of the Committee on the Working of the
Abortion Act* (Chairman, Mrs Justice Lane) Cmnd 5579 (3 vols.) (London: 1974)
Vol. 1, 196. (Cited hereinafter as 'Lane Vol. 1, 2, 3', respectively); *Abortion: An
Ethical Discussion* (Church of England Board for Social Responsibility)
(Westminster: 1965) 13.

3 Means 2, 336–337.

4 Cyril C. Means Jr, 'The Law of New York concerning abortion and the status of the foetus, 1664–1968: a case of cessation of constitutionality' (1968) 14 *NY L.F.* 411. Cited hereinafter as 'Means 1'.

5 (1327) Y.B. Mich. 1 Edw. 3, f. 23 pl. 18, translated in Means 2 at 337.

6 (1348) Y.B. Mich. 22 Edw. 3, translated in Means 2 at 339.

7 Sir William Staunford, *Les Plees del Coron* (London: 1557) Book 1, Ch. 13; William Lambard, *Eirenarcha* (London: 1581) Book 1, Ch. 21.

8 Robert M. Byrn, 'An American tragedy: the Supreme Court on abortion' (1973) 41 *Fordham L.R.* 807, 817–819; Joseph W. Dellapenna, 'The history of abortion; technology, morality, and law' (1979) 40 *University of Pittsburgh L.R.* 359, 366–370.

9 'If one strikes a pregnant woman or gives her a poison in order to procure an abortion, if the foetus is already formed or quickened, especially if it is quickened, he commits homicide' (Bracton, *De Legibus et Consuetudinibus Angliae (c.* 1250) f. 121. (4 vols.) (Cambridge, Mass: 1968, ed. George E. Woodbine, transl. Samuel E. Thorne) Vol. 2, 341).

10 'He, too, in strictness is a homicide who has pressed upon a pregnant woman or has given her poison or has struck her in order to procure an abortion or to prevent conception, if the foetus was already formed and quickened, and similarly he who has given or accepted poison with the intention of preventing procreation or conception. A woman also commits homicide if, by a potion or the like, she destroys a quickened child in her womb' (*Fleta (c.* 1290) Vol. 2, Book 1, Ch. 23. *Publications of the Selden Society* (London: 1955, ed. and transl. H. G. Richardson and G. O. Sayles) Vol. 72, 60).

11 With reference to abortion resulting in stillbirth, Staunford's words are, 'this is not a felony, neither shall he forfeit anything', which Means interprets to exclude liability for both felony and misprision: see Means 2, 341. However, forfeiture was a penalty for felony rather than for lesser offences and neither Staunford nor Lambard excludes lesser penalties, whether for abortion resulting in stillbirth or death after live-birth: see Edward Hyde East, *A Treatise on the Pleas of the Crown* (2 vols.) (London: 1803) Vol. 1, 227–228. Moreover, neither author purported to provide a comprehensive treatment of criminal law: see William Hawkins, *A Treatise of the Pleas of the Crown* (2 vols.) (London: 1716) Vol. 1, Preface.

   Staunford, like the courts deciding the anonymous cases, was clearly swayed by difficulties of proof: *loc. cit.* n. 7 *supra*; see also e.g. East, *op. cit.* Vol. 1, 227–228; D. Seaborne Davies, 'Child-killing in English law' (1937) 1 *Mod. L.R.* 203, 209; *R. v. Kwok Chak Ming (No. 2)* [1963] H.K.L.R. 350 at 354 (Full Ct.).

12 R. H. Helmholz, 'Infanticide in the province of Canterbury during the fifteenth century' (1975) 2 *Hist. Child. Quart.* 379.

13 *Ibid.*, 386.

14 *Ibid.* Damme, writing about the history of child murder, observed that none of the cases she came across before the secular courts involved death by overlaying. She concluded: 'Perhaps the crime of infanticide by overlaying and other means, which are so difficult to detect and for which intent is nearly impossible to ascertain, was left to the church' Catherine Damme, 'Infanticide: the worth of an infant under law' (1978) 22 *Med. Hist.* 1, 10. The same could be said of abortion. Even if the offence were exclusively ecclesiastical, however, it was still an offence under English law for, as Matthew Hale observed in the *Proemium* to his *History of the Pleas of the Crown* (2 vols.) (London: [1685]), both 'ecclesiastical' and 'temporal' jurisdictions are derived from the Crown.

15 See William Holdsworth, *A History of English Law* (17 vols.) (London: 1938) Vol. 11, 555–580.

16 Dellapenna, *op. cit.* n. 8 *supra*, 382–386. He states, on p. 383, that there appear to have been no prosecutions for abortion in the church courts after 1547. See, however, *Before the Bawdy Court* (London: 1972, ed. Paul Hair) 258, comment 7.

17 (1505) (King's Bench) Public Record Office (hereinafter called P.R.O.), ref: Coram Rege Rolls, 974, Rex m. 4.

18 (King's Bench) P.R.O., ref: Ancient Indictments, 434, 12, cited in R. F. Hunnisett

(ed. and transl.), 'Calendar of Nottinghamshire coroners' inquests 1485–1558' in *Record Series of the Thoroton Society* (Nottingham: 1966) Vol. 25, 8, inquest 10.

19 *Ibid.*, 8–9.

20 Moreover, in 1586 the Court of Queen's Bench regarded offering to supply abortifacients as a sufficient ground for binding the offeror to be of good behaviour: *Cockaine* v. *Witnam* Cro. Eliz. 49.

21 *Calendar of Assize Records, Surrey Indictments, Elizabeth I* (London: 1980, ed. J. S. Cockburn) 512, case 3146.

22 'Secundum Juratores pro domina Regina present[es] quod Margareta Webb nuper de Godalmyn in Comitatu predicto Spynster decimo die Augusti Anno Regni Domine nostre Elizabethe dei gratia Anglie Francie et Hibernie Regine fidei defensorisque quadragesimo primo vi et ar' apud Godalmyn' predict' in Com' predict' deum prae oculis suis non habens sed instigacione diabolica seducta quondam venenum vocatum rattesbane [*sic*] comebat ea intencione infantem in ventre ipsius Margarete ad spoliandum et distruendum. Et sic predicta Margareta ratione comedendi verenum predictum eandem infantem in ventre suo adtunc et ibidem spoliauit et distruit in pernitiocissimum exemplum omnium malefact' in consimili casu delinquend' contra pacem domine Regine nostre Coronam et dignitatem suas' (P.R.O. ref: ASSI 35/44/7 m. 18).

23 The general pardon from which the defendant benefited appears to have been 43 Eliz. 1 c. 19, enacted in 1601 and entitled 'An Acte for the Queenes Majesties moste gracious generall and free Pardon', *The Statutes of the Realm* (London: 1819 edn) Vol. 4, Part 2, 1010. Dr Hunnisett and Professor Cockburn believe that Webb was pardoned *after* conviction (personal communication from Dr Hunnisett, August 1984).

24 Edward Foss, *A Biographical Dictionary of the Judges of England* (London: 1870) 293.

25 *Ibid.*, 213.

26 (1601) Gould. 176; 75 Eng. Rep. 1075.

27 (1601) Gould. 176; 75 Eng. Rep. 1076.

28 *Gentleman's Magazine*, August 1732, 931. With rare exceptions, no Midland Circuit assize records prior to 1818 have survived.

29 *Ibid.*

30 *Ibid.* The absence of any reference to quickening in this indictment, in that against Webb (see text at n. 22 *supra*) and in the presentments studied by Helmholz (*loc. cit.* n. 12 *supra*) cast some doubt on its legal significance.

31 *Ibid.*

32 *Ibid.*

33 *Ibid.*, 931–932.

34 *Ibid.*, 932.

35 *Ibid.*

36 *Quarter Sessions Minute Book* 1755. (Notts. R.O., ref: Q.S.M. 1/27.)

37 *Ibid.*

38 *Ibid.*

39 'If a woman be quick with childe, and by a potion or otherwise killeth it in her wombe; or if a man beat her, whereby the childe dieth in her body, and she is delivered of a dead childe, this is a great misprision, and no murder: but if the childe be borne alive, and dieth of the potion, battery, or other cause, this is murder: for in law it is accounted a reasonable creature, *in rerum natura*, when it is born alive (3 *Co. Inst.* 50 (London: 1641)). At 3 *Co. Inst.* 36 he writes: 'misprision in a large sense is taken for many great offences which are neither treason nor felony . . .'. See also 3 *Co. Inst.* 139, where he describes misprision as 'some heynous offence under the degree of felony'. On the current status of the offence of causing a child's death after delivery by prenatal injury, see Jennifer Temkin, 'Prenatal injury, homicide and the draft criminal code' [1984] 45 *Cambridge L.J.* Pt 3, 414.

40 William Hawkins, *op. cit.* n. 11 *supra*, Vol. 2, Book 1, Ch. 31, Sect. 16; William Blackstone, *Commentaries on the Laws of England* (4 vols.) (Oxford: 1765–1769) Vol. 1, 129; Vol. 4, 198, Edward Hyde East, *op. cit.* n. 11 *supra*, Vol. 1, 227–230; Wm Oldnall Russell, *A Treatise on Crimes and Misdemeanors* (2 vols.) (London:

1819) Vol. 1, 617–618; 796. See also Thomas Wood, *An Institute of the Laws of England* (2 vols.) (London: 1720) Book 1, Ch. 1, 17, Sect. I. Richard Burn, *The Justice of the Peace and Parish Officer* (London: 3rd edn, 1756) 380, Sect. 16.

41 Sir Matthew Hale, *Pleas of the Crown: or A Methodical Summary of the Principal Matters relating to that Subject* (London: 1682). The Preface asserts that the work was 'well accepted and esteemed by divers of the most eminent lawyers' and that its author took it with him on circuit.

42 *Ibid.*, 53.

43 Hale, *op. cit.* n. 14 *supra*, Vol. 1, 433. In the *Proemium*, he refers to ecclesiastical offences as crimes, but declares 'yet these I shall not meddle with at this time', which tends to support the natural assumption that the words 'great crime' refer to a secular offence – an assumption which was, moreover, apparently made by later commentators: see e.g. East, *loc. cit.* n. 11 *supra*.

44 (1748) 1 Vesey 86.

45 *Ibid.* See also *Beale v. Beale* (1713) 1 P. WMS. 244 at 246; 24 Eng. Rep. 373, *per* Harcourt L.C.

46 Edward Umfreville, *Lex Coronatoria: or the Law and Practice of the Office of Coroner* (Bristol: 1822, ed. Joseph Baker Grindon).

47 *Ibid.*, 234–235.

48 *Ibid.*, 235–237.

49 J. Chitty, *A Practical Treatise on the Criminal Law* (4 vols.) (London: 1816) Vol. 3, 798–801. See also text at n. 68 *infra*. In 1788, the first English work on legal medicine also referred to abortion as a crime (Samuel Farr, *Elements of Medical Jurisprudence* (London: 1788) 71).

50 Audrey Eccles, *Obstetrics and Gynaecology in Tudor and Stuart England* (London: 1982) 67. Another historian, noting the persistent condemnation of abortion by the Church, concludes that abortifacient potions were widely known about and used in the Middle Ages (B. D. H. Miller, 'She who hath drunk any potion . . .' (1962) 31 *Medium Aevum* 191).

It should be remembered, however, that while prosecutions for abortion seem few, fetal life was indirectly protected by prosecutions, for murder, of those who killed the mother whilst attempting to procure abortion. For instances of such prosecutions see Hale, *op. cit.* n. 14 *supra*, Vol. 1, 429–430; *Tinkler's Case* (1781) reported by East, *op. cit.* n. 11 *supra*, Vol. 1, 354–356.

51 Robert V. Schnucker, 'Elizabethan birth control and puritan attitudes' (1975) 4 *J. Interdisc. Hist.* 655, 656.

52 G. R. Quaife, *Wanton Wenches and Wayward Wives* (London: 1979) 120. See also Lawrence Stone, *The Family, Sex and Marriage in England 1500–1800* (Harmondsworth, revised edn, 1979) 325; E. A. Wrigley, 'Family limitation in pre-industrial England' (1966) 19 *Econ. Hist. Rev.* 82, 104–105.

53 (1832) 1 Moo. C.C. 356 at 365.

54 *Ibid.*

55 A legal journal reported that one of the judges, Vaughan B., was clearly of the opinion that it was a 'high misdemeanour' in a woman to take poison to procure abortion, though it added that a careful examination had not shown that either common or statute law had made voluntary abortion criminal. 'Trial of William [*sic*] Russell for the murder of Mary Wormsley. No. 2' (1832) 2 *Leg. Exam.* 35, 36.

56 (1857) Dears. and Bell 288 at 290. Both *Russell* and *Gaylor* were distinguished in *R. v. Fretwell* (1862) Le. & Ca. 161 on the ground that Fretwell did not desire the deceased woman to take the poison. The court did not, therefore, find it necessary to decide whether the deceased was *felo de se*. Nevertheless, Erle J. said (at 164) that the court in *Russell* had found that the woman was *felo de se* because she had been guilty of a misdemeanour in taking the poison to procure abortion. For further dicta, albeit conflicting, as to the common-law liability of the woman who procured her own abortion, see *R. v. Wilson* (1856) Dears. and Bell 127 at 128, *per* Coleridge J.; *ibid.*, *per* Jervis C.J.

57 (1890) 24 Q.B.D. 420 at 422–423. Cf. *R. v. Bourne* [1939] 1 K.B. 687 at 690; [1938] 3 All E.R. 615 at 620 *per* Macnaghten J.; Francis Wharton, *A Treatise on the Criminal*

Law (Philadelphia: 3rd edn, 1855), where the author goes so far as to state (at 541) that the criminality of abortion, even before quickening, was a 'settled doctrine of the common law'. Cf. 12th edn (3 vols.) (Philadelphia: 1932, ed. J. C. Ruppenthal) Vol. 1, 1073–1075. Only a few of the courts in the United States which considered the question went as far as Wharton: the majority followed Coke. See Means 1, 426–428, and authorities there cited.

58 See text at n. 49 *supra.*

59 Both Bills are reproduced in *Sessional Papers of the House of Lords* (1801–1833) Vol. 5, Pt 1 (1802–1803) 85; 99, respectively.

60 For the progress of the Bill in the House of Lords see the *Journals of the House of Lords* Vol. 44 (1802–1804) 82; 85; 89; 95; 109; 146; 155.

61 *The Times*, 18 March 1803.

62 *Ibid.*

63 *Ibid.*

64 *Ibid.* For the passage of the Bill through the House of Commons, see the *Journals of the House of Commons* Vol. 58 (1802–1803) 221; 232; 240; 243; 246; 250.

65 *The Times*, 18 March 1803.

66 (1803) 36 Parl. Hist. 1245.

67 *Ibid.* He specifically aimed to amend the Coventry Act (22 & 23 Car. II. c. 1). A conviction for wounding under this Act required proof of a 'lying-in-wait', and he instanced a case where 'an atrocious offender' had been recently acquitted for want of such proof *(ibid.).*

68 *The Times*, 29 March 1803. The report continues: 'There was *another* crime highly atrocious . . .' (1803) 36 Parl. Hist. 1246). (Emphasis added.) By implication, therefore, he regarded abortion in the same light.

69 'The remarkable trial . . . of William Pizzy and Mary Codd . . .' (1810) 6 *Edin. Med. Surg. J.* 244, 245.

70 *Ibid.* On the Act generally see Leon Radzinowicz, *A History of English Criminal Law and its Administration from 1750* (London: 1948) Vol. 1, 430–436.

71 *The Times*, 29 March 1803.

72 *Ibid.* See also *The Annual Register, or a View of the History, Politics and Literature for the Year 1803* (London: 1805) Ch. 9, 109.

73 The procurement of abortion by such methods may still, however, have been prohibited by common law.

74 The ambit of the words 'or other means whatsoever' would probably be limited by the *ejusdem generis* rule of interpretation to instrumental methods: see *R.* v. *Skellon* (1913) 33 N.Z.L.R. 102 (C.A.). Similarly, the words 'or other noxious and destructive substance or thing' in cl. 1 would appear to be confined to potional methods.

75 (1818) 1 B. & Ald. 405; 106 Eng. Rep. 149 (K.B.).

76 *The Times*, 30 April 1803.

77 For the progress of the Bill in the House of Lords, see the *Journals of the House of Lords* Vol. 44 (1802–1804) 111; 151; 156; 170; 172; 187; 265.

78 For the progress of the Bill through the House of Commons, see the *Journals of the House of Commons* Vol. 58 (1802–1803) 424; 514; 516; 523; 543.

79 See e.g. *Webb's Case, loc. cit.* n. 21 *supra* Bracton, *loc. cit.* n. 9 *supra.* Other treatises expressly cited the biblical prohibition against taking human life: see e.g. Coke, *op. cit.* n. 39 *supra*, 50; and Blackstone wrote that life was a gift from God, a right inherent by nature in each individual which began, in law, as soon as the infant stirred in the womb *(op. cit.* n. 40 *supra*, Vol. 1, 129).

80 Glanville Williams, *The Sanctity of Life and the Criminal Law* (London: 1958) 206. See also John M. Finnis, 'Three schemes of regulation', in *The Morality of Abortion* (London: 1970, ed. John T. Noonan) 172, 175–177. In *R.* v. *Smith* (1942), Crown counsel conceded that one could not 'procure the miscarriage' of a dead fetus adding, 'The whole purpose of the legislation is to prevent the destruction of the child's life . . .' (*Taylor's Principles and Practice of Medical Jurisprudence* (2 vols.) (London: 11th edn, 1956, ed. Sydney Smith and Keith Simpson) Vol. 2, 99).

81 Quoted from Ellenborough's obituary in *The Courier*, 18 October 1818, located among the *Ellenborough Papers*: PRO., ref: 30/12.

82 Ellenborough admitted that in his formative years he had been greatly influenced by Paley, who had been chaplain to his father Edmund Law, Bishop of Carlisle. See John Lord Campbell, *The Lives of the Lord Chief Justices of England* (4 vols.) (London: 3rd edn, 1874) Vol. 4, 148, 201n. See also the *Dictionary of National Biography* (1909, ed. Sidney Lee) Vol. 11, 657, 661.

83 (1810) 17 Parl. Deb., H.L., 200.

84 *The Crown Circuit Companion* (London: 10th edn, 1836) 64.

85 *The Anatomy of the Gravid Uterus* (Glasgow: 1799) 58n.

86 'Thoughts on the means of alleviating the miseries attendant upon common prostitution' (1799) 6–7, quoted by Angus McLaren, *Birth Control in Nineteenth-Century England* (London: 1978) 32. McLaren asserts that, in restricting the law, the ruling classes were policing the reproductive behaviour of the lower orders (*Reproductive Rituals* (London: 1984) 113). He also states that Ellenborough restricted the law against abortion because he relaxed the law against child murder (*ibid.*, 136). Another author asserts that the aim of the restriction was 'demographic aggression' (Wendell W. Watters, *Compulsory Parenthood* (Toronto: 1976) 81). Neither assertion gains support from the legislative evidence, and the former assertion is weakened by the fact that Ellenborough's Bill did not originally propose to repeal the presumption of stillbirth: see text at nn. 68–78 *supra*.

87 Samuel Farr, *loc. cit.* n. 49 *supra*. (Emphasis added.)

88 *Reproductive Rituals* (1984) 111. He states that although the social and economic conditions of the late eighteenth century did not encourage abortion – industrialisation produced a demand for child labour – it still had a role to play in spacing births (*Birth Control in Nineteenth-Century England* (1978) 36). He also writes that, before quickening, women regarded neither the fetus as alive nor themselves as pregnant and that abortion before quickening was, therefore, regarded merely as restoring menstruation (*ibid.*, 35). If so, the common law's apparent failure to prohibit pre-quickening abortion would have done little to challenge such a belief.

89 *Ibid.*, 31–32.

90 *Op. cit.* n. 49 *supra*, 23–24. Farr was still uncertain, however, about the exact process of generation; whether the 'germen' was formed in the ovary, or whether the semen contained a 'homunculus' for which the mother merely provided a 'nidus'. He wrote that the first rudiments of the human body were not a human creature, but only a foundation upon which a 'human superstructure' was raised (*ibid.*, 17–19). Perhaps this uncertainty as to the status of the early fetus helps to explain the distinction drawn in Ellenborough's Act between abortion before and after quickening. On the irrelevance of quickening see Thomas Denman, *An Introduction to the Practice of Midwifery* (2 vols.) (London: 1794) Vol. 1, 268; Burns, *op. cit.* n. 85 *supra*, 115.

91 *Op. cit.* n. 87 *supra*, 69.

92 See text at n. 87 *supra*.

93 (1784) 6 *Med. Obs. Inq.* 266.

94 *Ibid.*, 272.

95 *Ibid.*, 273.

96 *Medical Ethics* (Manchester: 1803) 80.

97 *Ibid.*, 79. It is interesting that a place was found for this condemnation of abortion in a book that was essentially about medical etiquette rather than medical ethics. See Ivan Waddington, 'The development of medical ethics – a sociological analysis' (1975) 19 *Med. Hist.* 36, 39.

98 Irvine Loudon, *Medical Care and the General Practitioner 1750–1850* (Oxford: 1986) 13.

99 F. F. Cartwright, *A Social History of Medicine* (London: 1977) 50–52.

100 *Birth Control in Nineteenth-Century England* (1978) 33.

101 *Ibid.*, 31; 33.

Chapter 2

1 9 Geo. IV c. 31.
2 7 Will. IV & I Vict. c. 85.
3 Section 8 provided that a sentence of imprisonment could be aggravated by hard labour and by solitary confinement.
4 Sections 58 and 59 are reproduced in the Appendices, p. 167.
5 (1828) 18 Parl. Deb., H.L., 1171–1172.
6 *Ibid.*, 1173–1174.
7 *Ibid.*, 1357.
8 *Ibid.*, 1442–1445.
9 (1828) 19 Parl. Deb., H.C., 350–351.
10 *Ibid.*, 350.
11 'The remarkable trial . . . of William Pizzy and Mary Codd . . .' (1810) 6 *Edin. Med. Surg. J.* 249. See also J. A. Paris and J. S. M. Fonblanque, *Medical Jurisprudence* (3 vols.) (London: 1823) Vol. 3, 90–91.
12 'Law lecture' (1832–33) 3 *Leg. Exam.* 279, 286. The influence of medical opinion is also suggested by Lansdowne's proposal to abolish the penalty of dissection for murder. He said that he had been in correspondence with medical men who had objected that the stigma attaching to dissection dissuaded people from leaving their bodies to science (*op. cit.* n. 5 *supra*, 1357). See also *ibid.*, 1445.
13 'Second Report from His Majesty's Commissioners on Criminal Law' Parl. Pap. (1836) XXXVI, 183, 205–220.
14 'Correspondence . . .' Parl. Pap. (1837) XXXI, 31, 39.
15 *Ibid.*, 41. Similarly, Dr Hutchinson observed that charges for abortion were rare because prosecutors felt the penalty too severe and pitied the women involved, and because witnesses committed perjury to prevent conviction. He added, 'That, however, feticide is so rare an action in England, can hardly be supposed . . . .'. 'On feticide' (1820) 43 *Lond. Med. Phys. J.* 1; 90, 97.
16 *Op. cit.* n. 14 *supra*, 43.
17 *Anonymous* (1811) 3 Camp. 73 at 77; 170 Eng. Rep. 1310 at 1312.
18 *Op. cit.* n. 14 *supra*, 50.
19 Parl. Pap. (1837) II 707, 709 [Bill 180].
20 (1837) 38 Parl. Deb., H.L., 1773, 1775.
21 *Ibid.*, 1776.
22 *Ibid.*, 1778.
23 *Ibid.*, 1784.
24 *Ibid.*
25 (1828) 1 Moo. C.C. 216, overruling *Anonymous, loc. cit.* n. 17 *supra*, on this point.
26 (1837) 38 Parl. Deb., H.C., 1915, 1916.
27 Based largely on the *Index-Catalogue of the Library of the Office of the Surgeon-General* (Washington D.C.).
28 *An Introduction to the Practice of Midwifery* (2 vols.) (London: 1794) Vol. 1, 268.
29 John Burns, *The Anatomy of the Gravid Uterus* (Glasgow: 1799) 115.
30 *Op. cit.* n. 11 *supra*, 248. Cf. the testimony of the medical witnesses in *Anonymous* (1811) 3 Camp. 73, who (at 76) differed as to the time when the fetus was quick and had a distinct existence.
31 Royston, 'Historical sketch of the progress of medicine in the year 1809' (1810) 24 *Lond. Med. Phys. J.* 1, 38n.
32 See *R. v. Wycherley* (1838) 8 C. & P. 262 at 264n.
33 A. T. Thomson, 'Lectures on medical jurisprudence' (1836–1837) 1 *Lancet* 625, 626.
34 *Ibid.*
35 *First Lines of the Practice of Midwifery* (London: 1831) 134. See also John Gordon Smith, *The Principles of Forensic Medicine* (London: 2nd ed, 1824) 312; 315–316; 467–468.
36 Severn, *loc. cit.* n. 35 *supra*.

37 *A Manual of Medical Jurisprudence, And State Medicine* (London: 2nd ed, 1836) 268. See also *ibid.*, 281–282; Thomas Stewart Traill, *Outlines of a Course of Lectures on Medical Jurisprudence* (Edinburgh: 1836) 28.

38 Theodric Romeyn Beck, *Elements of Medical Jurisprudence* (London: 2nd edn, 1825) 140.

39 'Trial of William [*sic*] Russell for the murder of Mary Wormsley. No. 2' (1832) 2 *Leg. Exam.* 10, 12.

40 *Ibid.*, 12–13. In the following year it observed: 'Medical men, however, still quarrell [*sic*] with the present law, in making a distinction between quick and not quick with child; a distinction which they say does not exist in nature: and they say that the popular idea of quick and not quick is a vulgar error' (*op. cit.* n. 12 *supra*, 286–287). Shortly after, the significance of quickening was also undermined in the context of the law relating to the reprieve of capitally convicted women, when Gurney B. ruled that 'quick with child' means 'having conceived' (*R. v. Wycherley* (1838) 8 C. & P. 262). The reporter of the case added an interesting note on a new method of detecting early pregnancy (*ibid.*, 264n. (a)–265).

41 (1846) 1 Den. C.C. 187.

42 'Second Report of Her Majesty's Commissioners for Revising and Consolidating the Criminal Law' Parl. Pap. (1846) XXIV, 107.

43 *Ibid.*, 147.

44 *Ibid.*, n.1.

45 See text at nn. 23–26 *supra*.

46 For two anonymous cases in which proof of pregnancy was required see Alfred S. Taylor, *A Manual of Medical Jurisprudence* (London: 1844) 596. Cf. *R. v. Haynes*, *ibid.* (2nd edn, 1846) 520.

47 *Op. cit.* n. 43 *supra*, 147.

48 *R. v. Wilson* (1856) Dears. & Bell 127. The reporter of an earlier case wrote that Lansdowne's Act did not appear to punish self-abortion: *R. v. Enoch* (1833) 5 C. & P. 539, 541n.

49 See authorities cited in ch. 1, nn. 17; 21; 39–43; 56.

50 *R. v. Gaylor* (1857) Dears. & Bell 288 at 290. It was later held, however, that a non-pregnant woman could incur liability for conspiracy to produce her miscarriage (*R. v. Whitchurch* (1890) 24 Q.B.D. 420) and for aiding others to procure her miscarriage (*R. v. Sockett* (1908) 24 T.L.R. 893). These cases reinforce the contention that the law did not regard the woman as the victim of the offence. See also *R. v. Tyrrell* (1894) 10 T.L.R. 167.

51 Section 59, 'Offences Against the Person Bill' Parl. Pap. (1859) II, 363, 380 [Bill 111].

52 (1857) Dears. & Bell 127. Followed in *R. v. Farrow* (1857) Dears. & Bell 164.

53 Though not, it was later held, if the means were supplied unwillingly: *R. v. Fretwell* (1862) Le. & Ca. 161.

54 If the defendant had committed the statutory felony of causing to be taken, he could be charged with constructive murder. If not, he could still be charged as an accessory before the fact to the woman's suicide. *R. v. Russell* (1832) 1 Moo. C.C. 356; *R. v. Gaylor* (1857) Dears. & Bell 288.

55 *Op. cit.* n. 29 *supra*, 57–58.

56 John Burns, *The Principles of Midwifery* (London: 3rd edn, 1814) 211. (Footnote omitted.)

57 *Ibid.*, 211n.

58 *Op. cit.* n. 35 *supra*, 134–135.

59 'Criminal abortion' (1857) 15 *Med. Tim. Gaz.* 524.

60 *A Treatise on Forensic Medicine* (London: 1815) 3.

61 *Ibid.*, 5.

62 George Edward Male, *An Epitome of Judicial or Forensic Medicine* (London: 1816) 116–117.

63 *The Principles of Forensic Medicine* (1821) 295–296.

64 *Op. cit.* n. 38 *supra*.

65 *Ibid.*, 143–149.

66 *Ibid.*, 149. Not even spontaneous abortion was free from risk: 'Even in cases where miscarriage results from involuntary causes, and where every prudential measure has been adopted for obviating its consequences, it is well known that the mother frequently falls a victim' (*ibid.*).

67 *Ibid.*, 150.

68 *Op. cit.* n. 37 *supra*, 270.

69 *Ibid.*, 270–271.

70 *Op. cit.* n. 33 *supra*, 627.

71 *Ibid.*, 629.

72 *Op. cit.* n. 46 *supra*, 591.

73 *Ibid.*, 592.

74 *R.* v. *James* (1853), 7 *Med. Tim. Gaz.* 101, 102.

75 *Op. cit.* n. 39 *supra*, 10.

76 *Ibid.*, 10–11. See also Archibald Alison, *Principles of the Criminal Law of Scotland* (Edinburgh: 1832) 628.

77 'The mind instinctively recoils at the idea of the destruction of human life, however imperfectly and immaturely it may be developed, and extends the same cherishing feeling to embryo humanity and to humanity worn out and sunk into useless dotage. This universal sentiment is of itself sufficient to justify penal enactments for the repression of abortion' (*op. cit.* n. 39 *supra*, 10.)

78 See text at Chapter 1 nn. 79–81. See also n. 49 *supra*. Rejecting the view that female safety was the primary concern of the legislation, Williams observes that qualified abortionists have been punished as severely as the unqualified (*The Sanctity of Life and the Criminal Law* (London: 1958) 140).

79 Ricci states that several medical subjects were well rounded out by the end of the nineteenth century and, significantly, that embryology assumed a leading role. The greatest contributor was the discoverer of the ovum, von Baer, but other significant contributions were made by Barry, who in 1843 showed the fertilisation of rabbits eggs; Neuport, who saw sperm enter frogs eggs in 1854; and Hertwig, who in 1875 demonstrated that fertilisation is accomplished by the fusion of the male and female pronuclei. James V. Ricci, *One Hundred Years of Gynaecology 1800–1900* (Philadelphia: 1945) 10.

80 *Observations on Abortion* (London: 2nd edn, 1807) 85. To James Barlow it was a 'most cruel and inhuman' crime (1801 5 *Med. Phys. J.* 53).

81 *Op. cit.* n. 35 *supra*, 134. See also John Ramsbotham, *Practical Observations in Midwifery* (London: 2nd edn, 1842) 378–379.

82 *Op. cit.* n. 60 *supra*, 5–6.

83 *Ibid.*, 2.

84 *Ibid.*, 9–10.

85 *Op. cit.* n. 62 *supra*, 114–115.

86 *Op. cit.* n. 63 *supra*, 290.

87 *Op. cit.* n. 38 *supra*, 130.

88 *Op. cit.* n. 37 *supra*, 265.

89 *Ibid.*, 283. He noted that some medical writers, not sharing Percival's view that it was as wrong to destroy the 'first spark' of life as an adult (see text at Chapter 1 n. 97), argued that a woman should not be convicted of the murder of a non-viable fetus. Ryan replied that 'no human being is justified in causing abortion before the seventh month, because no one can, in the present state of science, positively declare that a foetus before that time cannot arrive at maturity, or at the adult age' (*ibid.*). However, Ryan had written some years earlier that a woman who destroyed the fetus soon after conception was 'assuredly less criminal' than one who did so at a stage when the fetus, if left undisturbed, might reach maturity. The former destroyed an 'imperfect' being, the latter a 'perfect' being which nature destined for her family and society (*A Manual of Midwifery* (London: 3rd edn, 1831) 216). Similarly, Hutchinson thought abortion 'much less heinous' than infanticide : *op. cit.* n. 15 *supra*, 90.

McLaren makes the point that the abolition of quickening also served the regulars' interests by depriving the woman of the power of deciding whether the fetus was alive (*Reproductive Rituals* (London: 1984) 142).

90   Thomas Radford, 'The value of embryonic and foetal life, legally, socially, and obstetrically considered' (1848) 1 *Brit. Rec. Obst. Med. Surg.* 6, 10. See also Aliquis, 'Thoughts on the present state of the law respecting the procuring of abortion' (1853) 7 *Med. Tim. Gaz.* 149. Dr George Greaves wrote that since the 1837 Act scientific advance and the reports of abortion trials had made self-abortion increasingly possible ('Observations on some of the causes of infanticide' (1862–1863) *Trans. Manchester Stat. Soc.* 2, 12).

Medical opinion condemned abortion whether deliberate or merely negligent. Greaves, for example, maintained: 'life, and above all, the life of an immortal being, is the most precious work of God; . . . the destruction of it, either by design or by wilful neglect, at however early a moment of its existence, is one of the gravest crimes of which man can be guilty . . .' (*ibid.*, 22). Deliberate abortion was 'unquestionably a form of murder' ('On the laws referring to child-murder and criminal abortion, with suggestions for their amendment' (1863–1864) *Trans. Manchester Stat. Soc.* 19, 30).

91   In 1859 Dr Clay wrote that criminal abortion by regular practitioners was very frequent ('Statistics and observations on the liability to abortion' (1859) 6 *Glas. Med. J.* 408, 409). See also Ryan, *op. cit.* n. 37 *supra*, 272.

92   Burns, *op. cit.* n. 80 *supra*, 84.

93   *Op. cit.* n. 60 *supra*, 5–6. He observed that some made this 'iniquitous practice' their profession and daily advertised their services to women (*ibid.*, 10).

94   *Op. cit.* n. 15 *supra*, 90.

95   *Ibid.*, 91.

96   'Observations on criminal abortion' (1837) 2 *Lond. Med. Surg. J.* 881.

97   *Ibid.*, 882.

98   *Op. cit.* n. 46 *supra* (2nd edn, 1846) 518.

99   *Op. cit.* n. 90 *supra*, 53, 55.

100 *Loc. cit.* n. 59 *supra*.

101 'Correspondence: on criminal abortion' (1844) 8 *Prov. Med. Surg. J.* 80, 81 ('Investigator'). The law, he added, encouraged the crime: abortion was preferable to the workhouse (*ibid.*).

102 'Attempt to procure abortion by mechanical means' (1846) 2 *Lond. Med. Gaz.* 831, 832.

103 *Op. cit.* n. 90 *supra*, 54.

104 *Op. cit.* n. 46 *supra* (3rd edn, 1849) 548.

105 *Ibid.* (1st edn, 1844) 591.

106 *Ibid.* (5th edn, 1854) 527. See *ibid* (12th edn, 1891, ed. Thomas Stevenson) 543 for a total concession of the allegation.

107 'The charge of criminal abortion before the Lambeth Police-Court' [1853] 1 *Lancet* 432.

108 *Ibid.*

109 *Ibid.*, 433.

110 *Ibid.* The same case spurred another journal, which stressed that the accused were irregulars, to insist upon powers to punish those who misrepresented themselves as regulars ('The case of criminal abortion' (1853) 7 *Med. Tim. Gaz.* 67, 68). On the profession's rejection of liberalism, libertarianism, and *laissez-faire* as applied to medicine, see Jeffrey Lionel Berlant, *Profession and Monopoly* (Berkeley: 1975) 147–167.

111 'The practice of procuring criminal abortion' [1853] 1 *Lancet* 475.

112 *Ibid.*

113 *Ibid.* (Emphasis in original.) As early as 1815, it will be recalled, Bartley noted that some made this 'iniquitous practice their profession' (*op. cit.* n. 60 *supra*, 10). See also Hutchinson, *op. cit.* n. 15 *supra*, 97.

114 *Loc. cit.* n. 111 *supra*.

115 *Ibid.*
116 'The frequency of criminal abortion' [1853] 2 *Lancet* 101–102. Referring to the conviction of irregulars for abortion the journal remarked: 'Experience has proved the difficulty of procuring conviction for offences of this nature; and many disclosures lead to the horrible conclusion that they are of fearful frequency' (*ibid.*, 40). See also William Burke Ryan, 'Child-murder in its sanitary and social bearings' (1858) 4 *San. Rev. J. Pub. Health.* 165, 174; Hinds, *loc. cit.* n. 59 *supra*. Greaves wrote that the police suspected an organised system of feticide in certain parts of London. 'Observations on some of the causes of infanticide' (1862–1863) *Trans. Manchester Stat. Soc.* 2, 11.
   The profession would also appear to have regarded infanticide as a growing evil and to have pressed for legislative intervention: see George K. Behlmer, 'Deadly motherhood: infanticide and medical opinion in mid-Victorian England' (1979) 34 *J. Hist. Med.* 403. On the role of the American medical profession in encouraging the restriction of U.S. abortion laws in the nineteenth century, see James C. Mohr, *Abortion in America* (Oxford: 1978). Kristin Luker, *Abortion and the Politics of Motherhood* (Berkeley, CA: 1984) Ch. 2.
117 Ernest Muirhead Little, *History of the British Medical Association 1832–1932* (London: [1932]) 64–66. For a summary of the advantages and disadvantages of the Act for the profession see Irvine Loudon, *Medical Care and the General Practitioner 1750–1850* (Oxford: 1986) Ch. 14.
118 'Recent trials' (1858) 17 *Med. Tim. Gaz.* 658, 659.
119 'An abortive career' [1859] 1 *Lancet* 114.
120 'Criminal abortion' [1861] 1 *Lancet* 272.
121 'More abortionists' *ibid.*, 294, 295.
122 *Ibid.*, 295. See also, 'The week' [1860] 1 *Med. Tim. Gaz.* 371; 555. Regulars sought not only to suppress abortion by irregulars but also to replace the Jury of Matrons, whose function it was to decide whether a condemned woman was pregnant: see e.g. Radford, *op. cit.* n. 90 *supra*, 7–9.
123 *Loc. cit.* n. 121 *supra*. (Emphasis in original.)
124 *Ibid.* See also 'Abortion and its procurers' [1862] 2 *Lancet* 627; 'Alleged abortion mongers' [1863] 1 *Lancet* 614. A survey of the *British Medical Journal* from 1857 to 1862 reveals that the B.M.A. was more concerned with the issue of medical reform in general than with abortion in particular. (Nevertheless, the journal's attitude to abortionists is reflected in its description of one as 'Another of those hideous excrescences of civilisation . . .' ('The week' [1862] 1 *Brit. Med. J.* 97). For a more extensive discussion of the problem, see George Greaves, 'On the laws referring to child-murder and criminal abortion, with suggestions for their amendment' (1863–1864) *Trans. Manchester Stat. Soc.* 19).
125 Support for the idea of a link between the restriction of the abortion laws and the furtherance of the interests of the medical profession is provided by McLaren *op. cit.* n. 89 *supra*, Ch. 5.
126 See Loudon, *op. cit.* n. 117 *supra*, 18.
127 *The People's Health 1830–1910* (London: 1979) 73–78. Similarly, Lionel Rose asserts that abortion was 'very widely practised' (*The Massacre of the Innocents* (London: 1986) 86). See also Patricia Knight, 'Women and abortion in Victorian and Edwardian England' (1977) 3–4 *Hist. Workshop* 57; and, more generally, McLaren, *op. cit.* n. 89 *supra*, 53; 81; 117; 123–126; 135; 231–250.
128 Smith, *op. cit.* n. 127 *supra*, 77–78.
129 R. Sauer, 'Infanticide and abortion in nineteenth-century Britain' (1978) 32 *Pop. Stud.* 81.
130 *Ibid.*, 83.
131 *Ibid.*, 88.
132 *Ibid.*, 92. See also Edward Shorter, *A History of Women's Bodies* (London: 1982) 191–199. On the development of scientific medicine in the last century, including the advances in antisepsis and anaesthesia, see A. J. Youngson, *The Scientific Revolution in Victorian Medicine* (London: 1979).

Chapter 3

1 'Charge of procuring abortion' [1938] 2 *Brit. Med. J.* 97.
2 *Ibid.*
3 *Ibid.*, 199.
4 *Ibid.*, 202.
5 *Ibid.*
6 *Ibid.* Bourne's defence is summarised in [1939] 1 K.B. 687 at 688–689.
7 *Op. cit.* n. 1 *supra*, 202.
8 *The Times*, 20 July 1938.
9 [1939] 1 K.B. 689–690; [1938] 3 All E.R. 615 at 616; [1939] L.R. 471. The three reports differ in material respects.
10 [1939] 1 K.B. 691; [1938] 3 All E.R. 617.
11 [1939] 1 K.B. 691. See also [1938] 3 All E.R. 617; [1939] L.R. 471.
12 [1939] 1 K.B. 692. See also [1938] 3 All E.R. 617; [1939] L.R. 471.
13 [1939] 1 K.B. 693. See also [1939] 3 All E.R. 618–619; [1939] L.R. 472.
14 [1939] 1 K.B. 694. See also [1938] 3 All E.R. 619; [1939] L.R. 472. If the woman's life was threatened by the continuation of the pregnancy, the doctor need not wait until she was in immediate danger but was duty bound to operate ([1939] 1 K.B. 693). See also [1938] 3 All E.R. 618; [1939] L.R. 472. The judge also went so far as to state that a doctor whose refusal to operate on religious grounds led to the woman's death might incur liability for manslaughter by negligence ([1939] 1 K.B. 693). See also [1938] 3 All E.R. 618–619.
15 [1939] 1 K.B. 694. See also [1938] 3 All E.R. 619; [1939] L.R. 472.
16 [1939] 1 K.B. 694–695. See also [1938] 3 All E.R. 619.
17 [1938] 3 All E.R. 620. See also [1939] L.R. 472.
18 [1939] 1 K.B. 695. See also [1938] 3 All E.R. 621; [1939] L.R. 472.
19 L. J. F. Smith, The abortion controversy 1936–1977: a case study in emergence of law (Ph.D. thesis, University of Edinburgh, 1979) 17.
20 *Ibid.*, 25.
21 [1898] 2 *Brit. Med. J.* 59; 122.
22 *Ibid.*, 129. The defendant, who had not advanced this defence, was convicted. Similarly, in a Canadian case, Lamont J. refused an application for extradition for alleged illegal abortion as he could not say from the evidence that the operation had not been necessary to preserve the woman's life and was therefore not unlawful within s. 303 of the Criminal Code 1906. *Re McCready* (1909) 14 C.C.C. 481 at 485.
23 (1858) 17 *Med. Tim. Gaz.* 658.
24 *Ibid.* Similarly, in a later abortion trial, a medical witness testified openly that there was nothing in the woman's condition which justified abortion (*R. v. Poole* (1873), [1873] 1 *Lancet* 422).
25 *Loc. cit.* n. 23 *supra*.
26 *Ibid.*
27 *R. v. Bell* [1929] 1 *Brit. Med. J.* 1061. For a civil action brought after the non-consensual removal of a pregnant uterus where the law relating to abortion was not raised, see *Cull v. Royal Surrey County Hospital and Butler* [1932] 1 *Brit. Med. J.* 1195.
28 'Death after operation to terminate pregnancy' [1933] 2 *Brit. Med. J.* 549.
29 *Ibid.*, 550.
30 Quoted in *Taylor's Principles and Practice of Medical Jurisprudence* (2 vols.) (London: 5th edn, 1905, ed. F. J. Smith) Vol. 2, 154.
31 *Ibid.* Moreover, as early as 1846 the Commissioners for Revising and Consolidating the Criminal Law, in their second report, had included, as art. 16 of their Draft Bill, a proviso which stated that no act specified in the preceding article, which proscribed abortion, would be punishable if done in good faith with the intention of saving the life of the woman (Parl. Pap. (1846) XXIV, 148). (A note added that the proviso seemed expedient: it was contained in other codes but did not seem to have been adverted to in English treatises (*ibid.*).)

Further, in the Criminal Code (Indictable Offences) Bill 1878, drafted by Stephen, s. 23, on 'Necessity', provided that nothing therein should justify any person in any act or omission by which the death of any pregnant woman was likely to be caused, in order that her child might be born alive (Parl. Pap. (1878) II, 5, 33 [Bill 178]). Moreover, a proviso to s. 168(a)(iii), which punished the destruction of a child during birth, excepted destruction carried out in good faith for the purpose of preserving the life of the mother (*ibid.*, 88). See also Criminal Code (Indictable Offences) Bill 1879 s. 212 (Parl. Pap. (1878–79) II, 175, 267. [Bill 117]); Sir James Fitzjames Stephen, *A History of the Criminal Law* (3 vols.) (London: 1883) Vol. 2, 110. Cf. *idem, Digest of the Criminal Law* (London: 4th edn, 1887) 24n., 25; *General View of the Criminal Law of England* (London: 2nd edn, 1890) 77.

32 'The ethical, legal, and medical aspects of abortion' [1927] 1 *Lancet* 230–231.

33 *Ibid.*, 231.

34 *Ibid.*

35 *Ibid.*

36 *Ibid.*

37 'The law relating to abortion' [1938] 1 *Brit. Med. J.* 408.

38 *Ibid.*, 410.

39 *Ibid.*

40 (1928–29) 72 Parl. Deb., H.L., 441. See also *ibid.*, 669 *per* Lord Darling. Whether Hailsham's reference to the doctor's 'duty' connoted a moral or a legal obligation is unclear.

41 Sir William Oldnall Russell, *A Treatise On Crimes and Misdemeanors* (3 vols. in 2) (London: 7th edn, 1909, ed. William Feilden Craies and Leonard William Kershaw) Vol. 1, 830. It is not clear whether this word, which appeared in all the anti-abortion provisions from 1803 to 1861 (with the exception of s. 2 of Ellenborough's Act) was intended to except therapeutic abortion. See Bernard M. Dickens, *Abortion and the Law* (1966) 39. More generally, see E. Y. Exshaw, 'Some illustrations of the application and meaning of "unlawful" in criminal law' [1959] *Crim. L.R.* 503.

42 [1939] 1 K.B. 694. See also [1938] 3 All E.R. 619; [1939] L.R. 472.

43 [1939] 1 K.B. 694. See also [1938] 3 All E.R. 619; [1939] L.R. 472.

44 [1939] 1 K.B. 693. See also [1938] 3 All E.R. 618–619.

45 *R.* v. *Bergmann and Ferguson* [1948] 1 *Brit. Med. J.* 1008.

46 *R.* v. *Newton and Stungo* [1958] *Crim. L.R.* 469; [1958] 1 *Brit. Med. J.* 1242. For the view that Macnaghten J. should have based his decision on the principle of necessity see John V. Barry (as he then was) 'The law of therapeutic abortion' (1937–1938) 3 *Proc. Med. Leg. Soc. Vict.* 211. (Barry's article was referred to by Menhennit J. in *R.* v. *Davidson* (1969) V.R. 667. For the application of the principle in Commonwealth jurisdictions generally, see Bernard M. Dickens and Rebecca J. Cook, 'The development of Commonwealth abortion laws' (1979) 28 *Int. Comp. L. Q.* 424, 434–441.) For the view that Macnaghten J. did apply the principle see Glanville Williams, *The Sanctity of Life and the Criminal Law* (London: 1958) 152; D. Seaborne Davies 'The law of abortion and necessity' (1938) 2 *Mod. L.R.* 126.

47 'Therapeutic abortion: report by a special B.M.A. committee' [1966] 2 *Brit. Med. J.* 40, See also e.g. Dickens, *op. cit.* n. 41 *supra*, 39.

48 Alfred Derek Farr, Medical developments and religious belief with special reference to the 18th and 19th centuries (Ph.D. thesis, Open University, 1977) 292.

49 'Lectures on the theory and practice of midwifery' [1827–1828] 2 *Lancet* 129, 134. Similarly, Severn wrote that embryotomy was justifiable to preserve the woman from 'inevitable injury' (*First Lines of the Practice of Midwifery* (London: 1831) 83).

50 Blundell, *op. cit.* n. 49 *supra*, 129.

51 'Dr. Radford on the operation of craniotomy' (1844) 8 *Prov. Med. Surg. J.* 510.

52 'The value of embryonic and foetal life, legally, socially and obstetrically considered' (1848) 1 *Brit. Rec. Obst. Med. Surg.* 87.

53 *Ibid.*

54 *Ibid.*

55 *Ibid.*, 88.

56 *Ibid.* In a later paper he wrote that the mortality statistics for craniotomy were worthless as hundreds of such cases had been 'silently consigned to the grave'. 'Remarks on the Caesarian section, craniotomy, and the induction of premature labour' (1851) 12 *Lond. Med. Gaz.* 583, 587.

57 *Op. cit.* n. 52 *supra*, 89. Whether Radford's opposition to destructive operations was disinterested is open to question, since their restriction would have redounded to his benefit as a specialist in the Caesarian.

58 Francis H. Ramsbotham, *The Principles and Practice of Obstetric Medicine and Surgery* (London: 5th edn, 1867) 306 n.

59 *Ibid.*, 306.

60 *Ibid.*, 306–307.

61 *Ibid.*, 307. See also the appendix on 'Obstetric morality' in Fleetwood Churchill, *On the Theory and Practice of Midwifery* (London: 5th edn, 1866) 786.

62 *Historical Review of British Obstetrics and Gynaecology, 1800–1950* (Edinburgh: 1954, ed. J. M. Munro-Kerr, R. W. Johnstone and Miles H. Phillips) 35. For a brief history of the induction of labour, see *ibid.*, 33–35; 81–82; 130–131.

63 *An Introduction to the Practice of Midwifery* (2 vols.) (London: 1794) Vol. 2, 215.

64 *Ibid.* Ramsbotham wrote that the operation was first performed by a Dr Macaulay around the time of the conference in 1756 (*op. cit.* n. 58 *supra*, 329n.).

65 *Op. cit.* n. 63 *supra*, Vol. 2, 215–220.

66 (1801) 5 *Med. Phys. J.* 40. Similarly, Burns, though condemning abortion as murder, excepted those 'necessary attempts' which were occasionally made to induce labour before or after viability when the safety of the mother or child demanded it (*Observations on Abortion* (London: 2nd edn, 1807) 85). The question of the desirability of medical abortion had been raised as early as the eighteenth century by William Cooper. 'A case of the Caesarian section' (1772) 4 *Med. Obs. Inq.* 261, 271.

67 F. B. Smith, *The People's Health 1830–1910* (London: 1979) 15–16.

68 *Op. cit.* n. 58 *supra* (1st edn, 1841) 380.

69 *Ibid.*, 373.

70 *Ibid.*, 374n.

71 *Ibid.*, 373–374. Fleetwood Churchill devoted the first essay in his *Researches on Operative Midwifery* (Dublin: 1841) to the induction of labour. He said it had been performed so often and so successfully since Denman's time that it had taken its place among the regular obstetric operations in the various systems of British writers and teachers (*ibid.*, 1, 2).

72 *Op. cit.* n. 58 *supra*, 337. Cf. Radford, text at n. 53 *supra*.

73 (1859) 1 *Trans. Obs. Soc. Lond.* 21.

74 *Ibid.*, 46. That the majority of practitioners condoned abortion was conceded by Radford, who wrote: 'In England it was first suggested and practised, and at the present period the greater number of British practitioners recognise it as a valuable operation' (*op. cit.* n. 52 *supra*, 81). However, he called for its prohibition by statute as the 'door for evil purposes is already too open' (*ibid.*, 82). For the view that induction was only justifiable after viability, see Samuel Merriman, *A Synopsis of the Various Kinds of Difficult Parturition with Practical Remarks on the Management of Labours* (London: 3rd edn, 1820) 171.

75 *Op. cit.* n. 73 *supra*, 48.

76 *Ibid.*, 26. However, the operation was still in its infancy, and although its value had long been acknowledged in the British Isles, where it had most frequently been performed, it was still practised to a very limited extent (*ibid.*, 44–45).

77 'A lecture on the induction of premature labour' [1852] 2 *Lancet* 297.

78 *Ibid.*, 299.

79 *Op. cit.* n. 73 *supra*, 50. Similarly, a decade earlier Henry Oldham, lecturer in midwifery at Guy's Hospital, wrote that although the life of the child was secondary to that of the mother, 'it is only secondary to it, and something of the

same anxiety to preserve it, and the same resolute will to work out resources for doing so, ought to enter into all midwifery operations' ('Clinical lecture on the induction of abortion in a case of contracted vagina from cicatrization' (1849) 9 *Lond. Med. Gaz.* 45, 49). Again, in 1865 Dr Radford observed that few, if any, medical men still subscribed to Dr Osborn's assessment of the fetus as nearly a 'non-entity' and his consequently low estimation of fetal life. See William Osborn, *Essays on the Practice of Midwifery in Natural and Difficult Labours* (London: 1792) 187, 200–213; Thomas Radford, *Observations on the Caesarian Section* (Manchester: 1865) 56.

80 'On the induction of premature labour before the seventh month of pregnancy' (1854) 16 *Med. Tim. Gaz.* 475, 476. He, however, felt that the operation was the most important improvement ever introduced into midwifery and was warranted by a range of indications (*ibid.*).
81 *Op. cit.* n. 73 *supra*, 46.
82 *Op. cit.* n. 56 *supra*, 585.
83 *Op. cit.* n. 73 *supra*, 46.
84 *Op. cit.* n. 77 *supra*, 298.
85 *A Manual of Medical Jurisprudence* (London: 1844) 453. (Emphasis in original.)
86 *Op. cit.* n. 30 *supra* (2nd edn, 1873) Vol. 2, 201.
87 Charles Meymott Tidy, *Legal Medicine* (2 vols.) (London: 1883) Vol. 2, 158.
88 W. Bathurst Woodman and Charles Meymott Tidy, *A Handy-Book of Forensic Medicine and Toxicology* (London: 1877) 745.
89 *Ibid.*
90 Robert Reid Rentoul, *The Causes and Treatment of Abortion* (London: 1889) 251.
91 'The Legitimate Induction of Abortion' [1898] 1 *Lancet* 235. (Emphases in original.)
92 *Ibid.*, 235–236.
93 *Ibid.*, 235. Only rarely did obstetrical writings cite the law as a possible obstacle to induction: see e.g. Michael Ryan, *A Manual of Midwifery* (3rd edn, 1831) 206.
94 *Op. cit.* n. 91 *supra*, 236.
95 *Ibid.*
96 *Ibid.*, 235.
97 *Ibid.*
98 Stanley B. Atkinson, 'When abortion is justifiable' (1906) 15 *Congr. Int. Méd.*, *Lisbonne*, Sect. 16, 190–191.
99 *Op. cit.* n. 30 *supra* (4th edn, 1894, ed. Thomas Stevenson) Vol. 2, 187.
100 *Op. cit.* n. 90 *supra*, 251.
101 *Ibid.*, 16.
102 *Ibid.*
103 *Ibid.*, 251.
104 R. P. Ranken Lyle, 'The ethical and scientific aspects of the prevention, conservation, and destruction of intra-uterine life' (1926) 33 *Edin. Med. J. Trans. Med. Chir. Soc.* 34, 35.
105 *Ibid.*
106 *Ibid.*, 36.
107 See Sir John Phillips, 'The induction of abortion' [1921] 1 *Lancet* 266, for the view that it was preferable to abortion in cases of pelvic deformity.
108 S. MacVie, 'Mother versus child . . .' (1898–1899) 24 *Trans. Edin. Obs. Soc.* 123.
109 *Ibid.*, 128.
110 *Ibid.*, 127.
111 'Discussion on indications and methods for termination of pregnancy before the viability of the child' [1926] 2 *Brit. Med. J.* 237.
112 *Ibid.*, 237–239.
113 *Ibid.*, 239.
114 *Ibid.*, 237.
115 *Ibid.*
116 *Ibid.*

117 *Ibid.*
118 *Ibid.*, 240.
119 *Ibid.*
120 *Ibid.* For a fuller exposition of her views see 'The sociological and medical aspects of induction of abortion' (1936) 44 *J. State Med.* 332.
121 *Op. cit.* n. 111 *supra*, 245.
122 *Ibid.*, 246.
123 *Ibid.*, 248.
124 *Ibid.*
125 *Ibid.*, 238.
126 John S. Fairbairn, 'An address on abortion' [1927] 1 *Lancet* 217.
127 *Ibid.*
128 *Ibid.*
129 *Ibid.*, 217–218.
130 *Ibid.*, 218.
131 *Ibid.*
132 *Ibid.*, 219.
133 *Ibid.*, 220.
134 *Ibid.*, 230.
135 *Ibid.*, 233.
136 *Ibid.*, 232. Similarly, the *Lancet* – although observing that a doctor who used his best skill in the medical interest of his patient was in no danger of prosecution – cautioned that, with the possible exception of rape, the social and economic circumstances surrounding pregnancy were to be ignored by the doctor: 'The question for him in each case is the physical and mental safety of his patient' ('Abortion: lawful and unlawful' [1927] 1 *Lancet* 237, 238).
137 *Op. cit.* n. 111 *supra*, 239. Even earlier, Sir John Phillips had cited 'mental aberration' (*op. cit.* n. 107 *supra*, 267).
138 *Op. cit.* n. 111 *supra*, 239.
139 'The plea of insanity', *ibid.*, 244, 245.
140 *Ibid.*
141 *Ibid.*
142 'Ethical, legal and medical aspects of abortion' [1927] 1 *Lancet* 221.
143 J. R. Lord, 'The induction of abortion in the treatment and prophylaxis of mental disorder' (1927) 73 *J. Ment. Sci.* 390.
144 *Ibid.*, 396.
145 *Ibid.*
146 *Ibid.*
147 *Ibid.*, 395.
148 *Ibid.*, 396.
149 *Ibid.* For other discussions of the mental health indication see H. S. Davidson, 'Therapeutic abortion with special reference to the methods of induction' (1926–1927) 86 *Trans. Edin. Obs. Soc.* 185, 189; Andrew McAllister, 'The induction of abortion' (1929) 4 *Postgrad. Med. J.* 73, 78; Sydney Smith, 'Abortion: a discussion on its social, legal, and ethical aspects' (1931–1932) 91 *Trans. Edin. Obs. Soc.* 109, 111; A. Leyland Robinson, 'The effect of reproduction upon insanity' (1933) 40 *J. Obs. Gyn. Brit. Emp.* 39.
150 R. Percy Smith, 'Induction of premature labour in relation to mental disease' [1928] 1 *Brit. Med. J.* 9.
151 *Ibid.*, 11–12.
152 *Ibid.*, 12.
153 'Discussion on the Medical Indications for the Induction of Abortion and Premature Labour' (1929) 52 *Trans. Med. Soc. Lond.* 284.
154 *Ibid.*, 294–296.
155 *Ibid.*, 297.
156 *Ibid.*, 298.
157 *Ibid.*, 297.

158 *Ibid.*
159 *Report of the Committee on Medical Aspects of Abortion* (London: 1936).
160 *Ibid.*, 15–17.
161 *Ibid.*, 16.
162 *Ibid.*, 16–17.
163 *Ibid.*, 11–19.
164 *Ibid.*, 18. (Emphasis in original.)
165 *Ibid.*
166 *Ibid.*, 18–19. The Committee did, however, concede that eugenic abortion was generally regarded by medical men as falling outside the scope of therapeutic abortion (*ibid.*, 18).
167 *Ibid.*, 25.
168 In the view of one medical body, the change was due to a greater preoccupation with the mother's quality of life. In its Memorandum to the Inter-Departmental Committee on Abortion, which reported in 1939, the British College of Obstetricians and Gynaecologists observed: 'During the present century there has occurred a gradual and universal change in the attitude of the medical profession and of public opinion towards the status of therapeutic abortion'. It continued, 'The operation is now done in this country to prevent future ill[-]health and not only when the mother's life is endangered. No doubt,' it added, 'the underlying reason for the radical change in the national, as well as in the medical outlook, is the recognition of the importance of good health in the potential mother' (P.R.O., ref: M.H. 71/23/56/3). Lord Dawson attributed any change to an increasing emphasis on preventive medicine and on the good of the community ('Illegal operations' [1938] 2 *Brit. Med. J.* 1273, 1274).
169 *Op. cit.* n. 126 *supra*, 232.
170 'Medico-legal aspects of abortion' [1928] 1 *Brit. Med. J.* 452.
171 *Op. cit.* n. 126 *supra*, 219.
172 *Ibid.*
173 *Ibid.*, 219.
174 *Ibid.*, 232.
175 *Op. cit.* n. 111 *supra*, 237.
176 *Op. cit.* n. 126 *supra*, 218.
177 *Ibid.*
178 *Op. cit.* n. 153 *supra*, 284.
179 *Ibid.*, 286.
180 *Ibid.*, 287–288.
181 *Ibid.*, 288.
182 *Ibid.*, 286–287.
183 *Ibid.*, 287–288.
184 *Ibid.*, 287.
185 *Ibid.*, 288.
186 *Ibid.*, 288–289. Cf. Phillips's fifty-seven cases in thirty-five years of private practice (*loc. cit.* n. 107 *supra*).
187 *Op. cit.* n. 153 *supra*, 300. He later said that it was hardly justifiable to refuse abortion if the patient, having been informed of the risk to health in a given case, desired it ((1932) 25 *Proc. Roy. Soc. Med.* 247, 259).
   Beckwith Whitehouse observed in the same year that there was no doubt that abortions were being performed for reasons which, twenty-five years earlier, would have condemned the operator to the 'obstetric underworld' ('The indications for the induction of abortion' [1932] 2 *Brit. Med. J.* 337). He said that there was a consensus with regard to the 'major' indications (such as heart disease), and that, at least in the teaching hospitals, abortions were few. (In ten years he had performed sixty-three abortions, and for eight London hospitals the figure was 267 in five years.) However, a growing number of abortions were being done for 'minor' indications, to preserve not life but health (*ibid.*, 338). Moreover, these indications, which included eugenic and economic grounds, had been relied upon

by reputable doctors (*ibid.*, 340). If the profession was agreed that it should adopt broader views, he concluded, then it should do so, provided it was done openly: they should have nothing in common with the 'abortion-monger' (*ibid.*).

188 *Op. cit.* n. 143 *supra*, 394.

189 It appears that the authorities were aware that therapeutic abortion was performed. As early as 1908 a comment in the files of the Home Office noted that abortions to preserve life and health were 'numerous' (P.R.O., ref: H.O.45/13291/165493). Another stated that abnormal children were sometimes destroyed after birth (*ibid.*, 165493/15).

Whether Bourne instigated his prosecution is not wholly free from doubt. He gave an undertaking to the girl's father that he would keep the operation secret and at the trial the Attorney-General stated that he did not suggest that the defendant had broken this undertaking: *op. cit.* n. 1 *supra*, 199. (An anonymous letter was received by the police on 14 June informing them that the operation was to be performed that day and asking if they condoned it (Lilian Wyles, *A Woman at Scotland Yard* (London: 1952) 230).) However, it is difficult to see how this undertaking was preserved by a request to be arrested, and Bourne's letter to Dr Malleson reveals his intention to invite prosecution: see also, for example, his autobiography, *A Doctor's Creed* (London: 1962) 98–99. Finally, a colleague of Bourne's was told by him that he had informed the police. The colleague (who wishes to remain anonymous) was also told that, although he wanted to martyr himself, his counsel dissuaded him from pleading guilty because, even if he had received a nominal sentence, the General Medical Council would have had no option but to erase his name from the Medical Register (interview).

190 'Correspondence: *Rex.* v. *Bourne*' [1938] 2 *Lancet* 280.

191 Only two years before, the B.M.A. Committee of which he had been a member had reported that it was generally believed that a doctor who terminated pregnancy in the honest belief that it was necessary to safeguard life or health was free from the risk of conviction (*op. cit.* n. 159 *supra*, 10). See also 'When is abortion lawful?' [1937] 1 *Brit. Med. J.* 393, 394. He later wrote that he had challenged the law for the benefit of the country doctor, whose position between a demanding patient and possible misconstrual of his actions by gossips or the police could be very difficult (*loc. cit.* n. 190 *supra*).

192 P.R.O., ref: M.H. 71/27/161/2.

193 *Ibid.*, 3.

Chapter 4

1 Keigh Hindell and Madeleine Simms, *Abortion Law Reformed* (London: 1971); L. J. F. Smith, The abortion controversy 1936–1977: a case study in emergence of law (Ph.D. thesis, University of Edinburgh, 1979).

2 See Chapter 3, nn. 9–18; 45; 46 *supra*.

3 Section 2(1)(a), 2(1)(b), 2(1)(c), respectively.

4 Section 1(4) provided that abortion on the ground of rape would require a certificate from a registered medical practitioner consulted freshly after the alleged assault that there was then evidence of sexual assault; s. 1(5) that abortion on a girl under 16 would require her express consent in addition to any necessary consent of her parent or guardian [Bill 29].

5 (1965–66) 270 Parl. Deb., H.L., 113. [Bill 5.] (1966–67) 274 Parl. Deb., H.L., 44. [Bill 4.]

6 Hindell and Simms, *op. cit.* n. 1 *supra*, 158.

7 *Ibid.*, 159.

8 *Ibid.*, 160.

9 (1966–67) 729 Parl. Deb., H.C., 1459.

10 'The Royal Medico–Psychological Association's memorandum on therapeutic abortion' (1966) 112 *Brit. J. Psych.* 1071.
11 *Ibid.*, 1071–1072.
12 *Ibid.*, 1071.
13 *Ibid.*, 1072.
14 *Ibid.*, 1073.
15 *Ibid.*, 1072.
16 *Ibid.*, 1071.
17 The strength of psychiatrists' support for reform of the law was underlined in a survey by the Society of Clinical Psychiatrists of its 300 members. The first 100 replies showed 80% in favour of relaxation, twenty-four supporting abortion on request in the first trimester, and fifty-six abortion on the basis of an evaluation which included the woman's social situation ('Correspondence: Termination of Pregnancy Bill' [1967] 2 *Brit. Med. J.* 53 (Howells)). Further, to counter any suggestion that the R.M.-P.A.'s Memorandum was unrepresentative, the Association's Public Relations Committee Chairman wrote to the *Lancet* pointing out that it had been drawn up in June 1966 by a Special Committee chaired by the President and approved by the Council. The recommendations were based on the knowledge of a group of senior psychiatrists who considered many expert views. The only dissentient view had been that of Dr Myre Sim ('Correspondence: legalising abortion' [1966] 2 *Lancet* 1315 (Sargant)). In June 1967 a deputation from the Association, whose membership totalled 3000, told the Home Office that the great majority of British psychiatrists supported Steel's Bill as it then stood: 60% supported the Bill and 25% favoured even more relaxed legislation, while 15% favoured the legislation of existing case-law ('News and notes: attitude of psychiatrists to Abortion Bill' [1967] 2 *Brit. Med. J.* 778).
18 The tone of the A.R.M., held in July 1965 at Swansea, which moved that the Council should set up the Committee and ask the Government not to introduce legislation until it had reported, reflects concern that professional views would not be heard. The proposer of the successful motion urged: 'This was a medical matter. It was doctors who advised their patients, undertook the necessary treatment, and bore the ultimate responsibility. It should therefore be their duty, right, and indeed privilege to advise the Government on any reform of the law' ([1965] 2 *Brit. Med. J.* Supp. 54).
19 'Therapeutic abortion: report by B.M.A. Special Committee' [1966] 2 *Brit. Med. J.* 40, 44. Cf. the more restrictive recommendations in an interim report of the Committee produced in January, in anticipation of the introduction of Silkin's Bill in February 1966 ('Proceedings of Council: therapeutic abortion' [1966] 1 *Brit. Med. J.* Supp. 19). Even this report was regarded by A.L.R.A. as surprisingly liberal: 'it was much less critical than they expected in view of the elderly and conservative nature of the Committee' (Hindell and Simms, *op. cit.* n. 1 *supra*, 141).
20 [1966] 2 *Brit. Med. J.* 41. As early as 1953, a B.M.A. press statement had declared that there was considerable uncertainty as to the law among its members and had called for clarification ('Therapeutic abortion' [1953] 1 *Brit. Med. J.* Supp. 62, 63).
21 *Report of the Inter-Departmental Committee on Abortion* (Chairman, Normal Birkett K.C.) (London: 1939). Its terms of reference were: 'To enquire into the prevalence of abortion, and the law relating thereto, and to consider what steps can be taken by more effective enforcement of the law or otherwise to secure the reduction of maternal mortality and morbidity arising from the cause'.
22 [1966] 2 *Brit. Med. J.* 41.
23 *Ibid.*
24 *Ibid.*
25 *Ibid.*, 42.
26 *Ibid.* In the interim report, by contrast, the Committee recommended acceptance of rape as an indication in Silkin's Bill because it was qualified by the requirement of a medical certificate of evidence of sexual assault ([1966] 1 *Brit. Med. J.* Supp. 19, 20).

27 [1966] 2 *Brit. Med. J.* 42.
28 *Ibid.*, 42–43.
29 *Ibid.* The report was discussed by the B.M.A. Council in July 1966, when the undesirability of disclosing notifications to the police was stressed, as was 'abortion on demand' ('Proceedings of Council: therapeutic abortion' [1966] 2 *Brit. Med. J.* Supp. 10). Although this book limits itself to the reports of the medical bodies for its assessment of professional opinion, and does not survey opinion polls, it is noteworthy that, according to two such polls, the report was not unrepresentative. An A.L.R.A. poll, to which 750 replied, showed that 75% thought abortion should be available on the N.H.S. and that 70% supported relaxation of the law to allow abortion for therapeutic, eugenic and humanitarian indications. Again, in June 1967 a National Opinion Poll (N.O.P.) random survey of 1180 G.P.s found that, of the 65.5% replying, two-thirds favoured the grounds for abortion contained in Steel's Bill as amended by the Standing Committee, or wanted even greater relaxation. Of those who replied, 59% felt the main provisions of the Bill generally satisfactory and 6% felt they were not wide enough ('Notes and news: general practitioners and the Abortion Bill' [1967] 1 *Lancet* 1233).
30 'Legalized abortion: report by the Council of the Royal College of Obstetricians and Gynaecologists' [1966] 1 *Brit. Med. J.* 850, 852.
31 *Ibid.*
32 *Ibid.*
33 *Ibid.*, 853. On second reading, Silkin revealed that, on the previous weekend, he had met gynecologists to discuss the terms of his Bill ((1966–67) 274 Parl. Deb., H.L., 604).
34 [1966] 1 *Brit. Med. J.* 852.
35 *Ibid.*
36 *Ibid.*
37 *Ibid.* See also 'Abortion law' [1965] 1 *Brit. Med. J.* 1009, 1010; 'Legislation on abortion' [1966] 1 *Brit. Med. J.* 559, 560; 'Correspondence: abortion law reform' [1966] 1 *Brit. Med. J.* 422, 423 (Potts); 1050 (Bushby).
38 [1966] 1 *Brit. Med. J.* 852. Similarly, in a survey of Midlands gynaecologists carried out by Mr Wilfrid Mills, concern for autonomy was again evident: only three out of sixty-eight disagreed with a Memorandum which declared at one point: 'Many gynaecologists feel that the medical profession (and in particular the family doctor) is at present best able to reach the proper decision in each case, and that any change in the laws that might appear to give a patient a right to demand an abortion must be resisted. We consider that the present state of the law in England is satisfactory for discharge of this onerous duty by the medical profession . . .'. Moreover, codification of acceptable indications would complicate these consultations by 'introducing the new factor of legality' ([1966] 1 *Brit. Med. J.* 355).
39 Hindell and Simms, *op. cit.* n. 1 *supra*, 166.
40 'Abortion law reform: memorandum prepared by a subcommittee of the Medical Women's Federation' [1966] 2 *Brit. Med. J.* 1512. The broad scope for therapeutic abortion envisaged by the report is suggested by its repeated reference to the prevention of 'undesired and undesirable' pregnancies (*ibid.*, 1513).
41 *Ibid.*, 1512.
42 *Ibid.*, 1512–1513.
43 *Ibid.* There were two minority reports. One regarded abortion as murder (*ibid.*, 1513– 1514, Appendix A). The second urged that the right to decide whether to continue with a pregnancy belonged exclusively to the woman (*ibid.*, 1514, Appendix B).
44 'Medical Termination of Pregnancy Bill: views of the British Medical Association and the Royal College of Obstetricians and Gynaecologists' [1966] 2 *Brit. Med. J.* 1649.
45 *Ibid.* (Emphases in original.)
46 *Ibid.*

47 *Ibid.*, 1650.
48 *Ibid.*
49 'Abortion law' [1966] 2 *Brit. Med. J.* 1607, 1608. See also 'Tangled Bill' [1967] 1 *Brit. Med. J.* 519.
50 Hindell and Simms, *op. cit.* n. 1 *supra*, 174.
51 *Ibid.*
52 *Ibid.*, 178.
53 'Abortion law reform' [1966] 2 *Brit. Med. J.* Supp. 191.
54 Hindell and Simms, *op. cit.* n. 1 *supra*, 176.
55 *Ibid.*
56 *Ibid.*, 176–177. Again, in April 1968 Baird, commenting on an N.O.P. survey which showed 65% of G.P.s to be in favour of a new law at least as permissive as the Abortion Act 1967, opposed as unrealistic the 'persistent attempt to draw an artificial distinction between 'social' and 'medical' indications . . .' ('Correspondence: ethics and abortion' [1968] 2 *Brit. Med. J.* 173). For a fuller exposition of his views, see 'A fifth freedom?' [1965] 2 *Brit. Med. J.* 1141.
57 Hindell and Simms, *op. cit.* n. 1 *supra*, 177. The influence of the medical profession is also suggested by this book's comment that A.L.R.A. found Steel to be 'inexperienced in dealing with . . . the grand eminences of the medical profession' (*ibid.*, 157).
58 *Ibid.*, 177.
59 *Ibid.*, 179.
60 (1966–1967) X Parl. Deb., H.C., Standing Committee F, 107. At the beginning of the Committee stage the B.M.A. sent a copy of the joint report to every member of the Standing Committee and the Association's divisional secretaries were invited to consider writing to their M.P.s on the Committee to reinforce the policy behind the report ('Annual report of Council: therapeutic abortion' [1967] 2 *Brit. Med. J.* Supp. 66).
61 (1966–1967) X Parl. Deb., H.C., Standing Committee F, 108–109.
62 *Ibid.*, 109. The Memorandum recommended that the Minister should set up a panel of doctors, including gynecologists and psychiatrists, who would provide the second opinion ('Abortion law reform: memorandum by the Law Society and British Academy of Forensic Sciences' [1967] 1 *Brit. Med. J.* 294).
63 (1966–1967) X Parl. Deb., H.C., Standing Committee F, 110.
64 *Ibid.*, 114.
65 *Ibid.*, 113.
66 *Ibid.*, 111.
67 *Ibid.*, 115.
68 *Ibid.*, 120–121.
69 *Ibid.*, 121.
70 Hindell and Simms, *op. cit.* n. 1 *supra*, 174–179; 151; 153.
71 (1966–1967) X Parl. Deb., H.C., Standing Committee F, 313.
72 *Ibid.*, 320–323.
73 *Ibid.*, 233–237.
74 *Ibid.*, 251.
75 *Ibid.*, 4–12. 'Equivalent status' covered equally experienced gynecologists who did not have an N.H.S. contract (*ibid.*, 10).
76 *Ibid.*, 5.
77 *Ibid.*, 6–7.
78 *Ibid.*, 12–13.
79 *Ibid.*, 14.
80 *Ibid.*, 60, 61.
81 *Ibid.*, 38–39.
82 *Ibid.*, 40.
83 *Ibid.*, 335.
84 *Ibid.*, 336–337.
85 *Ibid.*, 339–340.

86 *Ibid.*, 345.
87 *Ibid.*, 346–347.
88 *Ibid.*, 348.
89 *Ibid.*, 350. He did, however, accept an amendment moved by Braine deleting that part of the Bill allowing abortion to be performed in any registered nursing home (*ibid.*, 349).
90 *Ibid.*, 353.
91 *Ibid.*, 335–336.
92 *Ibid.*, 367, 376.
93 *Ibid.*, 398–401.
94 *Ibid.*, 433.
95 *Ibid.*, 459–473.
96 *Ibid.*, 491–499.
97 *Ibid.*, 499–501.
98 *Ibid.*, 511–512.
99 *Ibid.*, 541–543.
100 *Ibid.*, 549, 550.
101 *Ibid.*, 563–591.
102 Hindell and Simms, *op. cit.* n. 1 *supra*, 190.
103 *Ibid.*, 191. The Central Ethical Committee of the B.M.A. had discussed aspects of abortion in detail and had concluded that the first consideration was the health of the patient: 'In the view of the Committee the artificial termination of pregnancy is permissible only when it is in the interests of the health of the mother or where there is risk of serious abnormality of the foetus' ([1967] 1 *Brit. Med. J.* Supp. 66).
104 Hindell and Simms, *op. cit.* n. 1 *supra*, 191.
105 *Ibid.*, 192.
106 (1966–1967) 747 Parl. Deb., H.C., 449.
107 *Ibid.*, 455–456.
108 *Ibid.*, 457.
109 *Ibid.*, 457–458.
110 *Ibid.*, 458–459.
111 *Ibid.*, 461, 463.
112 *Ibid.*, 464.
113 *Ibid.*, 468, 469.
114 *Ibid.*, 529.
115 (1966–1967) 749 Parl. Deb., H.C., 899, 900.
116 *Ibid.*, 925–926.
117 *Ibid.*, 963–965.
118 *Ibid.*, 998.
119 (1966–1967) 750 Parl. Deb., H.C., 1241–1244.
120 *Ibid.*, 1249, 1250.
121 *Ibid.*, 1252–1253.
122 *Ibid.*, 1254.
123 *Ibid.*, 1268.
124 'Notes and news: psychiatric views on the Abortion Bill' [1967] 1 *Lancet* 1337. See also n. 17 *supra*.
125 'Therapeutic abortion' [1967] 1 *Brit. Med. J.* Supp. 66.
126 'A.R.M.: request for Royal Commission' [1967] 2 *Brit. Med. J.* Supp. 51, 53.
127 *Ibid.*, 52.
128 *Ibid.*, 53.
129 (1966–1967) 285 Parl. Deb., H.L., 942.
130 *Ibid.*, 950, 951.
131 *Ibid.*, 961.
132 *Ibid.*, 966. The medical peers were evenly divided: Lords Brock, Segal and Waverley supporting the amendment, and Lords Platt, Amulree and Lady Summerskill opposing it (*ibid.*, 965–968).
133 *Ibid.*, 994, 995.

134 *Ibid.*, 996–997.
135 *Ibid.*, 999, 1000.
136 *Ibid.*, 1006, 1007.
137 *Ibid.*, 1018. Other amendments passed in Committee included the revision of the conscience clause to require participation in cases of emergency (*ibid.*, 1076–1095) and the alteration of the title to the 'Abortion Bill' (*ibid.*, 1099–1103).
138 *Ibid.*, 1394, 1395–1396.
139 *Ibid.*, 1397.
140 *Ibid.*, 1398, 1402–1403.
141 *Ibid.*, 1440–1441.
142 *Ibid.*, 1471.
143 *Ibid.*, 1498–1509.
144 (1966–1967) 751 Parl. Deb., H.C., 1737–1782.
145 Abortion Act 1967 s. 7(2).

Chapter 5

1 'A lawyer looks at medical ethics' (1978) 46 *Med. Leg. J.* 18, 21–22. Similarly, Lord Denning M.R. said that the Act 'has been interpreted by some medical practitioners so loosely that abortion has become obtainable virtually on demand. Whenever a woman has an unwanted pregnancy, there are doctors who will say it involves a risk to her mental health' (*Royal College of Nursing of the United Kingdom* v. *Department of Health and Social Security* [1981] 1 All E.R. 554 (C.A.)).
2 The sources for this material were the *Cumulated Index Medicus* from 1960 to 1982 and the *British Medical Journal* and *Lancet* for the same period.
3 Office of Population Censuses and Surveys (O.P.C.S) *Abortion Statistics* (London: 1982) Table 2. There is some evidence that medical abortions were rising before the Act, both in the N.H.S. (see e.g. *Report of the Committee on the Working of the Abortion Act* (Chairman Mrs Justice Lane) Cmnd 5579 (3 vols.) (London: 1974) [hereinafter Lane] Vol. 1, 11, Table C1) and in private practice (see e.g. Peter Diggory, John Peel and Malcolm Potts, 'Preliminary assessment of the 1967 Abortion Act in practice' [1970] 1 *Lancet* 287, 289 Table IV). The total number of abortions before the Act is relevant to this issue and has been widely discussed (see e.g. C. B. Goodhart, 'On the incidence of illegal abortion' (1973) 27 *Pop. Stud.* 207) but is beyond the scope of this book.
4 'The Abortion Act in practice' [1969] 1 *Brit. Med. J.* 436, 437.
5 *Ibid.*
6 *Ibid.*, 436–437.
7 *Ibid.*, 436.
8 *Ibid.*
9 [1969] 2 *Brit. Med. J.* Supp. 14, 15.
10 *Ibid.*, 15.
11 *Ibid.*, 14.
12 'The Abortion Act' [1969] 1 *Brit. Med. J.* 241, 242.
13 'Appendix V: working of the Abortion Act – memorandum by a Special Panel of the Board of Education and Science' [1971] 2 *Brit. Med. J.* Supp. 87, 88.
14 'The Abortion Act 1967: findings of an inquiry into the first year's working of the Act conducted by the Royal College of Obstetricians and Gynaecologists' [1970] 2 *Brit. Med. J.* 529.
15 *Ibid.*, 534.
16 *Ibid.*, 530.
17 *Ibid.*, 534.
18 *Ibid.*, 533.
19 'Consultants' report on abortion' [1970] 2 *Brit. Med. J.* 491, 492.
20 'Personal view' [1970] 2 *Brit. Med. J.* 478. See also Chapter 6 *passim*.

21 E. E. Rawlings and A. A. Khan, 'Effects of the Abortion Law, 1967, on a gynaecological unit' [1971] 2 *Lancet* 1249, 1250–1251. (Emphasis in original.) See also text at Chapter 4 n. 61.

22 *'Unplanned Pregnancy': Report of a Working Party of the R.C.O.G.* (Chairman, Sir John Peel) (London: 1972) 35. See also Joan Lambert, 'Survey of 3,000 unwanted pregnancies' [1971] 4 *Brit. Med. J.* 156, 157.

23 *Op. cit.* n. 22 *supra*], 37. More recently, Sir John Peel stated: 'at the present time, let's face it, the Act is acting as abortion on demand' (interview, 18 March 1985). Similarly, Sir John Dewhurst said that, for practical purposes, anyone who wants an abortion can have one (interview, 21 February 1985).

24 'Annual report of Council: Appendix II: inquiry into the Working of the Abortion Act. B.M.A.'s memorandum of evidence to Mrs. Justice Lane's Committee' [1972] 1 *Brit. Med. J.* Supp. 33.

25 Lane, Vol. 1, 183–184 para. 603.

26 *Ibid.*, para. 605.

27 'Attitudes to abortion, [1974] 2 *Brit. Med. J.* 69–70.

28 See e.g. J. R. Ashton *et al.*, 'The Wessex abortion studies. I, Interdistrict variation in provision of abortion services' [1980] 1 *Lancet* 82, 85.

29 'Annual Report of Council: therapeutic abortion' [1968] 1 *Brit. Med. J.* Supp. 74. See also Chapter 4, n. 103.

30 *The Registrar-General's Statistical Review of England and Wales for the Year 1968: Supplement on Abortion* (London: 1969) Table 1(c).

31 *The Registrar-General's Statistical Review of England and Wales for the Year 1973: Supplement on Abortion* (London: 1974) Table 1A(3).

32 O.P.C.S., *Abortion Statistics* (1980), Table 1.1(iii).

33 Lane, Vol. 1, 69–70 para. 203. Mr Huntingford confirms that this is 'widely believed' in the profession, and attributes it to doctors' lack of adeptness at interpreting legal documents. Just as many doctors believed that the Act came into operation when the Bill was passed, he says, many believe there is a 'social clause'. His comments were based on his referral letters from G.P.s and he said that he was sure that, if all these letters were evaluated to see whether they fell within the Act, most of them would not, 'not in terms of a justification that a critic of the Act would like to see' (interview, 20 March 1985).

34 A. E. R. Buckle *et al.*, 'Vacuum aspiration of the uterus in therapeutic abortion' [1970] 2 *Brit. Med. J.* 456, 457 Table 2.

35 K. C. Loung *et al.*, 'Results in 1,000 cases of therapeutic abortion managed by vacuum aspiration' [1971] 4 *Brit. Med. J.* 477, 478 Table II.

36 A. E. R. Buckle and M. M. Anderson, 'Implementation of the Abortion Act: report on a year's working of abortion clinics and operating sessions' [1972] 3 *Brit. Med. J.* 381, 383 Table III. See also e.g. E. J. M. Hopkins and Sylvia Solomon, 'Abortion in a general practice' (1972) 208 *Practitioner* 528, 530–531.

37 *Experience With Abortion: A Case Study of North East Scotland* (Cambridge: 1973, ed. Gordon Horobin).

38 Ian MacGillivray and K. John Dennis, 'Gynaecological aspects' *ibid.*, 47, 57.

39 *Ibid.*, 56.

40 *Ibid.*, 57.

41 *Ibid.*

42 *Ibid.*, 59.

43 *Ibid.*

44 *Ibid.*

45 *Ibid.*, 59–60.

46 *Ibid.*, 57.

47 *Ibid.*, 56.

48 *Ibid.*, 57. Sir John Peel believes that abortions are now being done, even in 'large sections of the N.H.S.', for purely social reasons, 'and not even seriously-considered social reasons; even trivial inconveniences, and patients get abortions done' (interview). Professor Taylor said that 'virtually all' abortions

were now done for social reasons (interview, 11 March 1985); Dame Josephine Barnes said: 'The indications are as broad as the individual doctor likes to make them' (interview, 11 March 1985).

It is not suggested that non-medical reasons do not influence *refusals* to abort, but a refusal on such grounds would not involve a doctor in liability under the law against abortion.

The number of prosecutions for illegal abortion from 1973 to 1982 inclusive was small: 11, 17, 1, 5, 3, 4, 0, 5, 3, 1 (*Criminal Statistics England and Wales 1983* Cmnd 9349 (London: 1984) Table 5.9: 'Offenders found guilty at all courts or cautioned for indictable offences of violence against the person by offence').

49 Several surveys of both professional and lay opinion about abortion until 1972 are recorded in Lane, Vol. 2, Ch. 3. The present chapter draws only on major surveys carried out both before and after that date which deal with the indications for abortion used by practitioners.

50 Quoted in Lane, Vol. 2, 24 para. 42.

51 Ann Cartwright and Majorie Waite, 'General practitioners and abortion' (1971) 22 *J. Roy. Coll. Gen. Prac.* Supp. 1, 1.

52 *Ibid.*

53 Quoted in Jean Aitken-Swann, *Fertility Control and the Medical Profession* (London: 1977) 29–30.

54 *Ibid.*, 30.

55 *Loc. cit.* n. 53 *supra*.

56 *Ibid.*, 32–33.

57 *Ibid.*, 56–57.

58 *Ibid.*, 58.

59 *Ibid.*, 231, 233 Appendix A, Question 8.

60 *Ibid.*

61 *Ibid.*

62 *Ibid.*, 80.

63 *Ibid.*, 67. Only 12% would not always refer a woman who persisted (*ibid.*, 68).

64 *Ibid.*, 67.

65 *Ibid.*, 68.

66 *Ibid.*, 80.

67 *Loc. cit.* n. 14 *supra*.

68 Majorie Waite, *Consultant Gynaecologists and Birth Control* (London: 1974).

69 *Ibid.*, 8.

70 *Ibid.*, 12 Table 8.

71 *Ibid.*, 11–12.

72 *Ibid.*, 12.

73 *Ibid.*, 12 Table 8.

74 *Ibid.*, 13.

75 *Ibid.*, 14–15.

76 *Op. cit.* n. 53 *supra*, 120–121.

77 *Ibid.*, 119.

78 *Ibid.*, 119–120.

79 *Ibid.*, 127.

80 *Ibid.*, 129.

81 *Ibid.*

82 *Ibid.*, 130–131.

83 *Ibid.*, 132.

84 *Ibid.*, 133. Aitken-Swann uses the term 'liberal' and 'conservative' to mean 'the tendency to give answers to key questions which taken together indicate a greater or lesser willingness to perform abortions when there are no medical reasons to do so' (*ibid.*, 135).

85 *Ibid.*, 133.

86 *Ibid.*, 134. For a study of the decision-making process in relation to abortion, see Colin Farmer, 'Decision-making in therapeutic abortion' in *op. cit.* n. 37 *supra*, 333.

87 *Op. cit.* n. 53 *supra*, 135. Mr Huntingford said the shift in gynecologists' attitudes is pragmatic rather than philosophical: 'It's more that gynecologists have – I'm generalising – stopped fighting and, in a sense, I think it's easier for them not to fight and just to say "I'll do it, but I'll only do the number that I think I'm going to do"' (interview). Sir John Dewhurst said that it is probable that there has been a shift in attitudes and pointed to the fact that abortion has become standard practice with which gynecologists have tended to go along (interview). Sir John Peel said that, under pressure from the public, the profession had lowered its standards and that there had been a 'tremendous *volte face*' (interview). Dame Josephine Barnes said that, although gynecologists were concerned before the Act about a possible flood of abortions, most of them have come to accept it: there has been a 'general change of attitude', and she pointed to: the fact that abortion was legal; the improved techniques for abortion; a reduction in criminal abortions; and a greater awareness of the problems of pregnant women (interview). Similarly, Waite's study of psychiatrists' attitudes to abortion contains a suggestion that 'liberal' psychiatrists received more referrals, either because seeing large numbers of patients influenced them to become more liberal or because colleagues knew that they were willing to recommend abortion ('Consultant psychiatrists and abortion' [1974] 4 *Psychol. Med.* 74, 83). Again, for the view that confronting the problems of unwanted pregnancy increased the gynecologist's readiness to abort, see Diggory *et al.*, *op. cit.* n. 3 *supra*, 289–290.

88 *Op. cit.* n. 53 *supra*, 148.

89 *Ibid.*, 169.

90 John R. Ashton, 'The attitudes of Wessex women obtaining induced abortion outside their own region'. *Second Report of the Working Group set up by the Wessex R.H.A. with the University of Southampton to study the Provision of Induced Abortion and Abortion Related Services in Wessex* (Southampton: 1978) Vol. 2, Table B.15. A total of 180 of the Brighton abortions (81.8%) and 85 of the Southampton abortions (73.3%) were certified under ground 2 (risk to health) (*ibid.*, Table B.26).

91 *Ibid.*, 8.

92 Audrey Chamberlain, 'Consultant Gynaecologists' Attitudes to Induced Abortion in Wessex' *Third Report of the Working Group . . .* (Southampton: 1979).

93 *Ibid.*, 16.

94 *Loc. cit.* n. 87 *supra*.

95 *Ibid.*, 75.

96 *Ibid.*

97 *Ibid.*, 75–76.

98 *Ibid.*, 83–84. In 1971 the Society of Clinical Psychiatrists repeated a survey of its members' attitudes to abortion which had previously been conducted in 1967. Some 40% replied and the answers revealed a statistically significant shift to permissiveness. 'Correspondence: psychiatrists' attitudes to abortion' [1972] 1 *Brit. Med. J.* 110 (Little).

99 Waite, *op. cit.* n. 87 *supra*, 78.

100 *Ibid.*

101 *Loc. cit.* n. 1 *supra*.

102 (1966–1967) 732 Parl. Deb., H.C., 1067, 1075.

103 *Textbook of Criminal Law* (London: 2nd edn, 1983) 299. Cf. Lane, Vol. 1, 45 para. 118; 68–69 para. 201; 140 para. 464(ii); 71 Recommendation 2. The argument is referred to but not contradicted in the B.M.A.'s *Handbook of Medical Ethics* (London: 1980) 28. Mr Huntingford said that there is no condition which would make delivery safer than abortion before the fourteenth week; that he has never turned down a woman's request for abortion before that time; and that, although he applied the statistical argument (and is therefore at one extreme of the professional spectrum), he still has a duty to the individual woman which extends to determining whether she is ambivalent, and acquainting her with the risks (interview). See also text at Chapter 6 nn. 102–103. (Interestingly, the balancing of

risks in deciding whether to induce labour was recommended as early as 1844 by A. S. Taylor, *A Manual of Medical Jurisprudence* (London: 1844) 595).

104 T. G. A. Bowles and M. N. M. Bell, 'Abortion on demand or on request: is it legal?' (1980) 77 *Law Soc. Gaz.* 938.

105 Lane, Vol. 1, 68 para. 200. For attempts to restrict the Act see Chapter 6 *passim*. Mr Steel believes the statistical argument to be within the letter but not the spirit of the Act (personal communication, 23 April 1985).

106 [1974] 1 All E.R. 376 at 381 (C.A.).

107 [1978] 2 All E.R. 987 (Q.B.D.).

108 At 991. He added that it would be foolish of a judge to try to interfere with the discretion of doctors operating under the Act, unless possibly there were clear bad faith and an obvious attempt to commit an offence. Even then, he continued, the question would be whether the matter should be left to the Attorney-General (*ibid.*, 992). See also *Re F (in utero) The Independent* 10 February 1988 (C.A.)

109 [1981] 1 All E.R. 545 (Q.B.D.); 554 (C.A.); 563 (H.L.).

110 At 575. Later dicta have also suggested a broad interpretation of the policy of the Act: 'the Abortion Act 1967 has given mothers a right to terminate the lives of their unborn children and made it lawful for doctors to help abort them' (*McKay and another* v. *Essex Area Health Authority* [1982] 2 All E.R. 771 at 780 per Stephenson L.J.). See also *ibid.*, 790 per Griffiths L.J. Again, declining to follow the ruling of Jupp J. in *Udale* v. *Bloomsbury Area Health Authority* [1983] 2 All E.R. 522 that public policy precluded damages for the birth of an unwanted child, Pain J. said that abortion had been legalised 'over a wide field' and added: 'The policy of the state, as I see it, is to provide the widest freedom of choice. It makes available to the public the means of planning their families or planning to have no family. If plans go awry, it provides for the possibility of abortion' (*Thake* v. *Maurice and another* [1984] 2 All E.R. 513 at 526).

111 (1966–1967) 747 Parl. Deb., H.C., 461, 464.

112 (1966–1967) X Parl. Deb., H.C., Standing Committee F, 13.

113 S.I. 1968 No. 390.

114 The Abortion (Amendment) Regulations (1976) S.I. 1976 No. 15 s. 4. The notifying practitioner was also required, by s. 5, to state whether the certifying practitioners had seen or examined the patient. Moreover, 'Certificate A' now read that the opinion certified was given before treatment for abortion and related to 'the circumstances of the pregnant woman's individual case'.

115 See J. M. B. Crawford, 'Abortion: a logical oddity' (1976) 126 *New L.J.* 252, 253. See also 'Postscript' *ibid.*, 298, 299.

116 As amended by the Abortion (Amendment) Regulations (1969) S.I. 1969 No. 636.

117 The original failure to produce a certificate in *Smith* could only have helped to establish his lack of good faith ([1974] 1 All E.R. 376 at 380).

Howwever, Mr Kirby said that it was taken very seriously that the notifications are solely to the C.M.O., and added that they are not used for monitoring purposes. The Department of Health and Social Security's lay investigators do not normally have access to them and have only been allowed to see them on a small number of occasions when these related to the investigation of allegations of irregularity that had come to the Department's attention from other sources.

He said that there was no reason to believe that the information contained in the notification forms implied that doctors were interpreting the Act wrongly, but if it came to the Department's notice that a particular doctor was misinformed about the terms of the Act, a member of the C.M.O.'s staff would write to inform him of the requirements of the Act and the Regulations (interview, 3 April 1985).

118 Richard Crossman, 'The Abortion Law' *New Statesman*, 7 August 1970, 138. A policewoman with experience of enforcing the abortion law in the private sector wrote that without legal reform, the law requiring notification would be unenforceable (W.D. Ch. Insp. Brenda Reeve, 'The Abortion Act 1967 and

difficulties encountered in its enforcement' (1973) 12 *Police Coll. Mag.* 19, 22). She concluded that the number of abortions by doctors was then twice that notified, that many of the notified abortions did not fall within s. 1 of the Act, and that enforcement of the abortion law as a whole was very difficult and, without amendment, would remain 'virtually impossible' (*ibid.*, 23).

119 S.I. 1976 No. 15, s. 3. The D.H.S.S. refused to disclose the number of requests made since 1976 (interview).

120 'Legalized abortion: report by the Council of the Royal College of Obstetricians and Gynaecologists' [1966] 1 *Brit. Med. J.* 850, 853.

121 'Therapeutic abortion: report by a B.M.A. Special Committee' [1966] 2 *Brit. Med. J.* 40, 43.

122 'Proceedings of Council: Abortion Act' [1968] 1 *Brit. Med. J.* Supp. 56.

123 The number of prosecutions initiated by the D.H.S.S. for failure to notify properly was only three in 1981, resulting in two convictions: (1981–1982) 16 Parl. Deb., H.C., *285–286*). The figures for returned notifications are as follows:

1973:	3301
1974:	2242
1975:	1187
1976:	3307
1977:	3397
1978:	3680
1979:	3580
1980:	6053
1981 (Jan.–March incl.):	2340

Source: (1981–1982) 17 Parl. Deb., H.C., *459, 460* (Vaughan).

124 The Abortion (Amendment) Regulations (1980) S.I. 1980 No. 1724. The form states: 'This form is to be COMPLETED BY THE OPERATING PRACTITIONER' and sent to the C.M.O. Part 1 of the form requires the operator to certify that the particulars are correct to the best of his knowledge. (Capitals in original.)

125 (1981–1982) 995 Parl. Deb., H.C., *451–452* (Vaughan).

126 William Russell, 'Letter from Westminster' [1982] 1 *Brit. Med. J.* 603. However, Mr Huntingford says that when he completed only the section on non-medical grounds he was never challenged (personal communication, February 1985).

127 *Loc. cit.* n. 126 *supra.*

128 (1981–1982) 19 Parl. Deb., *29* (Havers).

129 The letter from the C.M.O. reads: 'Lest there be misunderstanding I should point out that non-medical factors alone do not provide legal justification for termination on the grounds you have entered on the form. Statistical factors must have a medical basis which must also be notified. There has to be a current medical condition which puts at risk the life, or physical or mental health of the patient, or the doctor must believe such a condition is a foreseeable consequence of the pregnancy'. Huntingford's reply (dated 7 October 1981) stated: 'I am sure that you would not wish me to certify that disease was present that did not exist. I carried out the abortion believing that it was safer to terminate the pregnancy than for it to continue so far as her physical and mental health were concerned.' He also expressed curiosity that the form in question should have been returned but not many previous ones completed in the same way.

The parts of the record of the police interview to which access has been obtained indicate that Mr Huntingford stated that the indication for the abortion was medical. The following extracts are taken from the interview:

Police ('P'): In your opinion was there a risk of injury to Miss 'C''s physical health greater than if the pregnancy were terminated?
Huntingford ('H'): Yes.
P: What was the condition that created that risk?
H: Primarily the pregnancy itself.

P: Was it present before the termination took place?

H: Yes, by definition.

P: Did you anticipate the condition would occur if Miss 'C''s pregnancy was not terminated?

H: Yes. . . .

P: Was your opinion under s. 1(1) of the Abortion Act 1967 in the case of Miss 'C' based on what is safer as a matter of statistics or on what was safer having regard to the condition of Miss 'C'?

H: My opinion was concerned with the condition of Miss 'C' based on, among other factors, the statistical record. . . .

P: Would you mind telling me what those other factors are?

H: My knowledge and experience of how she might react if the pregnancy were to continue and she either kept the baby or it was offered for adoption.

P: Are you referring to an anticipated medical or mental condition or risk?

H: Yes.

P: [Why did you state the main medical condition as 'NONE'?]

H: Because, in my opinion, there were no medical conditions present in the woman. . . .

P: In an earlier reply you stated that termination . . . was justified because, among other factors, you believed that there was an anticipated mental risk. Would you still have put 'NONE' in the column . . . referred to if it had referred to 'MEDICAL/MENTAL' condition(s) instead of 'MEDICAL' alone?

H: Yes.

Mr Huntingford says that the requirement of stating a medical condition has taken the profession back to hypocrisy: doctors have not returned to the 'charade' of psychiatric referral, but have assumed a new one of stating a medical condition. He also reveals that he has subsequently written 'None' but has not been challenged (interview).

130 On the administration of the Act by the D.H.S.S. see its evidence to the *Select Committee on the Abortion (Amendment) Bill* (1974–1975) H.C. 253 (i); (ii); (iii); (iv); (v); (xiv); and *First Report from the Select Committee on Abortion* (1975–1976) H.C. 573-II 196; 216; 244. See also Chapter 6, *passim*.

131 (1968–1969) 782 Parl. Deb., H.C., 948, 949–950.

132 (1968–1969) 786 Parl. Deb., H.C., 932. See also text at Chapter 4, n. 94. Reeve concluded that the many unnotified abortions performed by doctors were done in both approved and unapproved places (*op. cit.* n. 118 *supra*, 22; 23).

133 (1968–1969) 787 Parl. Deb., H.C., 414, 416.

134 'Outside the law' [1969] 2 *Lancet* 148.

135 'Abortion and money' [1975] 2 *Lancet* 315.

136 *Minutes of the General Medical Council, Committees, and Branch Councils* (1968–1982) Vols. CV–CXIX, esp. (1969) Vol. CVI, 91; (1970) Vol. CVII, 37; (1971) Vol. CVIII, 57; 89; (1973) Vol. CX, 68; 103; (1979) Vol. CXVI, 56; (1981) Vol. CXVIII, 148. For disciplinary action taken against doctors for alleged misconduct involving abortion see (1969) Vol. CVI, 109; 117; 119; 120; 139; (1970) Vol. CVII, 133; (1971) Vol. CVIII, 62; 106; (1972) Vol. CIX, 134; (1974) Vol. CXI, 73; (1975) Vol. CXII, 60; (1980) Vol. CVXVII, 126.

137 *Ibid.* (1970) Vol. CVII,. 117; (1972) Vol. CIX, 98; (1976) CXIII, 61; (1980) Vol. CXVII, 123.

138 C. R. A. Martin, *Law Relating to Medical Practice* (London: 2nd edn, 1979) 25.

139 Reliance on the criminal justice system to detect abuse is suggested in the Council's own notes of guidance to the profession: 'The termination of pregnancy is regulated by the law and doctors must observe the law in relation to such matters. A criminal conviction . . . for the termination of pregnancy in circumstances which contravene the law in itself affords grounds for a charge before the Professional Conduct Committee. (*Professional Conduct and Discipline: Fitness to Practise* (London: 1983) 11.)

Chapter 6

1 (1968–1969) 787 Parl. Deb., H.C., 411. [Abortion Law (Reform) Bill.] Interestingly, the preservation of the status of the profession was also an expressed aim of those who spoke against Steel's Medical Termination of Pregnancy Bill on second reading: (1966–1967) 732 Parl. Deb., H.C., 1080. However, the cause of reform was also not infrequently expressed in terms of enhancing the freedom of the profession.

2 (1966–1967) 787 Parl. Deb., H.C., 413.

3 *Ibid.*, 412.

4 *Ibid.*

5 *Ibid.*, 416.

6 *Ibid.*, 415.

7 (1969–1970) 795 Parl. Deb., H.C., 1653, 1654. [Bill 29.]

8 See e.g. 'Annual Report of Council: therapeutic abortion' [1968] 2 *Brit. Med. J.* Supp. 74; [1969] 3 *Brit. Med. J.* Supp. 25, 29. Cf. 'The first year of the Abortion Act' [1969] 1 *Lancet* 867, where the journal maintained that the way to stop abuse was to improve N.H.S. abortion provision and education on sexual and contraceptive practice.

9 (1969–1970) 795 Parl. Deb., H.C., 1694–1695. The *Lancet* objected that the proposal to discriminate between doctors interfered with clinical freedom and queried whether the Bill would really make any impact on abuse of the Act ('Mr. Irvine's Bill' [1970] 1 *Lancet* 343).

10 *Loc. cit.* n. 7 *supra.*

11 [Bill 22A.]

12 (1974) 873 Parl. Deb., H.C., 403–404.

13 (1974) Parl. Deb., H.C., Standing Committee C, 98–99.

14 *Ibid.*, 27.

15 'News and notes: Parliament' [1974] 3 *Brit. Med. J.* 355, 356.

16 Its exact terms of reference were: 'To review the operation of the Abortion Act 1967 and on the basis that the conditions for legal abortion contained in paragraphs (a) and (b) of subsection (1) and in subsections (2), (3) and (4) of section (1) of the Act remain unaltered, to make recommendations'.

17 *Report of the Committee on the Working of the Abortion Act* (Chairman Mrs Justice Lane) Cmnd 5579 (3 vols.) (London: 1974) [hereinafter Lane] Vol. 1, 71 Recommendation (1).

18 See text at Chapter 5 n. 25.

19 See text at Chapter 5 n. 33.

20 See text at Chapter 5 n. 24. See also 'Proceedings of Council: Board of Education and Science' [1974] 2 *Brit. Med. J.* Supp. 112, 113.

21 'The General Practitioner and the Abortion Act' (1972) 22 *J. Roy. Coll. Gen. Prac.* 543, 546.

22 'Attitudes to abortion' [1974] 2 *Brit. Med. J.* 69.

23 'Joint Consultants Committee: Abortion Act' [1974] 3 *Brit. Med. J.* 358.

24 Abortion (Amendment) Bill 1975. [Bill 19.]

25 (1974–1975) 885 Parl. Deb., H.C., 1757.

26 *Ibid.*, 1758.

27 *Ibid.*, 1758–1759.

28 *Ibid.*, 1760.

29 *Ibid.*, 1761–1762.

30 *Ibid.*, 1774, 1775.

31 *Ibid.*, 1763, 1764.

32 *Ibid.*, 1765–1766.

33 *Ibid.*, 1773, 1774.

34 *Ibid.*, 1793, 1794.

35 *Ibid.*, 1797, 1798.

36 *Ibid.*, 1806.
37 *Ibid.*, 1799.
38 *Ibid.*, 1802.
39 *Ibid.*, 1805.
40 *Ibid.*, 1805–1806.
41 *Ibid.*, 1822, 1823.
42 *Ibid.*, 1854, 1855.
43 *Ibid.*, 1858.
44 *Ibid.*, 1864–1868.
45 For its recommendations, see *Third Special Report from the Select Committee on the Abortion (Amendment) Bill* (1974–1975) H.C. 552. For their acceptance, see (1974–1975) 898 Parl. Deb., H.C., 244. (Castle.)
46 (1975–1976) 905 Parl. Deb., H.C., 100–109.
47 *Ibid.*, 147, 149.
48 *Ibid.*, 147.
49 'Proceedings of Council: Abortion (Amendment) Bill' [1975] 2 *Brit. Med. J.* 696.
50 *Ibid.* In May, a group of doctors and medical students staged a 'sit-in' at B.M.A. House, expressing concern at what they saw as the Association's silence on the Bill. 'Medical news' [1975] 2 *Brit. Med. J.* 512, 513.
51 *Loc. cit.* n. 49 *supra.*
52 *Ibid.*, 696–697. By 360 votes to 4, the Local Medical Committees conference passed a motion that it was 'firmly opposed' to the Bill ('Annual Conference of Representatives of Local Medical Committees: Abortion' [1975] 2 *Brit. Med. J.* 763–764).
53 'Working of the Abortion Act' [1975] 3 *Brit. Med. J.* 254.
54 *Ibid.*, 254–255. See Chapter 5 n. 114. For the evidence of the B.M.A., the Royal College of Psychiatrists, the Royal College of Pathologists, and the Association of Anaesthetists see *The Select Committee on the Abortion (Amendment) Bill* (1974–1975) H.C. 253 (ix); for that of the R.C.O.G., *ibid.*, (x); and for that of the Royal College of Nursing, the Association of Nurse Administrators, and the Health Visitors Association, *ibid.*, (xiii). The Committee's proposals were criticised by the *Lancet* as 'destructive' and as making it harder for a woman to obtain a skilful abortion ('Abortion' [1976] 2 *Lancet* 296). Similarly, a letter signed by 326 doctors claiming to represent a very broad band of medical opinion praised Lane, said the Select Committee was unrepresentative, and urged that the overwhelming majority of medical opinion was against any 'retrogressive' change in the law ('Correspondence: Select Committee on Abortion' *ibid.*, 306). Seventy-seven doctors later wrote to support these views (*ibid.*, 424 (Fairweather *et al.*)).
55 *Loc. cit.* n. 53 *supra.*
56 *Ibid.*, 255.
57 *Ibid.* For other expressions of concern, see for example 'Correspondence: Abortion (Amendment) Bill' [1975] 3 *Brit. Med. J.* 42 (Beatson Hurd *et al.*). One consultant gynecologist said that, in his part of the home counties, abortion was available on request in early pregnancy. He added that this was so generally understood by both doctors and the public that his role as a gynecologist was merely to decide whether the operation would be free or the patient referred to a clinic in the private sector (*ibid.*, 99 (Banwell)).
58 'Abortion on demand' [1976] 2 *Brit. Med. J.* 325 Supp.
59 *Ibid.*
60 *Ibid.*
61 'A criminal approach to abortion' [1975] 2 *Brit. Med. J.* 352.
62 *Ibid.*, 353. Similarly, in an editorial on abortion in April 1975 the *Lancet* declared that there would be no thriving private sector if there were adequate N.H.S. facilities. It also went so far as to state: 'perhaps this is one instance where, subject to such safeguards as careful counselling and a limit on late abortions, a woman's own wish should be the final arbiter' ('A smell of burning' [1975] 1 *Lancet* 844).

63 'Correspondence: working of the Abortion Act' [1975] 2 *Brit. Med. J.* 337 (Wilkes). Unfortunately, the details of the survey's methodology and response rate are not provided.

64 (1976–1977) 926 Parl. Deb., H.C., 1783–1784.

65 *Ibid.*, 1784–1785. For its proposals see *First Report of the Select Committee on Abortion* (1975–1976) Vol. 1. H.C. 573-I.

66 *Op. cit.* n. 64 *supra*, 1785–1786.

67 *Ibid.*, 1786–1787.

68 *Ibid.*, 1787.

69 *Ibid.*

70 *Ibid.*, 1789, 1790.

71 *Ibid.*, 1791.

72 *Ibid.*, 1793.

73 *Ibid.*, 1792.

74 *Ibid.*, 1795.

75 *Ibid.*, 1795–1796.

76 *Ibid.*, 1805, 1806–1807.

77 *Ibid.*, 1809.

78 *Ibid.*, 1809–1810.

79 *Ibid.*, 1810–1811.

80 *Ibid.*, 1811.

81 *Ibid.*, 1812.

82 *Ibid.*, 1813.

83 *Ibid.*, 1814.

84 *Ibid.*, 1797, 1799.

85 *Ibid.*

86 *Ibid.*, 1799–1801.

87 *Ibid.*, 1803.

88 'Annual Report of Council: Abortion (Amendment) Bill' [1977] 1 *Brit. Med. J.* 1100 Supp.

89 'Correspondence: amendment of the Abortion Act' (Lorraine and Lester); [1977] 1 *Brit. Med. J.* 575. Another group, Doctors for a Woman's Choice on Abortion, favoured reform to allow the woman the right to decide. 'Correspondence: Abortion Law Reform' [1978] 1 *Brit. Med. J.* 1968 (Bury).

90 'Benyon's progress' [1977] 2 *Lancet* 120–121.

91 *Ibid.*, 120.

92 *Ibid.*, 121.

93 *Ibid.* Cf. *ibid.*, 'Correspondence: abortion' 247 (Ridsdill Smith).

94 (1976–1977) Parl. Deb., H.C., Standing Committee C.

95 (1977–1978) 944 Parl. Deb., H.C., 1213–1217.

96 *Ibid.*, 1214.

97 *Ibid.*, 1217.

98 'Annual Report of Council: Abortion (Amendment) Bill' [1978] 1 *Brit. Med. J.* 1076.

99 *Ibid.*

100 [1978] 1 *Brit. Med. J.* 1642 Supp., motion 267. The debate was, however, heated. 'The week in Cardiff' [1978] 2 *Brit. Med. J.* 290, 294. See also 'Notes and news: views' [1978] 1 *Brit. Med. J.* 1492.

101 (1979–1980) 970 Parl. Deb., H.C., 891.

102 *Ibid.*, 892. See also Chapter 5 n. 103; the *Daily Telegraph* 21 July 1971. Similarly, Dr Anne Savage openly declared: 'I refer for termination anyone who requests it for . . . the law is generally regarded as being one of "abortion on demand" ' ([1979] 2 *Brit. Med. J.* 667). Again, J. B. Metcalfe wrote: 'Our job as doctors is to help the patient to decide what are the true interests of all concerned and then to carry out her decision' ('Correspondence: Abortion (Amendment) Bill' [1975] 3 *Brit. Med. J.* 160).

103 (1979–1980) 970 Parl. Deb., H.C., 892.

104 *Ibid.*, 893. See also Chapter 5 nn. 22–23.
105 (1979–1980) 970 Parl. Deb., H.C., 893–897. He was, however, prepared to withdraw this clause in committee if the Minister gave satisfactory assurances about the control of pregnancy advisory bureaux (*ibid.*, 898).
106 *Ibid.*, 898.
107 *Ibid.*, 898–899.
108 *Ibid.*, 900.
109 *Ibid.*, 904, 905–906.
110 *Ibid.*, 905.
111 *Ibid.*, 939, 941.
112 *Ibid.*, 943–944.
113 *Ibid.*, 951, 952.
114 *Ibid.*, 953, 954.
115 *Ibid.*
116 *Ibid.*, 980.
117 (1980) Parl. Deb., H.C., Standing Committee C.
118 (1979–1980) 978 Parl. Deb., H.C., 929.
119 'Abortion (Amendment) Bill: B.M.A.'s comments' [1979] 2 *Brit. Med. J.* 1163.
120 *Ibid.*, 1164.
121 *Ibid.*, 1163. See also 'Correspondence; abortion' [1979] 2 *Brit. Med. J.* 496 (Huntingford); 'Correspondence: Abortion (Amendment) Bill' [1980] 1 *Brit. Med. J.* 188 (Clarke); 248 (Paintin); 479 (Ashton).
122 [1979] 2 *Brit. Med. J.* 1166. The Scottish Council of the B.M.A. informed the Scottish Home and Health Department that the Act was being administered 'tolerably well and was in the medical interests of the mother, the unborn child, and the family unit'. No evidence was available to it that any change was necessary (*ibid.*).
123 'No case for an abortion Bill', *ibid.*, 230.
124 *Ibid.*
125 *Ibid.*
126 'Mr. Corrie's Bill: a step backwards' [1980] 1 *Lancet* 186.
127 *Ibid.*
128 'Correspondence: Abortion (Amendment) Bill' [1980] 1 *Lancet* 260.
129 'Alternative pathways for abortion services' [1980] 1 *Lancet* 1121.
130 'Abortion: a matter of clinical judgment' [1980] 280 *Brit. Med. J.* 269.
131 *Ibid.* See also T. L. T. Lewis, 'Legal abortion in England and Wales 1968–78' [1980] 280 *Brit. Med. J.* 295, 296.
132 *Loc. cit.* n. 130 *supra*. See also 'An emergency operation' [1968] 2 *Lancet* 495.
133 *Loc. cit.* n. 130 *supra*. (Footnote omitted.) As early as 1973, Hordern maintained that legal abortion was best considered as part of a spectrum of fertility control and that it would be needed, at least for the following few years, as an 'indispensable backstop' in cases of ineffective contraception ('Correspondence: latent morbidity in abortion' [1973] 2 *Brit. Med. J.* 368). See also 'The first year of the Abortion Act' [1969] 1 *Lancet* 867; 'Correspondence: deaths from abortion' 2 *Lancet* 547 (Arthure); John McEwan, 'The Abortion Act: a general practitioner's view' (1970) 204 *Practitioner* 427, 431; 'How safe is abortion?' [1971] 2 *Lancet* 1239–1240; Michael Brudenell, 'Gynaecological aftermaths of the 1967 Abortion Act' (1972) 65 *Proc. Roy. Soc. Med.* 155, 157–158; J. N. Rea, 'Social aspects of pregnancy, a general practitioner's view' (1972) 86 *Pub. Health* 165, 167; 'Correspondence: abortion on demand' [1972] 1 *Lancet* 45 (Grogono); 'Correspondence: termination of pregnancy' [1972] 2 *Brit. Med. J.* 228 (Bluett); 655 (Moxon); 3 *Brit. Med. J.* 700 (Bluett); 'Latent morbidity after abortion' [1973] 1 *Brit. Med. J.* 506; W. Dewi Rees, 'Personal view' *ibid.*, 228; Geoffrey Chamberlain, 'Usage of contraception and abortion' (1973) 92 *Roy. Soc. Health. J.*191, 194; H. Gordon, 'Is abortion a form of contraception?' *ibid.*, 194, 197; H. R. Arthur, 'Termination of pregnancy' *ibid.*, 204; Michael Maresh *et al.*, 'Why admit abortion patients?' [1974] 2 *Lancet* 888; 'Menstrual regulation' [1974] 1 *Lancet* 84; 'Correspondence: Abortion

(Amendment) Bill' [1975] 2 *Brit. Med. J.* 686 (Binning); 'Abortion' [1976] 2 *Lancet* 296; 'Correspondence: Abortion (Amendment) Bill' [1980] 280 *Brit. Med. J.* 248 (Paintin); 477 (McLaren); 479 (Elliott); 643 (Wong); 'Correspondence: abortion regarded as contraception' [1977] 2 *Lancet* 666 (Beaconsfield); 765 (Adam).

134 *Loc. cit.* n. 130 *supra.*

Chapter 7

1 'The influence of the Association on legislation' [1937] 1 *Brit. Med. J.* Supp. 42. For the influence of the emerging profession on legislation other than that regulating abortion, see W. H. McMenemy, 'The influence of medical societies on the development of medical practice in nineteenth-century Britain' in *The Evolution of Medical Practice in Britain* (London: 1961, ed. F. N. L. Poynter) 67; 69–70; 77. On the political influence of the British Medical Association see Harry Eckstein, *Pressure Group Politics: the Case of the B.M.A.* (London: 1960).

2 Philip Elliott, *The Sociology of the Professions* (London: 1972) Ch. 2. See also Noel and José Parry. *The Rise of the Medical Profession* (London: 1976) Chs. 6 and 7; Ivan Waddington, *The Medical Profession in the Industrial Revolution* (Dublin: 1984).

3 Irvine Loudon, *Medical Care and the General Practitioner 1750–1850* (Oxford: 1986) 18.

4 Personal communication from Dr Loudon, January 1985. In his book he explains that the breakdown of the tripartite division led to uncertainties over status and that although the G.P. could boast an all-round education, his status suffered from his involvement with pharmacy and obstetrics (*op. cit.* n. 3, *supra*, Ch. 9).

   On the displacement of midwives by man-midwives in the eighteenth century and the improving status of obstetricians in the nineteenth see Jean Donnison, *Midwives and Medical Men* (London: 1977) Chs. 2 and 3. Moreover, Sydney Smith says that in the first half of the last century forensic medicine was also establishing itself, and the place of medical opinion in the legal system became more important and more clearly defined ('The history and development of forensic medicine' [1951] 1 *Brit. Med. J.* 599, 605).

5 Eliot Freidson, *Profession of Medicine* (New York: 1975) 5.

6 See Howard S. Becker, *Outsiders* (New York: 1963) Ch. 8; Freidson, *op. cit.* n. 5 *supra*, 252ff. See also Joseph R. Gusfield, *Symbolic Crusade* (Urbana: 1963). This book does not address the various theories of law emergence in relation to the issue of abortion. See, however, L. J. F. Smith, The abortion controversy 1936–1977: a case study in emergence of law (Ph.D. thesis, University of Edinburgh, 1979) Ch. 6; Victoria Greenwood, The theft of the body: the sociology of the abortion law (M.A. thesis, University of Sheffield, 1973).

7 *Op. cit.* n. 5 *supra*, 82. Professional status may also help to explain the dearth of prosecutions of doctors for criminal abortion. Of high status criminals, one sociologist has written: 'Because of their social status they have a loud voice in determining what goes into the statutes and how the criminal law as it affects them is administered' (Edwin H. Sutherland, 'White collar criminality' in *White Collar Crime* (London: 1977, ed. Gilbert Geis and Robert F. Meier) 38, 45).

8 S. J. Macintyre, The medical profession and termination of pregnancy (M.Sc. thesis, University of London, 1977) 25. Cf. Madeleine Simms, 'Abortion law and medical freedom' (1974) 14 *Brit. J. Crim.* 118, 126–127.

9 This book's suggestion that a significant number of abortions since 1968 have been performed for non-medical reasons tends to support Macintyre's prediction of a broadening of the doctor's function in this area. See *op. cit.* n. 8 *supra*, 38–39.

10 Peter Bartram, *David Steel: His Life and Politics* (London: 1982) 85.

11 World Health Organization, *Basic Documents* (Geneva: 26th edn, 1976) 1.

12 I. M. Ingram, 'Abortion games: an inquiry into the working of the Abortion Act' [1971] 2 *Lancet* 969.

13 *Op. cit.* n. 5 *supra*, Chs. 7 and 16.
14 *Ibid.*, 248. See also Irving Kenneth Zola, 'Medicine as an institution of social control' (1972) 20 *Sociol. Rev.* 487.
15 *Ibid.*, 494–495. Freidson states that the medical profession has first claim to jurisdiction over the label of illness and anything to which it can be attached, regardless of its ability to deal with it effectively (*op. cit.* n. 5 *supra*, 251).
16 Peter Conrad and Joseph W. Schneider, *Deviance and Medicalization* (St Louis: 1980) 275. On another crime which has been medicalised, see Katherine O'Donovan, 'The medicalisation of infanticide' [1984] *Crim. L.R.* 259. For an examination of 'victimless' crimes see Edwin M. Schur, *Crimes Without Victims: Deviant Behaviour and Public Policy* (New Jersey: 1965).

The Birkett Committee concluded that the reasons for abortion were predominantly financial (*Report of the Inter-Departmental Committee on Abortion* (London: 1939) 118). (See also text at Chapter 4 n. 50). It added that a sound approach to the problem of criminal abortion was to attempt by social and economic measures to relieve the financial difficulties associated with birth and parenthood (*Report of the Inter-Departmental Committee on Abortion* 124).
17 *Op. cit.* n. 16 *supra*, 248–252. See also Ian Kennedy, *The Unmasking of Medicine* (London: 1983) Ch. 3; Sally Macintyre, 'To have or to have not – prevention and promotion of childbirth in gynaecological work' (1976) *Sociol. Rev. Monog.* 176, 186–191.
18 Thomas Szasz, *The Theology of Medicine* (Oxford: 1979) 77.
19 *Op. cit.* n. 5 *supra*, 252. See also P. M. Strong, 'Sociological imperialism and the profession of medicine' (1979) 13A *Soc. Sci. Med.* 199.
20 *Op. cit.* n. 5 *supra*, 206.

Subject index

Names index